THE MAN WHO SOLD THE WORLD

ALSO BY WILLIAM KLEINKNECHT

The New Ethnic Mobs:
The Changing Face of Organized Crime in America

THE MAN WHO SOLD THE WORLD

Ronald Reagan and the Betrayal of Main Street America

WILLIAM KLEINKNECHT

A Member of the Perseus Books Group
New York

Published by Nation Books
A Member of the Perseus Books Group

Books published by Nation Books are available at special discounts for bulk purchases in the United States by corporations, institutions, and other organizations. For more information, please contact the Special Markets Department at the Perseus Books Group, 2300 Chestnut Street, Suite 200, Philadelphia, PA 19103, or call (800) 810-4145, ext. 5000, or e-mail special.markets@perseusbooks.com.

Designed by Brent Wilcox

Library of Congress Cataloging-in-Publication Data
Kleinknecht, William, 1960–
The man who sold the world : Ronald Reagan and the betrayal of main street America / by William Kleinknecht.
p. cm.
ISBN 978-1-56858-410-2 (alk. paper)
1. Reagan, Ronald—Political and social views. 2. Reagan, Ronald—Ethics. 3. Reagan, Ronald—Influence. 4. United States—Politics and government—1981–1989. 5. United States—Economic policy—1981–1993. 6. United States—Social policy—1980–1993. 7. United States—Social conditions—1980– 8. City and town life—United States. 9. Social values—United States. 10. National characteristics, American. I. Title.
E877.2.K58 2009
973.927—dc22

2008041112

10 9 8 7 6 5 4 3 2 1

For Margarita

"It is easier for a camel to go through the eye of a needle, than for a rich man to enter into the kingdom of God."

—JESUS CHRIST

"I am absolutely convinced that no wealth in the world can help humanity forward, even in the hands of the most devoted worker in this cause. . . . Money only appeals to selfishness and irresistibly invites abuse. Can anyone imagine Moses, Jesus or Gandhi armed with the money-bags of Carnegie?"

—ALBERT EINSTEIN

"We're the party that wants to see an America in which people can still get rich."

—RONALD REAGAN

CONTENTS

INTRODUCTION

This book is borne of annoyance: a great bewilderment over the myth that continues to surround the presidency of Ronald Reagan. It gives voice to a vast swath of psychically disenfranchised Americans, millions of them, lumped most thickly in the urban areas on either coast, who never understood Reagan's appeal. For more than two decades they have stood by puzzled as this Hollywood actor and shill for General Electric, this obvious enemy of the common people he claimed to represent, this empty suit who believed in flying saucers and allowed an astrologer to guide his presidential scheduling, held sway over the American imagination.

Evidence is amassing to support their view. The bitter legacy of Reaganism—the subprime mortgage scandal, the near collapse of the financial system, widening income inequality, the emergence of Lockdown America, the obscene inflation of CEO compensation, the end of locally owned media, market crashes, blackouts, drug company scandals, rampant greed and materialism—is all around us. As D. H. Lawrence once wrote in another context, "The cataclysm has happened, we are among the ruins." But the controversy that once surrounded Reagan seems to have been banished from our public discourse. It is not that there is no public indignation over the state of our democracy. Americans are in wide agreement that the country has gone horribly off course, that Washington is now bought and paid for by corporations and is making little effort to solve the nation's most vexing problems. The great conundrum is this: *none of these unmistakable harbingers of American decline is being laid where it belongs—at the door of Ronald Reagan.*

In the two decades that have passed since Reagan left office, no nonacademic book has appeared making the case that his policies were destructive for America, even though that view is commonly held among members of the left-liberal intelligentsia. We have just finished a presidential campaign season marked by an unseemly competition among Republican aspirants to wrap themselves in the Reagan mantle. "I am a conservative Republican and I will remain so in the school of Ronald Reagan," proclaimed John McCain. "I took the exact same path Ronald Reagan took," insisted Mike Huckabee. In a *Time* magazine cover story headlined "What Would Ronnie Do? And Why the Republican Candidates Need to Reclaim the Reagan Legacy," political correspondent Karen Tumulty wrote admiringly that the former president "embodied the idea that progress comes from going up against the status quo."

The disconnect between the Reagan of myth and the Reagan of reality has been palpable in the media for years. Rarely in the history of the democratic world has a press corps been so blind to a leader's faults, so gullible in the face of a concerted effort by a small band of zealots to burnish an otherwise lusterless image. The so-called liberal media failed to utter a peep of protest in 2003 when *Esquire* magazine named Reagan "the greatest living American." This abjuring of all standards of evenhandedness by the media could not help but have a profound impact on public opinion. It explains how a 2001 poll by the Gallup Organization could find that Americans rate Reagan as the most popular former president, ahead of Kennedy, Lincoln, and Washington. His name adorns public landmarks across the country—the former Washington National Airport, any number of freeways, a medical center in Los Angeles, a Navy aircraft carrier, countless schools and office buildings, and a peak in New Hampshire's famous Presidential Mountain Range. A group called the Ronald Reagan Legacy Project has a goal of pinning his name to a landmark in every one of the nation's 3,067 counties, including a monument to rival the Lincoln Memorial on the Mall in Washington.

The apotheosis of Ronald Reagan was never more abject than in the coverage of his funeral. In death, as in the last years of his life, Reagan was revered in the media as a great patriot whose love of country and undying faith in American exceptionalism—the "shining city on a hill"—were his defining traits. He was lionized for his instinctive identification with the common man and for espousing the traditional values that had once been the backbone of the nation. He was hailed for an infectious optimism that restored the nation's faith in itself and put us on a path to the two longest spurts of economic growth in American history. The scant criticism of his domestic policies, almost none of it found in the electronic media, followed the same well-worn threads: his tax cuts and military buildup led to huge budget deficits, his administration was rife with ethical violations, his cuts in social welfare programs were seen by some as mean-spirited.

The script could not have been more adoring if it was written by Nancy Reagan herself. But it was also stunning in its myopia. For Ronald Reagan, when the layers of myth are peeled away, was arguably the least patriotic president in American history. He laid the foundation for a new global economic order in which nationhood would gradually become meaningless. He enacted policies that helped wipe out the high-paying jobs for the working class that were the real backbone of the country. This supposed guardian of traditional values was the architect of wrenching social change that swept across the country in the 1980s, the emergence of an eerie, overcommercialized, postmodern America that has left so much of the populace psychically adrift. Reagan propelled the transition to hypercapitalism, an epoch in which the forces of self-interest and profit seek to make a final rout of traditional human values. His legacy—mergers, deregulation, tax cuts for the wealthy, privatization, globalization—helped weaken the family and eradicate small-town life and the sense of community.

Not only the inner-city poor, but working-class and middle-class Americans in small towns across the country were the losers in the post-Reagan era. Because of deregulation, trucking concerns, bus companies, and airlines have eliminated much of their service to small rural communities, leaving them isolated and economically depressed in a society ever more dominated by the great population centers on either coast. Because of corporate consolidation, businesses are no longer owned locally and Main Street is gone. Companies made over many times by mergers and forced to tailor every decision to stock market prices have little loyalty to communities or people. Commerce becomes alien, unreliable, globalized. Plants are closed and companies are downsized, families uprooted, communities left without anchors. Reagan blithely ushered in an age of impermanence.

It is remarkable that Reagan took none of the blame for the corporate scandals that marred the last years of the American century and ushered in the millennium, since they were largely of his making. Without his tax, regulatory, and antitrust policies, there would have been no savings-and-loan bailout, no frenzy of mergers in the 1980s and 1990s, no unseemly scramble for overnight fortunes by arbitrageurs and raiders, no destructive obsession with quarterly earnings at the expense of long-term investment, no wholesale abandonment of ethics on the part of corporate executives. Nor would there have been an Enron or a subprime mortgage crisis, which sent shock waves through the global financial system and placed the country on the brink of its worst economic downturn since the Great Depression. The ultimate ramifications of the crisis are still not clear as of this writing.

The contagion of free-market purism has infected almost every sector of American life. It was hardly a surprise that so little of Reagan's real legacy was found in the journalism that followed his death. The very simplicity of the image the public took away from his funeral, that of a mythical Reagan riding off into the sunset of the country he loved, was itself a result of commercial values invading our most important institutions. The same government policies that fueled corporate mergers in other sectors propelled the increasing concentration of the media, which has resulted in a shallow and homogeneous presentation of the news that runs no risk of offending advertisers. In the days following Reagan's death, the media showed little interest in the minutiae of his presidency, dwelling instead on the Gipper's beatific smile, his sunny optimism, his long love affair with Nancy, the pageantry of the funeral, anything but his real effect on the world.

A typical moment was a *Dateline NBC* segment on Reagan's legacy in which correspondent John Hockenberry reported that in the late 1970s, America's torpor and self-doubt were swept away when "Ronald Reagan rode in from the West." Hockenberry gushed on with superlatives: Reagan was "larger than life," had "enduring popularity," was "a legend," "stuck to his guns," had a "personal touch"; his "achievements matched his soaring rhetoric"; "it would take more than a recession or James Bond adventure run amok, like the Iran-Contra scandal, to derail this president." Hockenberry and his guests spoke 114 sentences during the segment, only two of them containing criticism of Reagan's policies, and even those criticisms were dismissed in the same breath. Hockenberry said Reagan's policies "inflamed critics who claimed he did not grasp the complexity and contradictions of his own positions. But Reagan saw no contradictions. His feel for simplicity came from what seemed to be a basic sense of right and wrong, good and evil, and an old-fashioned ideal."

It cannot be disputed that there are legions of Reagan critics across the country. But why are they never seen on television or quoted in the media? Why is this dissenting view of Reagan's "heroism" never in the public eye? When CBS announced plans in 2003 to air *The Reagans,* a TV movie that presented Ron and Nancy in an unflattering light, there was such an outcry among Republicans—including a threatened advertising boycott—that the network canceled the showing and turned it over to Showtime, a cable network that had a fraction of the CBS audience. Television critics were quick to point out that it was unheard of for a network to pull the plug on a TV movie simply because of nit-picking over its accuracy. When it comes to media assessments of Ronald Reagan's presidency, the usual standards seem not to apply.

This book—focusing solely on domestic policy—is an effort to tell the story that architects of the Reagan propaganda machine have so zealously tried to suppress, an account of what the political cynicism and free-market zealotry of our fortieth president have done to America; how his legacy has decimated small-town life and undermined values that were once at the core of traditional conservatism; how it altered the American character by implanting an exaggerated sense of self-interest in every one of us at the expense of communitarian values. It is also an attempt to document the harm that Reagan's policies have brought to the average Americans who gave him such resounding victories at the polls. Reagan was fond of telling us that his entire life was shaped by the values instilled in him by his boyhood in Dixon, Illinois, a pastoral oasis with white picket fences, a tidy main street, and neighbors who looked out for one another. This identification with small-town America gave him the persona that was the key to his success in Hollywood and politics. "Reagan was Illinois come to California," wrote his most prolific biographer, Lou Cannon. "He was the wholesome citizen-hero who inhabits our democratic imaginations, an Everyman who was slow to anger but willing to fight for the right and correct wrongdoing when aroused." Reagan's speeches were filled with paeans to the common man: the farmer, the factory worker, the letter carrier, the fireman. He told them that they were the foundation of America. Their toil, their effort to build a more prosperous future for their families, was the backbone of our economy. It was a message that resonated with much of the country's lower and middle classes. Blue-collar whites from urban areas joined the rural folk in all the Dixons spread across the American heartland in delivering Reagan the presidency. They believed he was going to fight for them.

But therein lies the great myth of Reaganism, for his betrayal of the working people of America could not have been more complete. Thanks in large part to Reagan's policies, the two periods of economic expansion that followed his election did little for Americans in the middle and lower income brackets. While Reaganomics helped create huge fortunes for those at the top of the income ladder, it brought a reversal in the slow gains that the working class and the poor had made in the previous two decades. An exhaustive survey of wealth published by the Economic Policy Institute in January 2001—before the economic troubles that have plagued America in the wake of the Iraq War—painted a picture of rising inequality. Expressed in constant 1998 dollars, households whose wealth placed them in the bottom 40 percent of the country had seen none of the benefits of two decades of economic growth. Between 1962 and 1983, the average household net worth of that group had grown from $800 to $4,700. But by the time Reagan was out of office in 1989, that group had a negative net worth of $4,100; that is, they were in debt for that amount. Even during what has been described as the unbridled prosperity of the 1990s, that group has floundered, its household worth reaching only $1,100 by 1998. Trickle-down economics had proven to be a fallacy.

Nor were the benefits of the Reagan Revolution showered on the middle class. Between 1983 and 1989, the household worth of the middle 20 percent grew modestly, from $55,500 to $58,800, and then began declining, reaching $49,100 by 1995. Only in the second half of the 1990s did the middle 20 percent begin to see the benefits of prosperity, with its household worth climbing to $61,000 in 1998. Still, after the two longest spurts of economic growth in American history, the middle 20 percent of American households was on average only $5,500 richer.

The real winners in that economic growth were the wealthy. The top 1 percent of households saw its average net worth grow from $7.2 million to $9.1 million between 1983 and 1989, a 26.9 percent increase that far surpassed the 6 percent growth for the middle 20 percent. The next 9 percent at the top of the ladder saw its worth grow from $814,200 to $897,900, more than a 10 percent increase. And the wealthy continued to pull away from the rest of the pack in the ensuing years. The top 1 percent had a net worth of $10.2 million in 1998—a 42.2 percent increase from 1983—and the next 9 percent had an average worth of $1 million, a 24.4 percent increase from 1983. The middle 20 percent of households saw the net worth increase by only 9.9 percent in that decade and a half.

So for everyone except the already rich, there was no boom in the 1980s and 1990s. When the U.S. Census Bureau released new census figures in May 2002 on household income, the headlines in newspapers across the country expressed surprise that in many states inflation-adjusted median income had declined or had been essentially flat through the decade. The media had spent so much of the decade touting the lifestyles of the rich and famous, and heralding the benefits of prosperity, that they did not know how to react when the figures showed that, nationally, median household income had risen by only $1,200 in constant dollars between 1989 and 1999. And even that increase was attributable to the growth of two-income families and the trend toward more working hours. Some of the supposedly most prosperous states, like New York, Connecticut, and California, actually saw decreases in their inflation-adjusted median household income. Some economists and demographers theorized that the huge influx of low-income immigrants in key population centers had dragged down the median income numbers, but none went so far as to suggest that there was an enormous windfall for ordinary Americans that had somehow been missed in the numbers. The decade's prosperity had for the most part been limited to people at the top of the economic ladder.

Much has been made of the great democratization of the stock market in the 1990s. Conservatives have peddled the notion that regular Americans had shared in the stock market booms through their 401K and pension plans. But the numbers that emerged at the end of the century also belied those notions. While 52 percent of Americans in the $25,000-to-$49,900 income bracket owned stock in 1998, the monetary gains of the average household were insignificant compared to those of the rich, according to the Economic Policy Institute. Between 1983 and 1998, the average value of stock owned by the wealthiest 1 percent of the nation's households grew from $1.6 million to $2.5 million, while the value of stock owned by the next 9 percent of households increased from $100,000 to $291,000. But the stock owned by the middle 20 percent—including retirement funds—only increased from $1,600 to $9,200. The value of stock owned by the bottom 40 percent increased from $400 to $1,700. As the authors of the EPI report put it, the numbers showed that the stock market was of "little or no financial importance to the vast majority of U.S. households."

While recognizing the shortfalls of supply-side economics, even many liberals have reluctantly bought into the idea that the Keynesian regime was bankrupt by the 1970s. To one degree or another, they have come to accept the central fallacy of Reaganism: that the economic ills of the 1970s—the decline of manufacturing and the twin evils of high unemployment and galloping inflation—were the result of excessive regulation of business, out-of-control public spending, and a tax system that was choking our entrepreneurial spirit. But this is merely a testament to how effectively conservatism has infected the consciousness of Americans. No one—certainly not the mainstream media—seems to have noticed that Reagan's diagnosis of our economic problems has been debunked in its entirety, and not just by Keynesian economists.

In 1986, the Massachusetts Institute of Technology assembled a panel of experts in economics, technology, business management, political science, and other disciplines to mount an exhaustive study on the competitiveness of U.S. manufacturing. The findings of the MIT Commission on Industrial Productivity, as the panel was known, were debated before congressional committees and in conferences among corporate executives. The report's authors noted that in more than one hundred presentations and workshops conducted at major companies, the commissioners found that corporate executives were in widespread agreement with their conclusions.

And this is what they found: excessive taxes and regulation and high labor costs were not responsible for the loss of America's productive supremacy. Rather it was the myopia of U.S. industry, the refusal to sacrifice short-term profits in the interest of long-term investment in plant and equipment. The commission also faulted American business for not responding to the needs of customers and being much slower than their Japanese and European competitors in bringing new products to the market. Some loss of the world market was natural as Japanese and European countries rebuilt their industries after the devastation of World War II. But in studies of eight key industries—including automobiles, steel, and textiles—the commission found that most of the American firms had lost their competitive position because of poor decisions by executives, not because of macroeconomic factors like taxes and regulation.

The commission acknowledged that in some sectors of the economy a shortage of capital had hampered productive performance. But it said that when capital did become available, the industries tended to invest in areas that they viewed as more profitable than the retooling of factories and the development of new products. Perhaps most important, the commission concluded that the Reagan administration's encouragement of mergers and rampant speculation was feeding into exactly what was wrong with U.S. industry. "Only an extraordinary optimist could believe that the current wave of takeover activity is an efficient way to deal with the organizational deficiencies of American industries," the commission said in its report. "In at least one respect, its tendency to favor short-term horizons, we believe it is part of the problem, not part of the solution."

As is now well known, Reagan's supply-side policies failed to spur investment in plant and equipment. According to Harvard University economist Benjamin Friedman, the portion of national income invested in plant and equipment had been well over 3 percent in each of the three decades that preceded Reagan's election, but the period of 1980 to 1988 saw an investment rate of 2.3 percent. In none of the years that Reagan was in office did the rate exceed 3 percent. Instead, Reagan's policies led to two decades of mergers and speculation, which yielded huge fortunes for the upper class but entailed a loss of economic ground or meager benefits for most Americans.

While Reaganism has often been portrayed as the antithesis of the New Deal, it was more profoundly a repudiation of a long epoch of reform that, with some brief but notable interruptions, extended from the Populist era through the early 1970s. At the turn of the century, Progressivism brought about a political and cultural awakening whose reform impulses reached into every sector of American life: law, philosophy, economics, art, literature, education, the social sciences. The period brought about the creation of the Federal Trade Commission to protect the public from the most avaricious tendencies of big business, the enactment of important laws like the Pure Food and Drug Act of 1906, and the establishment of new rights like woman suffrage. Through an explosion of good-government groups, the average citizen began playing a greater role in public policy. Progressivism also spawned the concepts of business ethics and labor relations, the recognition that tending to the morale and working conditions of employees was smart management.

The combined sweep of Populism, Progressivism, and the New Deal opened the way for the remarkably affluent and egalitarian society that existed in the middle decades of the twentieth century, a golden era that has never been fully appreciated by liberals. Nor was it appreciated by Reagan, even though he was supposedly the embodiment of our halcyon past. With his incessant claim that reducing government intervention in the economy would return us to the good times of the midcentury, Reagan was conveniently forgetting that America's prosperity had reached its highest levels at a time when government activism—the legacy of Progressivism and the New Deal—was also at its peak. America came out of World War II with the common man a hero, the welfare state firmly ensconced, and the influence of labor unions at an all-time high. And yet it was also a period of high capital formation, rising profits, rising productivity, and increasing living standards for even the poor and the middle class. In 1957, even a left-leaning social critic like Max Lerner could call it "a people's capitalism."

Inequality and other social ills were still very much a fact of life in this people's capitalism. The epoch of the common man encompassed two periods of ascendant conservatism—the 1920s and 1950s—and at times coexisted with paroxysms of reaction like the Cold War, McCarthyism, Cointelpro, and the Jim Crow laws. People of color, women, gays, and other minorities were often not allowed to fully share in the gains of the white working class. The historian Howard Zinn has noted that there were more American blacks lynched during the Progressive era than any other time.

But alongside those unquestionable evils there arose a society more and more responsive to the needs of the lower classes, not just in the United States but in Europe. José Ortega y Gasset famously surveyed the rising power of the common man in his 1930 book, *The Revolt of the Masses,* arguing that the unprecedented influence of working people over the political, economic, and cultural affairs of Spain—what he called "the brutal empire of the masses"—was a crisis in the making, a threat to the wisdom, benevolence, and taste with which the aristocracy had shepherded the people. "You want the ordinary man to be master?" he warned in ominous tones. "Well, do not be surprised if he acts for himself, if he demands all forms of enjoyment, if he firmly asserts his will, if he refuses all kinds of service, if he ceases to be docile to anyone, if he considers his own person and his own leisure."

These dark portents were laid to rest with the emergence of New Deal liberalism and the great social democracies of western Europe, where the "brutal empire of the masses" turned out to be a more just society, where the working classes did indeed cease being docile and won higher wages, more leisure time, and greater government protection of their health, safety, and welfare.

Reagan stood against everything that had been achieved in this remarkable age of reform. His constant attacks on the inefficiency of government, a rallying cry taken up by legions of conservative politicians across the country, became a self-fulfilling prophecy. The more money that was taken away from government programs, the more ineffective they became, and the more ineffective they became, the more ridiculous government bureaucrats came to be seen in the public eye. Gradually government, and the broader realm of public service, has come to seem disreputable, disdained by the best and brightest college students planning their careers. And the image of government has been dragged down even further by the behavior of politicians, who, imbued with the same exaltation of self-interest that is the essence of Reaganism, increasingly treat public office as a vehicle for their own enrichment.

Reagan's brand of conservatism rippled across our society as thoroughly as did Progressivism, in ways that no one writer has fully explored. He disenfranchised the average citizen by inventing the soft-money machine that made large corporations the real power in Washington. He weakened the enforcement of labor laws and inspired union busters across the country by firing the more than eleven thousand striking air-traffic controllers and breaking their union in 1981. He empowered corporate executives to abandon the concept of loyalty to employees, shareholders, and communities and weakened the bargaining power of labor. He presided over the slow creep of commercial values into virtually every sphere of American life. Commercialism has invaded realms where it was once verboten: the nonprofit sector, law, health care, politics, public schools, public radio, and public television. Instead of public policy's influencing the corporation to fit the needs of society, society is shaped to fit the needs of the corporation.

That is not to say Reaganism represented a sudden rupturing of a liberal utopia. Reagan came into the White House at a time when it was widely acknowledged that Americans were in the midst of a spiritual and psychological crisis, not just unease caused by oil shortages, unemployment, and inflation, but a deeper ennui related to our very identity as a people. An array of social critics, among them Christopher Lasch, whose best-selling book *The Culture of Narcissism* appeared in 1979, attributed this bewilderment to the increasing self-absorption of Americans. The quest for sensory pleasure and personal liberation that for so many of the unenlightened had been the dominant ethos of the 1960s, laid the ground for the "Me Decade" of the 1970s, with its emphasis on health, personal well-being, and inner tranquility. The seventies were marked by a shift from public to private concerns, from antiwar protests and civil rights marches to Transcendental Meditation, macrobiotic diets, jogging, and other vehicles of "self-actualization." Americans had been withdrawing into themselves since the end of World War II, as the rapid suburbanization of the country and other social forces disrupted ties to family and neighborhood that were vital to our sense of identity, and more and more employees became faceless and powerless drones in the corridors of huge corporations. The new suburban middle class no longer sought fulfillment in God or community, but in material acquisition and the superficiality of status. By the 1970s, these trends had produced a spiritual crisis. Americans were stampeding to therapists to fill their inner emptiness. They had traded their country's shared sacrifice and sense of community for a culture of self-interest, what Lasch described as a "war of all against all."

Jimmy Carter recognized the disillusionment of his fellow citizens and sought, however feebly, to reawaken the communal spirit of America. With Lasch advising him, he delivered what has become known as the "malaise speech" in 1979. Often mocked as an exercise in hand-wringing that depressed rather than inspired the country, the speech—as of this writing—was the last fully honest message that a president ever delivered to the American people, and its diagnosis of our spiritual affliction could not have been more accurate:

> In a nation that was proud of hard work, strong families, close-knit communities, and our faith in God, too many of us now tend to worship self-indulgence and consumption. Human identity is no longer defined by what one does, but by what one owns. But we've discovered that owning things and consuming things does not satisfy our longing for meaning. We've learned that piling up material goods cannot fill the emptiness of lives which have no confidence or purpose.

It was a speech Americans did not want to hear. Ronald Reagan was far more attuned to the public mood. Rather than lament the shallow self-interest of many Americans, he celebrated it as a virtue. He echoed the credo of Adam Smith (or, more directly, the teachings of conservative economist Milton Friedman and his disciples in the University of Chicago School of Economics), which held that the bald pursuit of personal gain was the foundation of American prosperity. John F. Kennedy, in his inaugural speech, had urged Americans, "Ask not what your country can do for you. Ask what you can do for our country." Reagan turned that sentiment on its head, asking in his stock campaign speech, "Are you better off than you were four years ago?"

In the post-Reagan era, the talk of a spiritual crisis in America is no longer heard. We have accepted our psychic emptiness. Our socialization is now fully imbued with commercial values, consumption our greatest good. Many social critics in the immediate postwar era, ranging from the leftists Herbert Marcuse and C. Wright Mills to more moderate thinkers like William H. Whyte and David Riesman, were disturbed by the effect that corporate domination of society was having on the

American character. From infancy, Americans were programmed to be consumers. In what John Kenneth Galbraith called the "dependence effect," corporations not only manufactured goods but also had to manufacture the desire for those goods. If advertising—and society's value system—did not inculcate an ever-increasing propensity for consumption of automobiles, luxury homes, color televisions, and electric dishwashers, the American capitalist machine would shudder and come to a halt. This vision was haunting enough. The new corporate domination that Reagan unleashed on America is even more horrifying, for the products of our new information-based economy are no longer toasters and dishwashers but culture itself. For American capitalism to survive now, we must consume the effluvia of the entertainment industry, that vast synergy of books, movies, music, television shows, and video games, each in one way or another transmitting the ethos of materialism and consumption. The output of American capitalism is no longer in our driveways and our kitchens but in our heads.

In 1978, the Federal Trade Commission sought to enact regulations that would ban all television advertisements aimed at children under the age of seven. The proposal was prompted by studies showing that children that age cannot differentiate between programming and advertising. Despite support from the American Academy of Pediatrics, the National Congress of Parents and Teachers, the Consumers Union, and the Child Welfare League, the proposal was killed when Reagan and his appointee as FTC chairman, conservative economist James Miller III, came into office. Their allegiance was not to parents and children, but to the corporate interests lobbying against the regulation, including the National Association of Broadcasters, the Toy Manufacturers of America, and the Association of National Advertisers. Advertising aimed at young children now runs around the clock on Nickelodeon, the Disney Channel, and the Cartoon Network, as children spend unprecedented numbers of hours in front of the television set. Is it any wonder that children are more materialistic than ever, obsessed with status symbols, proudly wearing the brand names of corporations on their clothing? Teenagers no longer buy sneakers and T-shirts; they buy Nike and Abercrombie & Fitch.

It is ironic that Red State America, while uneasy about George W. Bush's foray into Iraq and the recklessness of his fiscal policies, delivered him victory in 2004 on the basis of his adherence to traditional values. Polls showed that among the voters who cared about values, the mindless and debased messages emanating from the entertainment industry were of paramount concern. How is it that Democrats could allow themselves to be identified with Hollywood trash? Mindless Hollywood blockbusters, the hyperviolence of the Schwarzenegger and Stallone movies, and the salaciousness and misogyny of gangster rap can hardly be blamed on the values of the 1960s counterculture. They are all products of the post-Reagan era, the result of major corporations—merged many times over in the age of deregulation—maximizing profit without a whit of concern for the integrity of American culture. Not only is the anger of rap music an outgrowth of the neglect of the inner city, but its emphasis on materialism and self-indulgence is perfectly in the spirit of Reaganism.

Considering the rampant materialism and corporate empowerment bred by Reagan's policies, it seems strange that he is considered a hero of American conservatism. So much of what Reaganism begot, with its upending of indigenous ways of life and its insistence that cultures everywhere adopt the same brand of commercialism, is an affront to what traditionally constituted conservative thought. Many of the seminal thinkers of the conservative movement in twentieth-century America, like Russell Kirk, Richard Weaver, and Friedrich A. Hayek, regarded major corporations as a threat to folkways and small-scale private property. It was, after all, not government but big corporations that did so much to wipe out agrarian culture. The former machinist or farmer now bagging groceries at Wal-Mart is not exactly a conservative icon.

Modern conservatism has its deepest roots in the Romantic movement of the eighteenth and early nineteenth centuries, whose adherents rebelled against the Enlightenment and the encroachment of science and secular values on the primacy of religion. They valued indigenous culture and human freedom over a society lorded over by reason and natural laws and the upheavals threatened by machine production and market capitalism. Thomas Carlyle, the eminent Scottish essayist and historian who has long inspired conservatives, lamented that the logic of mechanization had not only overtaken production but was bleeding into every aspect of human endeavor. "With individuals . . . natural strength avails little," he wrote in 1829. "No individual now hopes to accomplish the poorest enterprise single-handed and without mechanical aids; he must make interest with some existing corporation, and till his field with their oxen." Reagan claimed to stand for such individualism, but the spokesman for the ultimate corporate bureaucracy, General Electric, with its pioneering use of advertising and public relations to shape human desires, should fool real conservatives for only so long.

Reaganism stands for the type of conformity and homogeneity that would have riled the Romantics. Across the globe, the corporations empowered by Ronald Reagan peddle the same movies, music, and consumer goods—indeed, the same modes of lifestyle—to the peasants of Nepal that they do to the residents of Peoria. Ronald Reagan helped ensure that we in America are subject to the most stifling regimentation: cameras watch over us on public streets; police question us at sobriety checkpoints; we all buy the same frivolous consumer goods after getting credit from the same banks, but only after having our personal finances pored over by the same credit agencies; hitchhikers are arrested on the highways and the homeless ushered out of town squares. The bohemianism and political foment that once thrived on college campuses—to the disgust of former California governor Ronald Reagan, who dispatched state police to put down the cultural expression of the nation's youth—have largely disappeared. The television and radio spew mindless drivel—identical mindless drivel in city after city. Would conformity and regimentation have gladdened the hearts of the seminal conservative thinkers of the Romantic movement?

The appeal of Ronald Reagan to certain segments of the country is no mystery. America was deeply paranoid and insecure in the late 1970s, a time when oil shocks and resulting stagflation had threatened American prosperity to a degree not seen since the Great Depression. The invasion of Afghanistan by the Soviet Union and the seizure of the American hostages in Iran made us fear for our ability to stave off our enemies in a dangerous world. The economist Robert Heilbroner wrote of those years that "a great national illusion was gradually destroyed—the illusion that an invisible field surrounded the United States" that "held at bay the brutalities and irrationalities that seemed to be part of the life of other nations, but not our own."

Reagan was the perfect antidote to this gloominess and uncertainty. He seemed to personify the confidence and élan of America's past. It hardly mattered that he was misrepresenting that past as a laissez-faire utopia. What was important—at least to the 27 percent of eligible voters who pulled the lever for him in 1980, a year with record low turnout at the polls—was the intensity of his convictions. Such assuredness has deep resonance in American history. It is indeed the central tenet of the only important American-bred school of philosophy, pragmatism, which emphasized basing one's actions and ethics on personal experience rather than an abstract search for truth. "The true," wrote William James, a founder of the doctrine, "is the name for whatever proves itself to be good in the way of belief, and good, too, for definite and assignable reasons." In his famous essay *Self-Reliance,* Emerson had provided the foundation for pragmatism: "To believe your own thought, to believe that what is true for you in your private heart is true for all men—that is genius."

It is axiomatic that great men bend history to their will, and that the peculiarities of their own psychology, or their understanding—warped or not—of long-dead philosophers, can become the dominant ethos of an age. It is no less certain that the masses are more easily swayed by appeals to the emotions than to their intellects. Even a humanist like the theologian Reinhold Niebuhr could fault liberalism as the "gray spirit of compromise," lacking the fervency and power of myth. "Liberalism," he wrote, "is too intellectual and too little emotional to be a force in history."

But the genius of James and Emerson, while inspiring as philosophy and edifying to the individual in search of self-esteem and self-justification, while potentially electrifying on the campaign stump, is not necessarily a recipe for sound government or stewardship of something as complex as the American economy. In public policy, as in science, there are truths and there are untruths, and the wrong actions can have dire consequences. It has proven untrue that deeply slashing income taxes promotes investment and creates an increase in tax revenues; it has proven disastrously untrue that deregulating the financial sector benefits the consumer; it has proven tragically untrue that abandoning social-welfare spending and locking up millions of young black men solve the problems of the inner city. The fervency with which Reagan believed these things, and the riches they brought to certain Americans, did not make them true.

Our nation was founded on the principles of the Enlightenment, the idea of a society based on reason and democracy, not the perquisites of monarchs and aristocrats. The Progressive era and the New Deal rested on those principles. They brought intellect to bear on the most serious problems of society. Reaganism replaced Enlightenment thinking with a corrupted Romanticism that portrays free-market purism as an article of religious faith that is the real meaning of America. The answer to any of the economic challenges of the twenty-first century is to do nothing. Cut taxes, eviscerate all regulation of private enterprise, and trust the market to guide our fates.

With Reaganism has come an abandonment of all faith in reason and progress, and it has accrued manifestly to the detriment of the average American. It is the fate of that common lot of humanity that is the subject of this book.

CHAPTER 1

Forgotten Roots

It was as if the entire city of Dixon was holding its breath as the votes were counted. Citizens gathered by the thousands in front of a wooden platform in the middle of town, the local merchants, the clerks from the feed stores, the brawny men powdered with dust from the grain elevator, the sweaty workers from the steel plant down on the Rock River. They came, too, from the countryside, chugging along dirt roads in their pickup trucks, past the silos and cornfields and neat little farmhouses that spread out like an eternity on all sides of Dixon, until they reached the blacktop that would take them downtown. Most had spent their lives in precincts remote from the most important events of the world. They were not about to miss the festivities as one of their own, Dutch Reagan from Hennepin Avenue, was elected president of the United States.

Dutch had been little seen in his hometown since he gained Hollywood fame in the 1940s, but that hardly mattered now. Everyone wanted to lay claim to some piece of his memory. Among the revelers were dozens of people with placards hung from their necks with the words "Reagan Cousin." Vendors moved about the crowd selling Dutch chocolate ice cream and Dutch apple pie. Old-timers told stories of chance encounters with the great man: from his days as a lifeguard at Lowell Park, when he plucked distressed swimmers from the swift Rock River current; or the time in 1941 when he brought some Hollywood swells, including a young comedian named Bob Hope, to the Dixon Theater for a premiere of his film *International Squadron;* or the time he came for another movie premiere in 1950 and rode a white palomino in a parade down Galena Avenue.

Now Dixonites were poised to celebrate his triumph on a much larger stage. After the Dixon High School band led a torchlit parade across the newly renamed Ronald Reagan Bridge, and thousands of revelers danced to a country-and-western band and the high school's Twelve Bells junior and senior choir, then came the denouement. At exactly 7:15 p.m., on that first Tuesday in November 1980, an NBC anchor announced through a loudspeaker that Ronald Reagan had been projected the winner. A roar went up in the crowd, fireworks lit up the sky above the Rock River, and free beer began flowing at Republican and Democratic headquarters. The *Dixon Evening Telegraph* quickly ran off copies of an extra edition that, the paper proudly boasted, carried the first headlines in the world proclaiming Reagan's victory. Punctuating it all were the antics of two cowboys who trotted up and down Hennepin Avenue on horseback. Looking ignoble as it trailed behind them, silhouetted against the flashes of mortar in the dark November sky, was a riderless horse whose saddle was draped on either side with the words "Carter's Outta the Saddle."

Why Dixon should bear any enmity toward Carter was not immediately evident. Despite the runaway inflation, the oil shocks, and the distant troubles in Afghanistan and Iran, the previous decade had not been unkind to Dixon. The peanut farmer from Plains, Georgia, a fixture in his hometown even after he left the White House, did more for the common folk than would his "populist" successor. Contrary to conventional wisdom, much of the rural Midwest had regained hints of prosperity in the 1970s, with a slowing of the population exodus, and farming and manufacturing showing new signs of life. Dixon had shared in those good times. The city's median family income, adjusted for inflation, had grown by 9 percent in the decade, and the proportion of working people employed in manufacturing—the only route to decent wages for most Dixonites—had gone from 18 to 26 percent. The area's largest employer, the Northwest Steel and Wire Company in neighboring Sterling, was still humming in those days, with five thousand workers on its payroll.

Even the number of people with college degrees—not the associate degree available at Sauk Valley Community College, but a full bachelor's—had also seen a marked increase in Dixon.

Farmers in the region had perhaps the least to complain about. After the tough times of the 1960s, lowered trade barriers and the new dependency of the Soviet Union on the importation of American grain had brought about a boom in farm incomes and commodity prices in the 1970s. Farmland values had skyrocketed as banks and the federal government offered credit on the most lenient terms. In January 1981, the real assets of farmers—including land, livestock, machines, household furnishings, and crops, but not financial securities—were valued at $1,050 billion, up from $302 billion a decade earlier. In the countryside around Dixon, so much money could be made on land speculation and grain harvests that many farmers gave up their livestock; hogs and cattle began disappearing from the landscape, replaced by vast acres of corn and soybeans, loaded on trucks each autumn and driven to barges waiting on the Mississippi River. The bounty of the yeomen was also the bounty of the merchants in Dixon, many of whom dealt in feed and fertilizer and farm implements and the groceries and dry goods purchased greedily by the newly prosperous farmer. Galena Avenue, which rises to a steep hill in the middle of the business district, passes under Dixon's famous arch, and then plunges to the Rock River, was as bustling as at any time in its history.

But the region around Dixon was a conservative place, and the locals had no reason to doubt the economic nostrums of their prodigal son, who preached that a bloated federal government was standing in the way of America's renewal. Farmers with an innate distrust of distant Washington bureaucrats cheered his pledge to end the "quagmire of federal farm programs." Factory workers nodded in approval when Reagan said he would do away with environmental regulations that were costing jobs for people like themselves. And his pledge to end handouts to the "welfare queens" seemed only fair to the hardworking Dixonites. Of course, it was not only issues that drove Dixon into Reagan's camp—he picked up 5,755 votes to 1,445 for Carter—but the sheer excitement of having a local boy in the White House. The potential for a boost in tourism alone was enough to gladden the hearts of the local Babbittry. As the *Evening Telegraph* stated in its extra edition, the highway outside town would no longer be the "road to nowhere."

What most Dixonites did not know—and still have not figured out to this day—was that Reagan was no Jefferson Smith, Jimmy Stewart's character in *Mr. Smith Goes to Washington.* He was not an Everyman who was going to stand up for the people in a Washington bought and paid for by special interests. He had long before thrown in his lot with those special interests, the moguls of MCA, the executives of General Electric, and the Sun Belt millionaires who had ushered him into politics; his public persona, an approximation of Mr. Smith, was merely an ingenious bit of political theater that occasionally counted on the backdrop of wholesome little Dixon for maximum effect. It is hard to understand why more of the good people of Dixon have not understood this, because the signs were taking shape even before dawn had broken on the morning after his victory celebration.

The surest sign was the absence of Reagan himself. With Nancy at his side, Reagan made an election night telephone call to Dixon thanking the town for its support. He told a local radio station the next day that he would return triumphantly to his hometown. Everyone naturally assumed that visit would be in short order, and plans for the homecoming parade were put quietly into motion. The city fathers might not have been so optimistic if they had considered how often Reagan had actually come to Dixon in the past, and the timing of those visits. Before making a visit while campaigning for the 1980 Illinois primary, Reagan had been in town only once in the previous fifteen years, and that was in 1976, when he was waging a primary campaign against Gerald Ford and needed to accentuate his small-town roots. Some of his earlier visits had also carried the aroma of opportunism. That storied 1941 appearance was the brainchild of executives at Warner Brothers studio, who believed *International Squadron* could transform Reagan from a B-player into a star. To generate publicity, they came up with the idea of having Reagan accompany Louella Parsons, another Dixon native who also happened to be

Hollywood's most powerful gossip columnist, on a gala homecoming. The 1950 visit was for the same reason: a Universal publicist thought it would be a great stunt to promote the film *Louisa.*

So it was no surprise in 1980 that Dixon's homecoming parade would have to wait for an occasion that would serve the new president's political interests. Not only would the town not see Reagan in the jubilant days after his election; it would not see him in his first year in office, or his second, or his third. He finally came in 1984, when he was nearing reelection. In those giddy weeks of waiting for Carter to depart Washington, the Reagans did all their photo opportunities in California. Reagan greeted crowds at a church in affluent Bel Air a few days after the election and spent his days conducting business at the Beverly Wilshire Hotel. This was the community the First Couple really considered home, the place they would allow millionaires to buy them a retirement mansion after they left Washington, and the region they would one day choose for the Ronald Reagan Presidential Library.

The second snub was felt by Dixon High School's band, the Marching Dukes. Assuming the Dukes would be among the twenty high school bands marching in Reagan's inaugural parade, the school had ordered new uniforms, and the band had begun practicing its tunes. But then word came a month before the inauguration that the Dukes were not invited. The inaugural committee wanted the parade to be a slick television event, and only the top high school bands in the country—that is, those with enough money for flashy equipment and uniforms—would be invited. "We're concentrating entirely on television," said Robert Gray, the public relations man who was cochairman of the committee. "We've selected units on the basis of what will really portray well on television." The slight created such publicity that the committee relented and included the Dukes, but the episode left a bad taste in the mouths of some Dixonites.

That taste would only grow more bitter. The town that expected its fortunes to rise with the ascent of Reaganism quickly felt the sting of his fiscal policies. In keeping with his promise to reduce the size of government—to help pay for a major defense buildup and tax cuts for businesses and individuals—Reagan oversaw a dramatic rollback in domestic spending that quickly hit home in Illinois. His first budget cut deeply into the amount Illinois received in Medicaid, federal revenue sharing, education funding, and other aid, and the reductions did not take long to arrive on Dixon's doorstep.

An early casualty was the Dixon Developmental Center, a state-run home for the mentally retarded that was the city's largest employer. State budget cuts forced the closing of the center and the termination of its twelve hundred employees in 1983. Another round of funding cuts from the state helped produce a crisis in the Dixon schools, which by 1985 were so short on cash they were on the verge of eliminating their sports programs. The football team that once counted Ronald Reagan as a member, the high school band that played at his inauguration, the basketball team, the track team—these were all proud traditions that had survived even the Great Depression, but they were counted as luxuries in the fiscal straits created by Reagan's presidency. Helen Lawton, a Dixonite who had gone to high school with Reagan, sent him a letter asking if he could come up with money or lend his name to a fund-raising effort. He wrote her back, saying, "I deeply regret the problems facing Dixon schools, but there is little or nothing that can be done at the federal level." He later followed up with another letter telling her he was happy to hear her grandson would be able to continue on the school newspaper because the Dixon Kiwanis Club had donated money. "I am always pleased to see the private sector step in and help out," the letter said. The programs were saved when the voters approved a property tax increase in 1985, but the Dixon schools' financial struggle continues to this day.

More punishing for Dixon's residents was a steep recession—the steepest since the Depression—which was a direct outgrowth of Reagan's policies. In 1979, the Federal Reserve Board embarked on a plan to conquer double-digit inflation by dramatically tightening the nation's monetary reins. It was the nation's first full embrace of "monetarism," an economic doctrine that was part of the conservative revolution that swept Reagan into power, and the new president threw his support behind the experiment, even though it countenanced defeating inflation with the help of business failures, mass unemployment, and a disruption of the social fabric in communities like Dixon. The Fed's tight-money policies, together with Reagan's deficit spending, produced soaring interest rates and drove up the value of the dollar against other currencies. Almost overnight the high dollar left many U.S. manufacturers, already wounded by low-priced competition from overseas companies, at an even greater disadvantage in the marketplace.

The recession struck Dixon like a tidal wave. The region's biggest employer, Northwestern Steel and Wire Company, a massive edifice on the northern bank of the Rock River, was hemorrhaging money by the 1980s, unable to compete with cheap imported steel. It got so Peter Dillon, the company's president, could not even walk into a hardware store without confronting the dissolution of the company his grandfather had founded. "Every time I look at a sack of screws in the hardware store, I know that almost every one of those screws was made overseas," he told a reporter in 1984. As Dillon saw it, if nothing was done to make U.S. firms more competitive, "We're not going to have any manufacturing base. And to me that threatens our freedom." Reagan did nothing to make America's heavy industry more competitive. His idea of relief for big steel was tax cuts and reduced enforcement of regulations governing pollution and workplace safety. He also betrayed his following of free-market purists with some half-hearted attempts at limiting steel imports, at best buying the steel industry some short-lived breathing room.

Reagan had promised in his campaign to bring about a renewal of America's heavy industry, but his policies only hastened its decline. In 1982, domestic steel companies were running at 40 percent capacity, with three hundred thousand of their workers unemployed. Plants were closing at a rapid pace across the country, leaving massive hulks of real estate and great swaths of unemployed in Pittsburgh, Buffalo, Chicago's South Side, and many other cities. Big steel blamed its plight on high labor costs and the expense of complying with pollution controls and health and safety regulations, but the reality was far more complex. What had brought the steel industry so low was a paucity of investment in new technology. American firms had fallen behind their overseas competitors in modernizing plants so they could produce more efficiently and compete in the market for specialty steels. The salvation of American steel, as with other heavy manufacturing, lay in innovation, not just wage concessions and deregulation. But many steel companies, after losing money since the late 1970s, lacked the capital for such investment and were getting a cold shoulder from banks, which looked askance at the future viability of domestic steel production. Those companies that had access to capital were often plowing it into unrelated enterprises with better short-term profitability. A perfect example was U.S. Steel, which exhausted its cash reserve in the early 1980s with its $6.4-billion acquisition of Marathon Oil Company. Steel production by that point accounted for less than half the company's operations.

Only government could have provided the loan guarantees and other incentives for Big Steel to make the needed investment in its productive capacity. The precedents for such assistance were not hard to find. The federal government provided much of the funding that allowed railroads to spread across the continent in the 1800s. Government largesse played a major role in the creation of the domestic aviation industry, including the manufacture of the Boeing 747, the aircraft that would dominate international air travel. The postwar miracle of the Japanese economy could not have occurred if Japan's Ministry of International Trade and Industry had not helped direct investment into the most promising technologies. Even in the latter part of the Reagan administration, the lesson was learned anew when a government-subsidized consortium of technology companies, Sematech, combined research to enable the country to regain its lead in the manufacturing of semiconductors—at the same time transforming the economy of Austin, Texas, the consortium's base.

When Reagan imposed restrictions on steel imports in 1982, he justified the move by complaining that European governments were unfairly aiding their steel companies with public subsidies, including direct funding of capital. The corollary of that finding should have been obvious: government subsidies could also be effective in boosting the competitiveness of heavy industry in the United States. But Reagan and his aides mocked any notion of industrial policy as creeping socialism. Instead, through tax policy and deregulation, they subsidized mergers, speculation, and paper entrepreneurism, which generated fortunes on Wall Street but did little to invest in America's industrial future.

Having come into office promising a new direction, Reagan must be held accountable for the roads not taken. One of those roads, the acceptance of a government role in promoting industrial investment, might have saved the biggest employer in the region he once called home. Toward the end of his second term, Bill Clinton signed legislation to bring government aid to the steel industry. Under the Emergency Steel Loan Guarantee Act of 1999, Northwestern qualified for a $170-million government-guaranteed loan to modernize its production. But the help came too late. By then the company was down to fourteen hundred employees, its cash reserves were depleted, and no banks would back the 15 percent of the loan not guaranteed by the government. The final blow came in 2001, when dealers refused to ship the company any more of the scrap metal it was melting down and forging into steel in its new and promising "minimill" operation. Northwestern closed its doors after 120 years of operation, sending shockwaves through the region's economy. Retail businesses, school districts, real estate markets, health care facilities, and other sectors of the local economy were swept up in the fallout from Northwestern's long but steady decline. "We are going to feel this for a long time to come," Sterling mayor Ted Aggen said at the time of the closing.

But it wasn't just Northwestern Steel. Many other businesses in the Dixon area closed their doors or shed large portions of their workforce. The local carpenters' union reported in 1982 that 160 of its 216 construction workers were out of work, while the Lone Star Industries cement plant on the edge of Dixon laid off two-thirds of its 135 employees. While most Dixonites continued to support the president, if not all of his policies, many of the jobless began to realize he was not representing their interests. "Reagan's forgotten where he came from," Larry Sullivan, a Teamsters negotiator in Dixon, complained in 1984. "Out of the last twenty contracts I've negotiated, we only got a wage increase in three. The rest were hold-the-line contracts or give-backs." Lawrence Lally, an unemployed carpenter, quickly understood what has eluded so many other Dixonites. "He's no buddy of mine," Lally said of Reagan. "He hasn't done anything for anyone around here that I can tell. Seems like he spends more time in California on vacation than he does in the White House."

No Dixon constituency was more conservative and more supportive of the Reagan Revolution than family farmers. None to this day look more favorably on his memory. And yet none had a greater reason to feel betrayed by his policies. In the 1980s, farmers were faced with their worst crisis since the Depression, and Reagan only made the situation worse. Rather than make real efforts to save family farmers—that bedrock of rural America that should have been the core of his constituency—Reagan helped drive hundreds of thousands more of them into financial collapse while enriching agribusiness concerns like Cargill and Monsanto.

Worldwide recession put a damper on the demand for farm products in the early 1980s. The strong dollar—a product of the Fed's tight-money policies—priced U.S. farm products out of many foreign markets, a situation made even worse by the continuing fallout from Carter's embargo on grain shipments to the Soviet Union after the Afghanistan invasion. Farm commodity prices and farm income began a rapid descent. Most damaging of all, the enormous debt accrued by many farmers amid the speculation of the 1970s was suddenly an albatross. The Farmers Home Administration, the federal agency that had encouraged so much of the borrowing in the 1970s, became the Grim Reaper for many farmers the following decade, foreclosing on their loans and seizing their land.

In his rhetoric, Reagan's solution to the problem was the usual bromide: a reduction in federal farm programs and more free enterprise for the business of agriculture, which he said would be the salvation of the family farmer. "The answer to our farm problems cannot be found in sticking with discredited programs and increasing government controls," the president said in an address on farm policy in 1985. "The answer can only be found in our ability to help our entire agriculture industry stand on its own feet again." It was the height of disingenuousness, because his administration was about to embark on a program that would dramatically increase farm subsidies, for the benefit not of the small farmer but of the large landholder and the agribusiness. This sleight of hand was achieved through passage of the 1985 farm bill, which aimed to boost agricultural exports by lowering commodity prices to a point where they would be competitive on the world market. Corn, which at that time cost an average of $3.25 to grow, would be sold at as low as $1 a bushel by the middle of 1986. Farmers would be compensated for their losses with federal subsidies known as "deficiency payments."

The farm bill failed miserably in improving the competitive positions of American farmers. The U.S. share of the world wheat market, 44 percent in 1981–1982, fell to 26 percent before rebounding to 37 percent in 1988–1989. Coarse grains slipped from 54 percent to 39 percent and then rose again to 52 percent. More inexcusable, the deficiency payments amounted to a healthy subsidy for large farms but did little for middle-sized family farms, which defaulted on their loans in record numbers. The American Bankers Association reported that more than four hundred thousand American farm families lost their land between 1985 and 1989 alone. And yet the cost of federal farm programs grew from some $7.32 billion in 1984 to a record $25.8 billion in 1986—15 percent of the federal budget deficit for that year.

But it would be a mistake to call the policy a failure, since it performed mightily for agribusiness concerns, the constituency that really mattered to Reagan. Depressed grain and livestock prices meant a windfall for grain-trading companies like Cargill and Continental Grain, which essentially were getting their raw materials at a lower cost. These and other large agribusiness concerns saw their profits soar in that period. Food processing and wholesaling became one of the most profitable U.S. industries in the 1980s, second only to America's health industry in return on equity, averaging 18.4 percent over eleven years. The agribusiness giants were not passing on the low commodity prices to consumers; they were putting the money in their pockets. Whereas the prices paid to farmers dropped by 40 percent between 1980 and 1989, consumer food prices increased 36 percent in the same period. In the middle of America's farm crisis, Cargill, at the time the world's largest agribusiness, increased its profits by 66 percent to $409 million in 1986, its highest pretax profit in a dozen years. And it managed to do this at a time when its sales were flat. That $25.8-billion subsidy was a huge pot of corporate welfare for agribusiness.

While the problems of a troubled industry like steel defied easy solutions, there were sensible proposals for bailing out the family farmer without lining the pockets of agribusiness. Senator Tom Harkin of Iowa and Representative Bill Alexander of Arkansas proposed a competing farm bill in 1985 that would simply have set a minimum price for farm goods to give even small operators a fair return. It also would have taken some acreage out of production and promoted soil conservation. The bill had support from House Republicans from rural areas, but it met stiff resistance from the White House and strong lobbying from agribusiness concerns like Ralston Purina and the National Food Processors Association. It also did not help that it encountered opposition from some urban Democrats, who feared it would raise food prices for the poor. Harkin, acknowledging the possibility of a 4 percent price increase on supermarket shelves, said it was equivalent to the price increases that follow a boost in the minimum wage for urban workers. The legislation still would have required taxpayer subsidies, but the money would have flowed to small farmers instead of corporations. Clearly, if Reagan had supported Harkin's bill, if he was truly committed to the future of the family farms that surrounded his hometown, the measure would have become law.

With the rapid decline of its two most important sectors, manufacturing and agriculture, a dark cloud gathered over Dixon in the 1980s. Business began pulling out of the city's commercial district. Three of the four farm-implement businesses closed their doors. School enrollment dwindled and the district went deeply into debt. Much of the safety net carefully woven over the previous five decades to help distressed communities was left in tatters by Reagan's budget cuts: housing assistance, food stamps, and legal assistance for the poor were all cut to the bone. Reagan's budgets decimated an array of programs that had existed to promote rural economic development.

Rural development programs sponsored by the U.S. Department of Agriculture's Farmers Home Administration were cut by 69 percent from 1981 to 1987, going from $1.67 billion to $490 million. Business and industrial loans and community facilities loans aimed at rural areas were reduced by 85 percent. Few funds remained for the retraining of people who had lost their jobs in manufacturing.

No Dixonites interviewed for this book could remember anything Reagan did, even behind the scenes, to bring relief to his old community. When a private group was trying to raise $410,000 in the early 1990s to qualify for state funding for refurbishing the Dixon Theater, the ex-president donated $1,000. In 1984, a group of Dixon business owners desperate to reverse the town's fortunes formed a Hometown Heritage Foundation that offered a $10,000 bounty to anyone who lured a business with at least one thousand employees to Lee County. Just as he had refused to help Dixon's schools, Reagan agreed to be honorary chairman of the foundation's effort but made it clear he would be of no help in recruiting businesses. "He agreed to accept the post on the condition that his name not be used to attract business to the community," foundation director Bob Hamilton explained. Some might agree that a president should look out for the country as a whole and not favor any one community. But in Reagan's case, such pieties struck a false note. The president who once put in a call to a *Los Angeles Times* critic to help Buddy Ebsen, whose wife was happy to wear expensive jewelry loaned to her by Bulgari and who allowed oil company executives to redecorate the White House living quarters after he deregulated their industry—this is the man who suddenly was seized by a sense of ethics when it came to calling in some favors for his hometown.

The two decades since Reagan left office have not exactly brought about a renaissance in his hometown. If the 1990s were a time of prosperity, places like Dixon were somehow left out of the feast. No Lexus-driving investment bankers sip lattes in the Dixon Starbucks, because there is no Starbucks and no Lexus dealer. Anyone who wants to buy a Lexus has to drive an hour to Rockford. Dixon's sidewalks are not decorated with cobblestone and faux nineteenth-century streetlamps. There are no signs of redevelopment downtown, no waterfront esplanades or shimmering glass gallerias. Nor is there much retail activity on Galena Avenue, just state or county government buildings, a few nondescript office complexes, and a handful of taverns that don't seem to ever have anyone in them. Anyone who wants dry goods or groceries has to go to Walmart, which opened a store on the edge of Dixon in 2005.

For two decades, we have been regaled with tales of fabulous riches being made on either coast, the million-dollar bonuses on Wall Street and the dot.com millionaires in Silicon Valley. But none of that opulence has flowed to Dixon. The city's inflation-adjusted median family income, which had grown in the 1970s, actually declined by 9.1 percent between 1979 and 1999, the latter year being the peak of the nation's supposed economic boom, before the meltdown of the stock market. That is in stark contrast to more affluent communities in metropolitan areas, where the rich truly got richer. In Wilmette, a suburb of Chicago two hours to the east of Dixon, median family income grew by 29 percent in that period, going from $94,789 to $122,515 in constant 1999 dollars. It might be tempting to think that the nation as a whole is more like Wilmette than Dixon, but that is simply not the case. In fact, Dixon did a little better than the nation as a whole. Nationally, median family income fell by 19 percent in those two decades.

Dixon bears all of the dreary stamps of Reaganism: deregulated commerce, decimated labor unions, a starving public sector, privatization, corporate mergers, and the growth of temporary work. Government once would have shielded Dixon from the harshest predations of corporate America, but the town's fate is now subject to the vagaries of the market. Because deregulation relieved telecommunications companies of the requirement that they serve underdeveloped areas, broadband Internet service came to Dixon years after it was a staple of life in Wilmette. Without an automobile, there is no way in or out of Dixon these days. The city was never served by a passenger railroad, and the deregulation of bus companies allowed them to drop unprofitable routes. Greyhound, the last company to bring buses to Dixon, closed its terminal in 2001 and left town.

The city thought it had pulled off a coup in 1988, when the USF&G insurance giant decided to open an office in town and built a two-story brick office building in the middle of the commercial district on Galena Avenue. A drab square box with an unsightly concrete parking structure attached to its front, the building was hardly a good fit with the beaux arts facade of the historic Dixon Theater across the street or the nineteenth-century architecture of the nearby Lee County Courthouse. But at least USF&G's new building was a sign of vitality—that is, until the company abandoned it. The frenzy of merger activity that Reagan did so much to unleash came home to Dixon in 1998, when St. Paul insurance acquired USF&G with the express intention of laying off thousands of workers and shedding unprofitable insurance accounts. St. Paul quickly closed the Dixon office, leaving an empty office building in the middle of town.

In another sign of the times, the first floor of the insurance building has been occupied by Manpower Temporary Services, a company that makes money picking through the detritus of America's industrial economy. If a local manufacturer needs a supply of nonunion, low-wage workers who get no benefits and can be jettisoned quickly if business slows down, it goes to Manpower Temporary Services. The people who used to have dignity farming the land or producing steel now must grovel for whatever kind of labor Manpower will dish out on a temporary basis. On any given day, one can look through Manpower's windows and see men and women sitting at tables, staring vacantly at video screens training them for their next minimum wage position.

One company that utilizes Manpower's services is Rayovac, a battery manufacturer that opened a $20 million plant on Interstate 88 outside Dixon in 2003. Rayovac left its longtime home in Madison, Wisconsin, in large part so it could get rid of unionized production workers—whose pay averaged $13.50 an hour—and hire nonunion help in Dixon for $8.50. The state of Illinois came up with a $4.1-million package of incentives, including infrastructure work, to lure what was then the nation's third-largest battery maker. It even agreed to allow Rayovac to build its plant under a code name so local and state officials in Wisconsin—and Rayovac's employees—would not know about the move until it was happening. Dixonites were ecstatic about the new plant, especially when they saw its employee workout center and the big-screen television and desktop computers in the employee lounge. But the firm is no substitute for the high-wage employers of Dixon's past. The battery maker employs only three hundred people year-round, filling its seasonal employment needs with temp workers from Manpower.

On the second floor of USF&G's old building is the Dixon Chamber of Commerce. The Chamber's president, Jim Thompson, is an amiable man whose broad smile never seems to fade, even when he talks about the city's woes, what he calls "the hard pills to swallow." Thompson's father was a school chum of Ronald Reagan's and one of the townsfolk who put together the celebrations on those few occasions when Reagan the movie star made a homecoming. The wall next to Thompson's desk is plastered with photographs of the fortieth president from all phases of his life. But Thompson knows that memories of its most famous son are not enough to bring about his city's economic revival. His job is to bring businesses and well-paying jobs to the area, an effort that he said is hampered by the shortage of workers with college degrees or any other marketable skills. The first thing businesses ask when they consider moving into the area is whether there is an intelligent workforce, people with problem-solving skills and a knowledge of computers. "One of our real struggles we see in this area—and I think everywhere else in the country—is to acquire a quality and an educated enough workforce to be able to staff those positions," he said. "It takes a lot of training and education because the jobs have become a little more technical. We've seen robotics come in, we've seen automated factory lines. I wonder in another few years whether we are actually going to be able to find people to fill these jobs."

Not the way things are going. Educational opportunities in Dixon simply have not kept pace with those in more privileged areas of the country. The portion of Dixon's adults with a bachelor's degree or better had increased from 9 to 12 percent in the 1970s but then hit a plateau. Only 12.7 percent had finished college in 2000, virtually the same percentage as two decades earlier. Again, the picture was far brighter in the silk-stocking suburb of Wilmette, where the portion of adults with a college education increased from 54 percent in 1980 to 73 percent in 2000. In recent years, only 25 percent of Dixon High School's graduates reported on average that they were going on to a four-year college.

Everyone in Dixon knows the town has to do better training its young people for competition in the global economy, but the post-Reagan tradition of neglecting the public sector has meant that the funds simply are not available for the job. In the 1980s, state and federal aid to Dixon's schools dropped by 23 percent when adjusted for inflation. It rebounded slightly in the 1990s but in 2004 was still down significantly from its level the year Ronald Reagan was elected president. Overall spending for the schools, when local revenues are also included, grew to some degree, but Robert Brown, Dixon's superintendent of schools, said the increase has gone largely toward salaries and benefits, maintenance of the physical plant, and new requirements for special education. He said there has been virtually no expansion of mainstream educational programs in the last decade and a half.

Brown agreed to be interviewed about the schools as long as he was not asked to say anything negative about Ronald Reagan, a man who had meant so much to the community he serves. But he was not so reticent in discussing the lack of investment in the future of Dixon's children—the neglect of a system without enough computers, inadequate science labs, and a minimum of advanced-placement courses. Still struggling with the aftershocks of an economic crisis in 2003 in which officials instituted fees for school events and increased class sizes to keep from cutting programs, Dixon cannot even consider luxuries like new science labs. New education programs or an expanded teaching staff is out of the question. The implication is clear: Dixon's schools—and its children—will continue to fall behind. "We are in a world economy," Brown said. "We have to be able to compete. We need more time in the classroom. We need better tools. We need to be able to bring in outside resources. If we don't do that, we will not compete; we cannot compete on the dollars we are being given today."

Reagan's plan for bettering American education was privatization: give parents tax credits for money they spend on private school tuition and the public schools will improve their programming to compete. The proposal has become a rallying cry for conservatives across the country in the last two decades. But Brown, superintendent of the school system that educated a future president, said privatization is not the answer. "Then you've got the haves and the have-nots," he said. "If it's privatized, the better kids are going to go to the better schools. The better schools will not put up with special ed problems, will not put up with dysfunctional family problems, will not put up with the low-income problems. You're going to have the haves over here and the have-nots over there. If you're trying to run a democracy with that kind of spread, it's a formula for disaster."

With all that is disquieting about Dixon's schools and the future of its employment base, the city's leaders pin a lot of hopes on the local industry that has grown up around the adulation of Ronald Reagan. The shrines to Reagan, paid for by donations from wealthy businessmen, greet a visitor at every turn. A blown-up picture of young Reagan in his lifeguard suit even overlooks the pool in the local Comfort Inn. Reagan came to Dixon only once after he left the White House—a total of four visits between the 1960s and his death—but others have tended carefully to his flame. There are plaques in his memory at Lowell Park, in the public library, in City Hall, in the high school, and along the waterfront. A grim replica of the Berlin Wall, complete with cold war graffiti and rusty barbed wire, is in the middle of town, accompanied by yet another plaque with Reagan's immortal words, "Mr. Gorbachev, tear down this wall."

Hennepin Avenue, a charming street of Victorian and colonial homes that slopes southward from the Rock River, was dedicated as Reagan Way in 2002. Unlike other houses on the street, most of which could use a paint job or a new roof, the Reagan boyhood home, a modest wood-frame affair at number 816, is painstakingly refurbished. On an adjoining lot, a bronze statue of Reagan sits in the middle of a small park. Four blocks to the north, the old South Side School, which Reagan once attended, has been lavishly renovated as the Dixon Historic Center. Its chestnut woodwork has been fully restored, period furniture was gathered for Reagan's old classroom, visitors are greeted with a portrait of the president made entirely of jellybeans, and bronze statues of the Gipper greet visitors in the stairwells.

Only for the Reagan boyhood home and the historic center, private interests have donated more than $10 million to celebrate Reagan's heritage. The people behind that money are the usual specimens of ethically challenged businessmen who so happily genuflect before Reagan's image. The statue next to Reagan's home was donated by Dwayne O. Andreas, former chairman of Archer Daniels Midland, the agribusiness giant whose corrupt practices were revealed in federal court in 1998 when Andreas's son and another executive were convicted of price-fixing. Much of the rest was donated by Norman Wymbs, a wealthy Florida businessman who has been fanatical in his efforts to promote Reagan's image, writing two embarrassingly hagiographic biographies that he allowed Reagan to proofread before publication.

Just how devoted Wymbs is to the public trust was revealed in 2002, when President George W. Bush signed legislation allowing the federal government to purchase Reagan's boyhood home and operate it as a national historic site. As of 2006, the home was staffed entirely by volunteers, had no Web site, and was closed for most of the winter. Making it a national historic site would have allowed it to be professionally operated in perpetuity, erasing any questions of what would happen to it when the elderly Wymbs passed away. But Wymbs, who was the longtime chairman of the Ronald Reagan Home Foundation, rejected the government's offer of $420,000 for the property, saying it was a fraction of the $5 million he and other donors had put into it. "We're talking about work that has been done over twenty years," Wymbs said. "Everyone in town has contributed to this in one way or the other. And I can't go back to them and insult them by saying we're going to virtually give this away to the federal government."

It is hard to imagine a more specious rationalization for turning down the offer. Ostensibly, the purpose of the donors was to preserve the home and make it accessible to the public, a mission that the U.S. Department of the Interior would carry out more dependably in the long term than a small private foundation. It seems clear that Wymbs was irked that the government was not willing to have the taxpayers reimburse him for what he had put into the property. In his concern for his personal wealth and his disdain for our nation's government, he would have made Reagan proud.

In its quiet corner of the country, nestled among the hills rising from the Rock River, Dixon is still an outwardly pleasant community. The tulips bloom along Galena Avenue every spring, and the people exude a warmth reminiscent of Ronald Reagan at his best. But there is an eerie silence even in the center of town, a listlessness that reminds a visitor that the time in this country when such communities had relevance and vitality is coming to a close. It is not that Dixon is afflicted with grinding poverty like Youngstown or Flint. Young men don't kill each other over drug turf and babies aren't found in dumpsters. The town is simply without the energy and industry that once characterized the small-town Midwest. Everything that is inspiring or pleasing to the eye belongs to the past. The splendor of the Lee County Courthouse and the Dixon Theater, the handsome Victorian homes, even the great brick mills along the river—these all seem like vestiges of an ancient people who once inhabited this place but are now known only for their ruins, like the Mayans or the Sumerians. The society that has overtaken the magnificence of their civilization is spreading on the edges of town, a cheap tableau of fast-food restaurants, chain motels, Walmarts, and vinyl-clad modular homes. Move further out and a more pleasing vista beckons. The countryside looks much as it did fifty years ago. Lonely farmhouses and silos still stand like sentinels in the middle of vast horizons of agriculture. But knock on the doors of those farmhouses and the illusion crumbles. The paint is peeling and plastic covers the windows. Many are empty, and others are rented to people who have nothing to do with farming. That august property surrounding the home is among tens of thousands of acres belonging to a distant agribusiness concern. The Dixon of Reagan's youth has disappeared.

CHAPTER 2

Two Views of America

One morning in the spring of 1981, Tip O'Neill decided that the political fight of his life was over, and he had lost. It may have been only a brief lapse in his famous political ardor, but it was enough to kick the last leg out from under American liberalism.

Reporters had arrived in O'Neill's office just before noon expecting nothing more epoch shattering than their regular briefing with the Speaker of the House of Representatives. O'Neill had made a ritual of meeting with the press before taking to the floor of the House each day, and he used the sessions to masterful effect. He would settle himself behind a desk in the antebellum elegance of the Speaker's ceremonial room, his suit jacket studiously rumpled and a cigar jutting from his thick red fingers. With equal measures of charm and bravado, he would lash out at Ronald Reagan's latest affront to the workingman. It was more the performance of an old Irish ward heeler than a modern politician, but the reporters loved it. He was like a thespian playing the role of Reagan's gadfly to thunderous applause night after night, and then the show abruptly closed.

The months of raw politicking had taken a secret toll on the aging Speaker. Only his closest aides knew how effectively the public face had masked the inner exhaustion. The signs were there if anyone looked closely enough. His gait was slower, his eyes were puffy, and his cheeks, mottled with broken blood vessels, were more crimson than usual. Tip had never been a robust physical specimen. His body was always as pink and round as a brisket, a vestige of North Cambridge taverns and dinners of red meat and Scotch at Duke Ziebert's on Capitol Hill. His hair was a white mop which, like Tantalus, he was condemned to keep brushing futilely away from his eyes. He was loved for his political courage and his abiding concern for the workingman, not his angular physique. But on the morning of April 27, 1981, even those formidable assets, the energy and boundless enthusiasm that had sustained him throughout his public life, were about to fail him.

He could not have chosen a worse time to lose his political footing. With Reagan's election the previous November and the Republicans' new majority in the Senate, Democratic control of the House was the last liberal fortification blocking the advance of the Reagan Revolution. O'Neill, the highest-ranking member of the Democratic Party, had spent weeks attacking Reagan's program, which, he told reporters over and over, was hardly revolutionary, just a bald effort to slash programs for the poor and hand out generous tax relief to the wealthy. Now his first major battle with Reagan's minions was entering its decisive phase. The next day, the president was to address a joint session of Congress, the denouement of the administration's effort to coax moderate Democrats to defy their leadership and give Reagan's tax and budget proposals victory in the House. And the press, well aware that an epic struggle for America's values was being waged on the banks of the Potomac, was assembled the day before the speech to hear the Speaker's plan for repelling the Reagan onslaught.

Now sixty-eight years old and in politics for a half century, O'Neill was never one to shy away from a fight. He had cut his teeth in the clubhouses of Boston, where politics had always been a blood sport. He had been at odds with presidents before, most notably when he became the first member of the House leadership to turn his back on Lyndon Johnson's prosecution of the Vietnam War. Later, as House majority leader, he had played a major behind-the-scenes role in pressing for the impeachment of President Richard Nixon. But in those battles, he was up against beleaguered presidents slipping into political oblivion. This time he was fighting a new kind of enemy. Reagan's handlers, particularly Michael Deaver, the White House deputy chief of staff, had made deft use of Reagan's communications skills to sell the administration's policies. More than any administration before them, they turned the White House into a public relations machine. They kept Reagan's unscripted comments to the press at a minimum, carefully orchestrating news events where the actor's lines had been supplied in advance. In the words of James Lake, press secretary of Reagan's 1984 campaign, Reagan was "the ultimate presidential commodity . . . the right product."

The use of Madison Avenue techniques to sell presidents was not entirely new. Dwight Eisenhower kept an advertising firm on retainer throughout his first term. Nixon's use of television and advertising techniques were decisive in the 1968 election. But it was unprecedented for a president to be so thoroughly stage-managed by his staff. To a large measure, national policy had been reduced to a series of performances by a celluloid president, and so effectively that O'Neill was unable to compete. He came off as a rumpled, cigar-chomping old pol defending a system of big government that Americans had seemingly rejected at the polls, blaming it for the economic torpor of the 1970s. Reagan was a smooth, handsome, immaculately tailored movie star who had just won forty-two states by proclaiming "morning in America." To the degree that it was a contest of public relations, it was no contest at all.

Never before had O'Neill needed to compete on this level. He had spent his career as the consummate backroom politician, rising through the congressional leadership on the strength of his personality and a careful nurturing of political loyalties over three decades in the House. Even after his colleagues chose him as Speaker in 1977, he continued to act as a relic of the pretelevision age. He had little use for the staged news events and scripted sound bites that many of his colleagues used to put an artificial gloss on their images. O'Neill needed no gloss on his image. His unpolished mien was that of millions of workingmen on bar stools across America. He had become the most recognizable Speaker in history by perfectly enunciating the discontents of the working class.

It was a role that came naturally to him, for he was truly a child of the proletariat. He was raised in the blue-collar precincts of North Cambridge, Massachusetts, the son of a union bricklayer who had been elected to the local city council and later was appointed superintendent of sewers, a position that enabled him to dole out jobs to his friends and neighbors. It was this upbringing that had nourished O'Neill's view of government as a protector of America's poor. Because of his father's public employment, O'Neill's family was able to achieve something of a middle-class life. They moved into a comfortable home in one of North Cambridge's better neighborhoods, and Tip and his brother became the first members of the clan to attend college. In the world of O'Neill's youth, public employment was often Irish Americans' only way out of poverty. Barred from respectable office jobs by the prejudice of Boston's Anglo-American gentry, the Irish relied on jobs as policemen, schoolteachers, and sanitation men to carve out a piece of the American dream. "In those days," O'Neill said in his memoirs, "local politics boiled down to one thing—jobs."

O'Neill was elected to the Massachusetts Legislature in 1936, the middle of the Roosevelt era and the New Deal, when the capacities of the federal government to make a difference in the lives of the poor seemed limitless. Decades later, when he encountered a hostile question from an audience about government handouts, O'Neill became indignant that anyone would denigrate the historic role of the federal government. He would look out at a well-fed group of Rotarians or engineers and remind them that their very families had no doubt benefited from social legislation like the GI Bill of Rights and federally guaranteed housing loans, which had helped lift generations of working-class people into the idyll of the American middle class. Nothing frustrated O'Neill more than the lack of gratitude exhibited by the new middle class, which he felt was begrudging the poor the helping hand that had been extended to previous generations.

In his lifetime, O'Neill had watched the image of the poor come full circle. They had begun the century wrapped in the ignominy of social Darwinism, which had nourished a view of the lower classes as predestined by genetics and breeding to live in squalor. The doctrine had been promulgated by the economist Herbert Spencer in the midst of England's Industrial Revolution in the nineteenth century, but it achieved its greatest successes decades later in America, where it served as the perfect rationalization for the new class of capitalists amassing great fortunes in the Gilded Age. If men, women, and children labored for squalid sustenance in the mills of Lawrence and Paterson, while the rich built their mansions in Newport, social Darwinists counseled them not to worry: it was a matter of "natural selection" and "survival of the fittest." To intervene even with private acts of charity—let alone government largesse—would upset the balance of nature. Thus was the social equality that Tocqueville had celebrated as one of America's great treasures dismissed as a romantic fantasy, devoid of the imprimatur of science. America's poor disappeared in a haze of factory smoke. For the leisure class of Americans, the less fortunate were vulgar and uninteresting, appearing in popular fiction and theater only as urchins and moral reprobates. When newspapers delved into big-city slums, it was only to chronicle the appalling crimes of their residents.

But a succession of popular movements—Populism, Progressivism, and the New Deal—helped raise the estimation of the working class in the public imagination. Social Darwinism gave way in the first decades of the twentieth century to new reform impulses germinated in the fertile soil of the Gilded Age. The poor were no longer seen as genetic mediocrities but as victims of heartless industrial expansion and the rapid growth of American cities. Jacob Riis's *How the Other Half Lives,* a graphic survey of New York slums published in 1890, shocked the nation and led to a spate of legislation setting health standards for the city's tenements. Muckraking reporters like Ida Tarbell and Lincoln Steffens, writing for *McClure's* and other mass-circulation magazines with a huge impact on public opinion, exposed the evils of industrial trusts and big-city machines. The uplifting of the poor was in vogue for the first time since the Civil War. The patrician novels of Henry James and Edith Wharton gave way to the gritty realism of

Dreiser, Hemingway, Dos Passos, and Steinbeck, with their noble—and often tragic—portraits of America's laboring class. In the 1940 screen version of Steinbeck's *The Grapes of Wrath,* the penniless and nomadic Joad family became Americans idols. "We'll go on forever," Ma Joad tells her clan in the film's last seconds, "'cause we're the people."

Our greatest leaders made respect for the common man a bedrock American principle. Woodrow Wilson told us that anything that "dismays the humble man is against all the principles of progress." Franklin Delano Roosevelt, speaking words that would have horrified his Brahmin ancestors, declared that the test of our nation was "not whether we add more to the abundance of those who have much; it is whether we provide enough for those who have too little." His words resonated across America, in small towns and big cities, in the salons of the wealthy and the cramped quarters of the poor. Within two or three years of Roosevelt's election, wrote the social historian Frederick Lewis Allen,

> one man in three at a literary party in New York would be a communist sympathizer, passionately ready to join hands, in proletarian comradeship, with the factory hand or sharecropper whom a few years ago he had scorned as a member of Mencken's "booboisie"; daughters of patrician families were defiantly marching to the aid of striking garment workers, or raising money for the defense of Haywood Patterson in the long-drawn-out Scottsboro case; college intellectuals were nibbling at Marx, picketing Hearst newsreels, and—with a flash of humor—forming the Veterans of Future Wars.

Those paeans to the poor were not just idle words. Tip O'Neill's lifetime had also nearly coincided with what Richard Hofstadter had called the "Age of Reform," the epoch encompassing the Populist and Progressive eras and the New Deal, which had helped soften the jagged edges of American free enterprise. A reaction to the rapacious capitalism of the nineteenth century, these three movements sought to curtail the excesses of big business and better the lives of the less fortunate. Children were taken off the factory floor and exposed to the benefits of compulsory education, leisure time was bestowed on the workingman with the forty-hour workweek, unemployment insurance and welfare ensured sustenance for those unable to work, and labor unions were given the legal right to bargain for higher wages. "Without this sustained tradition of opposition and protest and reform," Hofstadter wrote, "the American system would have been . . . nothing but a jungle, and would probably have failed to develop into the remarkable system for production and distribution that it is."

By the 1950s, in no small measure because of these reforms, America could boast of what Max Lerner called "a people's capitalism," a world where even factory workers could afford the trappings of middle-class life, a sturdy suburban home, an automobile, vacations at Disneyland. Republican mythology would suggest that private entrepreneurship, not government spending or regulation, spurred an enormous creation of wealth that lifted all boats, even those of the working class. But blue-collar America never could have mimicked the lifestyles of the bourgeoisie had it not been for the New Deal's legitimizing of labor unions and government subsidies for housing and education. The consumption that propped up our enormous gains in productivity in the period behind 1948 and 1973 would not have been as prodigious without Social Security, unemployment insurance, and other social welfare spending, which yielded disposable income to classes of people who otherwise would have had a diminished role in postwar commerce. In the two decades after the war, America achieved the highest standard of living ever known to mankind at a time when a robust public sector was accepted as a given.

This was the world in which Tip O'Neill had grown and prospered as a politician, but that world was now being turned on its head. The entire concept of government as a champion of the neediest was under attack. Reagan was in the vanguard of a movement that portrayed federal largesse as the root of the nation's problems. The programs that O'Neill felt had done so much for his working-class brethren had, in the eyes of the Reagan cadres, destroyed the work ethic of the poor and turned them into a generation of welfare cheats.

The Reaganites' view of the lower classes would have made the most inveterate social Darwinists proud. Only the new view of the less fortunate was even more malign. Whereas the social Darwinists had regarded it as sad but inescapable that elements of the population were genetically predisposed to hardship, the Reagan administration suggested that people lived on meager welfare handouts because that was the life they preferred. Edwin Meese III, Reagan's longtime aide and adviser, once told an incredulous group of reporters that the administration "had considerable information that people go to soup kitchens because the food is free and that's easier than paying for it." In other words, the poor were a bunch of freeloaders.

Meese's remark stirred up a minor controversy, but he was just taking a cue from his boss. For five years before his election as president, Reagan had been regaling audiences with tales of "the welfare queen," the Chicago woman who he said "had eighty names, thirty addresses, twelve Social Security cards and is collecting veterans' benefits on four non-existing deceased husbands. . . . Her tax-free income is over $150,000." It was not just the baldest demagoguery but also a gross distortion of the facts. The woman, Linda Taylor, had been convicted in 1977 of using two aliases to collect checks totaling $8,000. But the anecdote was a powerful tool for arousing the anger of white working-class and middle-class voters who were coping with tough economic times. Indeed, Reagan found it so compelling that he continued using it in the White House, even after the press had revealed it to be a falsehood. He told the story to foreign leaders and even had the audacity to resurrect the anecdote in a 1981 meeting with the congressional black caucus, whose members left the Oval Office steaming.

The Reagan administration was bent on undoing layers of reforms and social welfare programs that had been put in place during the Progressive era, the New Deal, and Johnson's Great Society. David Stockman, Reagan's budget director, said of the Great Society legacy, "Substantial parts of it will have to be heaved overboard." On February 18, 1981, Reagan had fired the first shot over the bow of O'Neill and his fellow liberal Democrats by using his State of the Union address to unveil a fiscal plan that would eviscerate many social welfare programs. To the enthusiastic applause of Republicans in the chamber, Reagan proposed a $41.4-billion cut in the federal budget for 1982 that would include sharp reductions in food stamps, welfare, housing aid, unemployment insurance, and other programs for the poor. The cuts were designed to pare millions of Americans from the largest social welfare programs, with an estimated four hundred thousand households to be removed from the food stamp rolls alone.

At the same time, Reagan proposed a $7.2-billion increase in military spending, a sharp decrease in corporate taxes, and a 30 percent reduction in individual income taxes, the latter measure designed to deliver the greatest benefit to the wealthiest 20 percent of taxpayers. The tax for the highest income bracket was trimmed from 70 to 50 percent. The measures amounted to a huge corporate giveaway. Many large companies with huge profits, like General Electric, would pay zero taxes over the next several years, or even get money back from the federal government. By 1983 the portion of federal tax receipts derived from corporate income taxes would drop to an all-time low of 6.2 percent, down from 32.1 percent in 1952 and 12.5 percent in 1980. The government would be drowning in red ink. Supply-side theory, which promised that a reduction in taxes would spur investment and actually increase tax revenues, turned out to be a fallacy. The president who had promised to reduce the size of government had instead produced unprecedented deficits that would dominate fiscal decision making for the next two decades. None of this, of course, was apparent on February 18. Reagan's speech was met with enthusiastic applause from the floor, and a Washington Post–ABC News poll over the succeeding two days found that Americans supported the president's economic plan by a ratio of two to one.

But O'Neill continued to play the part of the spoiler. As he sat behind the president during the speech, he could not resist leaning over to remind Vice President George Bush how he had described supply-side economics a year earlier in the New Hampshire primary: "Voodoo economics, George. . . . You don't actually believe this shit, do you?" But O'Neill's smart-aleck ways could not alter the political arithmetic: with the Senate now in Republican hands for the first time since the Eisenhower years and the Democrats holding a fractious fifty-three-seat majority in the House, little stood in the way of Reagan's program.

O'Neill was the first to admit he had underestimated the new president. He had almost fallen off his chair with delight two years before, when he first learned that GOP leaders considered Reagan a favorite for the nomination. He and Leo Diehl, his chief of staff and lifelong friend, were having dinner in Duke Ziebert's with Maxwell Raab, a former cabinet member in the Eisenhower and Nixon administrations. The conversation naturally turned to the election. "Max said, 'Reagan's gonna be our next nominee,' and we all laughed. We pooh-poohed him," Diehl recalled. "We said we'd love to have him. We thought we had a soft touch. The guy was just a movie actor. O'Neill said, 'Max, we'll do everything we can to see that Reagan gets it.'"

By the fall of 1981, O'Neill had realized the magnitude of his error. He was mystified by the spell Reagan seemed to have cast over the American people. The president's legendary skills as a communicator had caught the imagination of a wide cross section of America. Many traditional Democrats had crossed party lines and voted for Reagan, so taken were they with his vision of a renewed America. O'Neill wished those defectors could see what he saw: a president wholly unfit to hold the office. O'Neill was cordial with Reagan in their frequent meetings in the Oval Office, but he was appalled by his lack of knowledge about the issues. He viewed him as little more than an actor reading lines. Like other congressional leaders, O'Neill was astonished that in his meetings with him, even if there were just a few people in the room, Reagan would read his lines from three-by-five index cards. Never before had O'Neill seen a president with such disdain for the details of governance.

But the public was not seeing what O'Neill saw. The Speaker's popularity seemed to be falling as quickly as Reagan's was rising. As the leader of the opposition, O'Neill was speaking out against Reagan's program almost every day. He had emerged in the public eye as the chief obstacle to Reagan's revolution. Sensing his vulnerability, Republican strategists attempted to portray O'Neill as an anachronism whose politics were linked to America's decay. They had learned the power of anti-O'Neill images during the 1980 campaign, when the GOP aired a commercial with an actor portraying O'Neill as a grumpy, cigar-chomping pol whose car was running out of gas on the highway. The Republicans found the commercial to be popular among blue-collar and middle-income workers across the country. A man who had always valued his connection to working people was suddenly looking like a pariah. In the 1981 budget battle with Reagan, hate mail began piling up in his office. There were so many negative letters and phone calls that his staff kept him from knowing about the full volume. The specter of Reagan followed O'Neill everywhere he went. It got so he could not go out in public without being vilified. In airports, strangers would shout insults like "Leave the president alone, you fat bastard." The harassment was one reason he stopped taking commercial flights and exercised a Speaker's right to travel in government aircraft.

O'Neill had made concessions to what seemed to be the popular will. In March 1981, he had met with the House Republican leadership and agreed to an expedited schedule for votes on the president's economic program. He pledged that the package of budget and tax cuts would come to a full vote of the House by August 1. He later regretted not taking the advice of the left wing of his party, which felt he was being too accommodating. He could easily have used procedural roadblocks to delay votes on the package indefinitely. But he worried that the Democrats would look like obstructionists in a time of economic crisis and lose still more seats in the 1982 congressional elections.

Despite his halfhearted efforts at compromise, O'Neill was still ruffling feathers, even within his own party. Moderate Democrats feared Reagan's popularity and wanted more accommodation with the White House. They felt that the Speaker, with his endless posturing in favor of social welfare programs, was out of step with the public mood. O'Neill's hold on his own party was loosening. Intimidated by Reagan's impressive approval rating after several months in office, many Democratic congressmen feared their leadership would be unable to protect them if they became identified as obstacles to the president's program in the midterm elections. Some of the members even began talking of a coup to remove O'Neill as Speaker. In April, Les Aspin, a Democratic congressman from Wisconsin who was later elected to the Senate, wrote in a letter to his constituents that "Tip is reeling on the ropes . . . he's in a fog . . . he's not part of what is happening, and has no idea where to go." Even the press, of whom O'Neill had always been a favorite, seemed to be turning against him. Not long after Aspin's letter, *Time* magazine ran an article that compared O'Neill to an old prizefighter, "too proud to quit."

But perhaps most disquieting for O'Neill, he was feeling the heat in his own district. "All politics is local" was one of O'Neill's most famous quotes, and he believed it in his heart. Unlike some congressional leaders who were more residents of Washington, D.C., than their home district, O'Neill was in North Cambridge every week. He shopped for groceries with his wife, Millie, in a local supermarket and was a fixture at barbecues and political dinners. Although his district covered the liberal, affluent precincts of Harvard University, he got his real support from the backstreets; these were the people whose opinions mattered. And in the first few months of 1981, his crude political antenna began telling him that even his constituents were growing weary of his obstructionism. People who had never before questioned O'Neill's wisdom were stopping him on the street and telling him to open himself to Reagan's ideas. The Speaker's son, Thomas P. O'Neill III, remembers one poignant moment when an old family friend named Brendan Fitzgerald stopped his father as he was walking up the steps to his home on Russell Street: "He was very pointed. He said, 'You know America elected the guy, you ought to listen to him.' Now you have to understand the history of the Fitzgeralds and the O'Neills. Brendan Fitzgerald's mother brought my mother up. She was Grandma Fitz to everybody. For Brendan, ten years younger than my dad, always a complete loyalist, to say that; it really shook him up."

In this season of conservatism, the Republicans had all of the momentum, and the Democrats began to appear rudderless. An already popular Reagan looked even better to the nation after his robust recovery from the bullet that a delusional young man named John Hinckley fired into his chest on March 30, 1981. He left the hospital with his approval rating in the stratosphere, only 18 percent of Americans disapproving of his job performance. The Democrats needed to redouble their efforts to counter the Reagan Revolution, but instead they waffled. During Congress's Easter recess, at a time when they should have been reassuring disaffected members of their party, O'Neill and fourteen other congressman took a two-week junket to New Zealand, Australia, and Hawaii. While the Democratic leaders were relaxing at poolside with little umbrellas in their drinks, Reagan and his lieutenants spent the Easter break furiously lobbying congressmen for votes. Their prime targets were the so-called Boll Weevils, Democratic congressmen from conservative southern states where support for the president was as strong as anywhere in the nation. The White House offered these nervous congressmen a powerful incentive to support its program: a promise that Reagan would not personally visit their districts to campaign against them in the 1982 election. The strategy was clearly working.

As he sat down to face the press on the morning of April 27, 1981, O'Neill was weary. Part of it was the inevitable deterioration of an old man. A painful prostate condition that he had battled throughout his Speakership, refusing to get the recommended surgery, had been flaring up in recent months. At one point, the pain was so severe he had been flown by helicopter to Bethesda Naval Hospital. But the greater pain was the deterioration of his political position. Everyone in the room knew he was losing the battle for votes. The math was obvious to all of them, most of all the Speaker himself. Still, no one in the room expected what was coming. They had come to see a brave battle cry but instead were about to witness an abject surrender.

In answer to a question about the prospects for Reagan's program, O'Neill uttered words that surprised the political establishment. His years of experience in Congress, he said, had taught him "when you fight and when you don't fight." In this case, it was time for a retreat: "I can read Congresses and I can read legislators and they go along with the will of the people, and the will of the people is to go along with the president."

O'Neill's white flag caught the rest of the House leadership unawares. Jim Jones, the House majority leader, publicly disavowed the Speaker's comment, and he joined about a dozen other top Democrats in giving O'Neill a dressing down the next day in a closed-door meeting at Blair House. O'Neill was appropriately contrite and even agreed to put out a statement recanting his surrender. All of this was, of course, to no avail. By July, Reagan's entire program of budget and tax cuts had cleared the House, with the help of dozens of Democrats who defied their leadership and crossed party lines. The three-year income tax cut had been trimmed from 30 to 25 percent, but Reagan's fiscal blueprint was otherwise triumphant.

In later years, O'Neill would regard the first few months of the Reagan administration as an anomaly, a brief low point in his own struggle for the common man. He wrote in his memoirs that a deep hatred of the poor had gripped the American middle class like a fever and then disappeared in about a year. Democrats won back twenty-six seats in the 1982 midterm elections, and they managed to restore money to many of the programs Reagan had slashed. After the Democrats also regained control of the Senate in the middle of Reagan's second term, in 1986, O'Neill told the press, "The Reagan Revolution is over."

He could not have been more wrong. The revolution was just beginning, and its effects would reverberate further than anyone could have imagined while Reagan was still in office. O'Neill was too close to the events of the 1980s, too wedded to the narrow arithmetic of congressional votes, to see how drastically Reagan was transforming the country. Even if the 1980s are viewed through the prism of fiscal policy—which was essentially the view that O'Neill took in his memoirs—Reagan had a profound impact. While failing to eviscerate fifty years of welfare programs overnight, he dramatically altered how Americans viewed the role of government and the poor. He forced advocates of social programs into rearguard actions to protect what already existed while making it politically impossible for new programs to emerge. And this trend has continued in the years since he left office. It has become received wisdom, even among many liberals, that the U.S. government, which waged war simultaneously in the Atlantic and Pacific in the 1940s, rebuilt the industrial capacity of Europe and Japan in the 1950s, developed railroads, the computer, the nuclear bomb and the Internet, and put a man on the moon, is a morass of inefficient bureaucrats that cannot be trusted to solve any of the domestic problems facing the United States in the twenty-first century.

But the Reagan Revolution involved far more than just the neutering of government. Reagan and his lieutenants were pursuing a far broader agenda than anyone was aware in the 1980s. Over the next two decades, the forces that Reagan unleashed or greatly accelerated—the huge transfers of wealth, the vast restructuring of American industry, the disappearance of business ethics, and the insecurity of workers, communities, and corporate shareholders—would produce enormous changes in society. It would generate vast new fortunes for some while leaving the majority of Americans, wide swaths of the poor and middle class, struggling to make ends meet in a new and uncertain world. Big government was not stripped away in the Reagan years; it was just redirected to the needs of private enterprise.

Tip O'Neill knew he was fighting a battle for America's soul in 1981, but he could not have been aware of the enormous stakes. He thought if he could save a few programs and get some tax revenues back in the budget, the revolution would be over. His liberalism was like a house in the middle of a great storm. He struggled valiantly to fortify the weakest wall from the onslaught, never noticing that the rest of the house had already blown away behind him.

Their differences were far more than just political. Though they claimed an affection toward one another, these two Irish Americans brimming with charm, from the same generation, from the same wrong side of the tracks, Ronald Reagan and Tip O'Neill could not spend too much time in the same room without quarreling. ("Don't give me that crap," O'Neill once thundered at the president of the

United States as Reagan told one of his anecdotes about malingering welfare recipients.) Even on a personal level, they were separated by distinct views of the world. In so many aspects of their lives, their experience of childhood and family, marriage and parenthood, friendship and community—all the values that weigh so heavily on the scales of character—there were profound differences between the two men.

Despite the death of his mother when he was an infant, O'Neill's family life had been stable and nurturing. His father, as O'Neill biographer John A. Farrell has written, was "tall and austere, disciplined and punctual, nicknamed 'Lord Fairfield' or 'the Governor' by his neighbors. . . . He shaved every night before dinner and sat in the same pew each Sunday." The elder O'Neill had sworn off alcohol as a young man, becoming president of the St. John's Catholic Total Abstinence Society in Cambridge. These patterns of stability, minus the abstinence, were passed on to his oldest son. The younger O'Neill was married to the same woman for more than fifty years, had strong relationships with his five children, and spent his entire life living within a few blocks of his childhood home in North Cambridge. His neighbors were like family, and his friendships and loyalties did not change over the decades. If old friends from his neighborhood wanted to talk to him, all they had to do was dial his office, and one of most powerful men in Washington would get on the phone. His world was the wooden three-decker homes of North Cambridge and Somerville, where neighbors had known each other for generations and siblings often reared their families in the same building. Tip O'Neill's son, Thomas P. O'Neill III, remembers his father taking the pulse of his constituency by chatting with longtime fixtures in the neighborhood—a barber named Frank Manelli or a shoemaker everyone knew simply as John the Cobbler. "Even Jimmy Carter got to know John the Cobbler," said O'Neill III. "He would say to my father, 'What does John the Cobbler think?'" This was the place that shaped the political values that O'Neill brought to Washington, a place where the views of John the Cobbler mattered.

Reagan once described his childhood as "one of those rare Huck Finn–Tom Sawyer idylls," but the reality was more complex. He was born in a rented apartment above a store in small-town Illinois, the child of a loving and religiously devout mother and a hard-drinking father whose gifts as a raconteur were not enough to keep him regularly employed as a store manager and salesman. His father's unemployment was of such duration that at one point during the Depression, the family would have starved had not the father and Reagan's brother, Neil, got employment from the Federal Emergency Relief Administration. (As Garry Wills put it, "The New Deal bailed the Reagans out.") In contrast to the rootedness of the O'Neills, the severe alcoholism of Reagan's father and his sales positions kept the family constantly on the move. The future president changed homes nearly a dozen times in his childhood, including five times in Dixon, the small Illinois town where he went to high school. This nomadic life left him with few lasting friendships. As a boy, he would play alone with lead soldiers for hours.

After Reagan left Dixon, he never returned for any length of time. He never again had any solid ties to any American community, no lifelong friends and no set of people to whom he had always been loyal. He was emblematic of the transience of American life in the second half of the twentieth century in that he really had no place to call home. After leaving the Midwest, he spent the first part of his professional life in Hollywood, a synthetic community made up of transplanted easterners and midwesterners who created an ersatz America on the studio lots of Universal and Paramount. He lived in the Los Angeles suburbs of Pasadena and Pacific Palisades but established no real ties in those communities. His first marriage, to the actress Jane Wyman, ended in divorce, and his relationship with his children withered. By late middle-age he had no one he could really call a close friend. The record is devoid of any references to people or institutions in California, apart from immediate family, that could always rely on Reagan. Even the small coterie of conservative businessmen in California who had bankrolled his early political career, including perhaps his closest friend, Los Angeles auto dealer Holmes Tuttle, found they had little access to Reagan once he entered the White House.

Much about Reagan's personality and even the vicissitudes of his politics can be explained by his father's alcoholism. Reagan and his brother, Neil, remembered Jack Reagan as being so drunk at times that he would walk through the screen door of their home rather than open it. As an eleven-year-old, Ronald once found his father passed out in the snow on the family's front porch and had to drag him inside and put him to bed. What happens to the personalities of children who grow up in such an environment is no mystery. Innumerable studies have shown that children of alcoholics tend to have low self-esteem and difficulty forming intimate relationships, afraid to express their feelings for fear they might be found wanting. And yet they crave acceptance and approval, some adopting the role of the clown and others merely exhibiting an excessive willingness to go along with the crowd and a chameleon's ability to adjust to their environment. Many also value self-reliance and place enormous importance on achievement, which for the better adjusted among them are positive attributes. These traits, every one of them, conform to what friends and other intimates have observed about Ronald Reagan.

They explain the paradox of Reagan, as a high school student in Dixon, being outgoing and popular, competitive on the football field, self-assured on the stage in school plays, and yet having no close male friends. Tall and handsome, he was the polite, all-American boy, eager to please and courteous to everyone while lifeguarding at Lowell Park outside Dixon. But he was also the boy no one outside his family really knew, the introspective lad who retreated into tales of heroism in motion pictures and in the adventure novels he borrowed from the Dixon library. He dated the beautiful Margaret Cleaver, daughter of a church pastor, but according to Reagan biographer Anne Edwards, she found his charm to be superficial and his real personality elusive. "His charm was overwhelming," Edwards wrote, "his kindness almost extreme." Many years later, Cleaver was reticent about explaining why she had broken off their engagement in college, although her comment to author Edmund Morris was revealing: "He had an inability to distinguish between fact and fancy."

With a sonorous voice that was a thespian's dream, with good looks and abundant charm, with an amazing memory for small bits of information, with a psychic need to transform himself from the shy, awkward boy playing alone with lead soldiers, Reagan was made for acting, and for politics. But he was also dangerously inchoate, willing to become whatever was required to please those around him or to serve his own self-interest. The Reagan of myth was an inner-directed man, forever motivated by the values he learned as a boy in the small-town Midwest. But the real Reagan was every bit the "other-directed" man famously described by the sociologist David Riesman, a new American character type taking cues from the crowd and the mass media rather than from family or clan.

The pattern was already in place on the day Reagan made his political debut as a freshman at Eureka College in 1928, when upper classmen recognized his gifts as a speaker and drafted him to make a speech in opposition to the college's president, Bert Wilson, who had angered students by proposing to cut back on the curriculum. Their plan was for him to deliver an oration firing up the student body to demand Wilson's resignation. As Reagan described the incident in his first biography, he was fed his lines by the older students, but he had already learned that the lines did not really matter, as long as the fire was one's own. "I discovered that night that an audience had a feel to it and in the parlance of the theater, the audience and I were together," Reagan recalled. "When I came to actually presenting the motion there was no need for parliamentary procedure: they came to their feet with a roar—even the faculty members present voted by acclamation. It was heady wine. Hell, with two more lines I could have had them riding through 'every Middlesex village and farm'—without horses yet."

Because of his family's indebtedness to the New Deal, Reagan had a strong emotional attachment to FDR and the Democratic Party. At the time he wrapped up a brief career as a radio announcer and packed his bags for Hollywood in 1937, the future lion of the conservative movement was still a passionate liberal. He was fired with the midwestern populism that was the birthright of any Illinois boy from a poor family, as suspicious of big business as he later would be of big government, and he pressed his political views on anyone who would listen. Other actors remembered Reagan hanging around studio cafeterias and hallways between shoots, engaging people in political arguments. But they were not exactly conversations. Even with the self-assured air of an actor and later a successful politician, Reagan remained famously inept at small talk and difficult to get to know personally—one former girlfriend of his Hollywood days "always had the feeling that I was with him but he wasn't with me." But he loved pontificating before a group, a compensation for his unease in more intimate settings. He always had a convincing statistic or anecdote at the ready, lifted from the newspaper clippings stuffed in his pockets or from the remarkable memory that was one of the less appreciated aspects of his political genius. "There were two things about Ronnie that impressed me, how much he liked to dance and how much he liked to talk," said the actress Doris Day, who dated him in the late 1940s. "When he wasn't dancing, he was talking. It wasn't really conversation, it was rather talking at you, sort of long discourses on subjects that interested him. I remember telling him that he should be touring the country making speeches."

A year after arriving in Hollywood, Reagan was recruited onto the board of the Screen Actors Guild and quickly became immersed in its affairs. Although he was as distrustful of communists as any other boy of the small-town Midwest, his dalliance with the labor movement and other liberal causes brought him into close contact with fellow travelers, who were as ubiquitous as fireplugs in Hollywood during the 1930s and early 1940s. On December 12, 1945, Reagan delivered a speech at a Hollywood Stadium event organized to raise alarm about the dangers of the atomic bomb. The event was sponsored by the Hollywood Independent Citizens Committee of Arts, Sciences and Professions, a successor to the Hollywood Democratic Committee, which had been formed by members of the film community to support the legacy of the New Deal. Reagan later joined HICCASP's board and also became active in the Hollywood branch of the American Veterans Committee, a group that was ostensibly dedicated to finding housing for returning servicemen but actually had a more subversive agenda. Reagan came off as a willing soldier of the left in this period. The FBI, which was already busy collecting files on suspected communists in the 1940s, listed Reagan as a sponsor of the Los Angeles Committee for a Democratic Far Eastern Policy and filed away a clip from the *People's World* of February 26, 1946, that described him as supporting a liberated Indochina and the overthrow of Chiang Kai-shek. He had also narrated a radio program that attacked the Ku Klux Klan.

Reagan admitted later that much of his liberal activism was just going along with the crowd. He wrote in his first autobiography that he was a "near hopeless hemophiliac liberal" in the 1940s, an "easy mark for speechmaking on the rubber-chicken and glass-tinkling circuits. . . . But, though I did not realize it then, both my material and my audiences were hand-picked, or at least I was being spoon-fed and steered more than a little bit." As Reagan remembered it, the people "steering" his activities and feeding him his lines were the communists, who lurked behind the facade of liberal organizations and whose real interest was in gaining control of the Hollywood propaganda machine. Reagan said he left both HICCASP and the American Veterans Committee after discovering, by 1947, that they were communist fronts. He broke with the veterans committee after a small far left contingent within the group attempted to organize a studio strike in the name of the full membership and, according to Reagan, tried to dupe him into playing a key role. His exit from HICCASP came when he and other noncommunist members of the organization's board, including Olivia de Havilland, James Roosevelt, and Dore Schary, grew disenchanted with the leftist element and sought a public statement from the board disavowing communism. Reagan said that when he joined Roosevelt in supporting the idea in a board meeting at the home of an unnamed "Hollywood celebrity," the bitter reaction opened his eyes to the true nature of Hollywood's leftist elite. "Well, sir, I found myself waist-high in epithets such as 'fascist' and 'capitalist scum' and 'enemy of the proletariat' and 'witch-hunter' and 'red-baiter' before I could say boo. . . . You can imagine what this did to my naivete." After the executive committee overwhelmingly rejected the proposal for an anticommunist statement, Reagan and the other dissidents resigned in July 1946.

No longer a dupe of the communists, Reagan now became an FBI informant. He recalled that three FBI agents showed up at his home one night in April 1947 and goaded him into providing information about communists in the Screen Actors Guild. The agents accomplished this, according to Reagan, by relating to him that at a meeting following his resignation from HICCASP, one of the communists had said, "What are we going to do about that sonofabitching bastard Reagan?" Reagan's FBI file, which biographers obtained under the Federal Freedom of Information Act in the 1980s, showed that Reagan was so busy an informant in the next few years that the bureau gave him a code name, T-10. He was especially valuable to the FBI by the time of his meeting with the three agents because a month earlier, in March 1947, he had replaced Robert Montgomery as SAG's president.

Reagan's metamorphosis, in the span of less than eighteen months, from dyed-in-the-wool leftist to FBI informant is highly revealing. It is not as if he merely grew disenchanted with the extremism of the communists but stayed on his populist course. Reagan's identification with the laboring classes began to wane at this point, and his allegiance to more powerful forces that could advance his own interests became the focal point of his ambitions. As head of the Screen Actors Guild, he began to promote the agenda of Hollywood executives as much as the rank and file of his union, beginning with his efforts to keep communists from gaining influence in the motion picture industry. In November 1947, at the SAG meeting that elected him to his first full term as president, he supported a resolution requiring that no one hold office in the union without signing an affidavit denying membership in the Communist Party. He also joined forces with Louis B. Mayer and other studio executives to stave off government meddling in the motion picture industry by making sure Hollywood cleaned its own house of communist influence. Reagan's partner in this effort was Roy Brewer, a powerful Hollywood labor leader and rabid anticommunist who had succeeded John Wayne as president of the Motion Picture Alliance for the Preservation of American Ideals, formed in 1944 to oppose not only communism but the New Deal, labor unions, and civil rights groups, all the liberal forces that just a few years earlier were at the core of Reagan's beliefs. The two cooperated on a number of anticommunist initiatives, including their service as founding vice presidents of the Motion Picture Industrial Council, a producers' group designed to promote a public image of Hollywood as dedicated to anticommunism.

Reagan has denied that he ever named names before Congress or participated in blacklisting. He was always insistent that no blacklisting ever occurred (which might explain how, in 1984, he could justify appointing Brewer, whom a *Los Angeles Times* reporter once called the "darkest figure of a dark age," to a key labor post in his administration). But the release of his FBI file in the 1980s and other documentation, including interviews given by Jack Dales, who was the executive director of SAG in this period, suggests that he played a major role in driving "subversives" from the industry. With Brewer, Reagan served on a committee within the Motion Picture Industrial Council responsible for "clearing" those accused of communist ties, which of course meant laying the ground for the banishment of those who could not be cleared. His FBI file notes approvingly that Reagan told an agent that "he has been made a member of a committee headed by L. B. Mayer, the purpose of which allegedly is to 'purge' the motion picture industry of Communist Party members." Reagan appeared as a "friendly witness" before the House Committee on Un-American Activities—meeting with committee counsel beforehand to discuss his testimony—and parroted the official statement of the producers that the government could make Hollywood's job easier by declaring the Communist Party an agent of a foreign power and banning its members from all occupations in this country. Dales, a devout anticommunist, expressed remorse in 1979 for forcing actors out of the industry, but he said Reagan had no such misgivings. "I think of people now," Dales said, "who I think were terribly mistreated—Larry Parks, Marcia Hunt. . . . I talked to Ronnie since, not recently, but since, and he has no doubts about the propriety of what we did. I do."

By this point, Reagan's political and social influences were no longer left-leaning actors or the rank and file of the Screen Actors Guild, but the moguls of Hollywood. A secret deal he cut with the Music Corporation of America provides the best evidence of who was feeding him his lines by the 1950s. Since the 1930s, the Screen Actors Guild had maintained a strict conflict-of-interest provision that barred its members from being represented by agents who were also involved in production. However, Reagan used his position as the union's leader in 1952 to sign a blanket waiver allowing the Music Corporation of America to both represent actors and produce an unlimited number of television shows. The deal included a secret agreement in which MCA would pay actors residuals for the reuse of their movies on television. But that little sop for actors was small change compared with the benefits the agreement yielded to MCA, which became a giant in entertainment production—it was nicknamed the Octopus—in succeeding years and made sure plenty of money flowed to Reagan. As his film career waned, Reagan became host of the MCA-created *General Electric Theater,* and the company secured him later roles in *Death Valley Days* and its own television production of an Ernest Hemingway story, *The Killers.* At one point, Reagan was a producer and co-owner of *General Electric Theater* at the same time that he was head of the actors' union, a clear conflict of interest. It was Taft Schreiber, MCA's vice president, who convinced Reagan to switch to the Republican Party and who joined a group of conservative businessmen in financing his successful run for California governor in 1966. And it was also Schreiber, along with Jules Stein, the founder of MCA, who helped persuade Twentieth Century-Fox to buy Reagan's ranch in Santa Monica at a grossly inflated price during the same period.

Reagan's later explanations for the conflicts of interest in his dealings with MCA were rife with falsity and evasion. In 1962, under questioning by a federal grand jury that was probing the MCA waiver, Reagan claimed falsely that blanket waivers had also been given to other agencies, and he denied any knowledge of MCA's agreement to give residuals to actors. His response to other questions in the grand jury, in the words of Garry Wills, was to "retreat toward constantly expanding areas of forgetfulness." Reagan came perilously close to being indicted in the affair, which spoke volumes about his supposed identification with the working people of America. His most memorable act as a union leader was the service he provided to management—and himself.

Reagan also had other influences pulling him away from his liberalism in the 1940s and 1950s. With his midwestern provincialism, he was never comfortable around nor fully accepted by the left-wing intelligentsia of Hollywood, which was dominated by urbane easterners. In his friendships, he tended to gravitate more toward westerners with more conservative attitudes. One of his best friends in the 1940s was the actor Dick Powell, an archconservative with whom Reagan would have political arguments deep into the night. Reagan would play the part of the New Dealer, while Powell would try to convert him to Republicanism, warning him that leftists were taking the Democratic Party away from pragmatists like FDR. Reagan also began spending more and more time with wealthy businessmen, most of whom had built their fortunes from the ground up and exhibited the kind of self-reliance that Reagan admired.

Reagan was especially fond of the drugstore magnate Justin Dart, whom he befriended in 1940 during the shooting of a film called *Brother Rat and a Baby.* Though they began their friendship on opposite sides of the political spectrum—Dart a conservative and Reagan a liberal—the two had much in common. Like the future president, Dart was the son of a salesman who had begun life in small-town Illinois and was a a bulldog on the athletic field in high school. After his father sold enough shirts to send his only son to prep school at the Mercersburg Academy in Pennsylvania, the strapping young Dart broke local track records, helped along by his habit of carrying a fifty-six-pound weight and a sixteen-pound hammer everywhere he went to develop strength. At Northwestern University, he played tackle on the football team and was chosen for the All-Big Ten Conference team in his junior and senior years.

Dart had come into his riches by marrying Ruth Walgreen, the daughter of Charles Walgreen, founder of an Illinois-based chain of drugstores. A shrewd businessman who claimed he had made a million dollars in just a few months by using his pharmacies to sell bourbon for "medicinal purposes" during Prohibition, Walgreen took the eager Dart under his wing and groomed him to be his successor. It was after Walgreen sent him to Phoenix to run one of his pharmacies in the late 1930s that Dart became friends with a young aspiring politician named Barry Goldwater. "The first time I saw Justin Dart he was jerking sodas trying to learn the drugstore business," Goldwater later recalled. But Dart would not be jerking sodas for long. He rapidly moved up the corporate ladder, becoming head of store operations in the 375-store chain in 1932, before leaving the firm thirteen years later and taking over the Rexall Drug and Chemical Company, which he turned into a conglomerate that included the manufacturers of Tupperware, Duracell batteries, and West End appliances. He also developed a fondness for showering conservative politicians with money. He not only used his wealth to help Goldwater get elected to the Senate in 1949 but also became a major player in the Republican Party seven years later by raising a tidy sum for Dwight Eisenhower's reelection.

When Reagan met him in 1940, Dart was in the process of leaving Ruth Walgreen, having filed for divorce about a year after her father's death, and he was dating Jane Bryan, an actress costarring with Reagan in *Brother Rat and a Baby.* Reagan was instantly attracted to Dart, a large, gruff man with outspoken views on almost any subject, but he agreed with him on almost nothing; the two argued bitterly in their frequent dinners at the Reagans' home. "The night we first met we fought like cats and dogs," Dart recalled. "My wife warned me not to talk politics with him." Reagan insisted that big business was the scourge of regular Americans, while Dart saw the devil in the bloated New Deal bureaucracy. He criticized Roosevelt's government programs as the pork of big-city bosses, which he saw as putting a drag on America's entrepreneurial energies by eating up the earnings of the wealthy. Reagan's friends from that period, including fellow actor Larry Williams, remember Dart having an enormous influence in swaying Reagan from his liberal views. Williams said Reagan acknowledged for the first time that government payrolls might be destructive to the country.

Reagan's enmity toward government would only grow, nurtured by a series of unhappy personal experiences in his Hollywood days. In the late 1940s, Reagan was increasingly frustrated by Warner Brothers' reluctance to cast him in anything but light romantic roles. He felt such typecasting, as he grew older, would be the death of his career. His frustration only deepened in 1948 when Jane Wyman filed for divorce and obtained custody of their two children. Despite earning $169,750 in 1946, Reagan found his finances suddenly precarious. In those days, marginal tax rates—those assessed against the top portion of a person's income, reached as high as 91 percent on the richest Americans to finance the war debt, and Reagan felt too large a chunk was coming out of his income. His frustration prompted him, as SAG's president, to propose that Congress approve a "human depreciation allowance" for actors and athletes, since their earning power had a short shelf life, but the proposal went nowhere. Reagan was candid in his memoirs about having had a gripe against government tax collectors ever since those years. David Stockman, the budget director in his first term, remembers Reagan saying that taxes had been so onerous in his Hollywood days that actors could afford to make only four movies a year before they crept into a punitive tax bracket. "So we all quit working after four pictures and went off to the country," Reagan told him. It is not going out too far on a limb to suppose that his later experience with Justice Department antitrust lawyers probing the MCA waiver only deepened his enmity toward government.

But it was during Reagan's employment with General Electric that he severed his last emotional ties with liberalism. MCA secured him an annual salary of $125,000 in 1954 to host *General Electric Theater* and be a goodwill ambassador for the company. Reagan virtually sold his identity to General Electric, becoming the public face of one of America's biggest corporations. He did not just mouth the lines that General Electric supplied him and go home for the day. He absorbed the company's values to the core. GE outfitted his Pacific Palisades home with its entire line of appliances and then ushered in the cameras to capture Ron and Nancy—the two were married in 1952—in their "home of the future." Reagan cheerfully accepted the company's censorship anytime one of the story lines on *General Electric Theater* even obliquely questioned the divinity of electronic gadgetry. He recalled in his memoirs "the time we came up with an exciting half-hour play based on the danger to a planeload of passengers lost in the fog with all the instruments out of whack. We needed someone to remind us GE made those instruments, sold them to the airlines, and said airlines would consider it tactless if GE told umpteen million potential passengers they might land the hard way."

In his eight years with the company, Reagan spent about a quarter of his time visiting 139 GE plants around the country, a goodwill mission that eventually came to include delivering speeches, first to the employees and later to outside groups like local chambers of commerce. By Reagan's own account, the antigovernment content of those speeches began with a simple warning to audiences that what he saw as the unfair taxation of Hollywood actors could spread to other business sectors. People would gather around him after his appearances and relate their own mistreatment by the government, and he began incorporating those complaints into his speeches. "I was seeing how government really operated and affected people in America, not how it was taught in schools," he said in his 1990 memoirs. He also began to nurture his conservatism with regular reading of William F. Buckley's *National Review,* a journal dedicated to the belief that the New Deal legacy of "collectivism" was stifling America's entrepreneurial energies. "The Speech," as his talk became known, soon contained all of the free-market, anticommunist rhetoric that would later mark Reagan's political campaigns.

By the time Reagan switched to the Republican Party in 1962, "The Speech" was so well honed that a career in politics seemed inevitable. Friends had been urging him to run for office since the mid-1950s, but he always resisted, undoubtedly not relishing the thought of giving up his lucrative position with General Electric for the relatively low pay of a senator or governor. But that picture changed in the spring of 1962, when General Electric decided to cancel *General Electric Theater,* ostensibly because it was losing out to *Bonanza* in the ratings. (Various historians have also pointed to the grand jury investigation of MCA and the increasing stridency of Reagan's speeches as other possible reasons for his termination by the company with only twenty-four hours' notice.) Reagan was suddenly an actor without a stage. He continued giving "The Speech," only now the venues were almost always political. What ultimately propelled him fully into the political arena was both the failed candidacy of Barry Goldwater and his friendships with a band of conservative businessmen who saw in him the perfect vehicle for bringing about the emancipation of private enterprise.

Chief among them was Holmes Tuttle, a wealthy owner of Ford dealerships who was one of the California GOP's biggest fund-raisers in the 1960s. Tuttle had met Reagan when he sold him a Ford coupe at his Los Angeles dealership in 1946, and they instantly became friends. Tuttle, like Dart, was the kind of man Reagan admired, a plainspoken, occasionally coarse millionaire with the libertarian spirit of the prairie. Tall, slim, and elegant, with a slow drawl reminiscent of the young Jimmy Stewart, he had been born in Oklahoma when it was still Indian territory and raised in the small dust-bowl town of Tuttle, named for his family. Tuttle started out as a stock boy in an Oklahoma City Ford plant in 1923 but ended up three years later in Los Angeles, where Charles E. Cook, then a Ford dealer and later a wealthy Los Angeles investor, gave him the job of parts dealer at his dealership. Tuttle eventually opened his own dealership, the first in in what would become a chain of franchises that made him one of the most successful auto dealers in the nation.

Tuttle, who was also a director of the Rexall Drug and Chemical Company, had been active with Dart in raising money for Eisenhower and, by the 1960s, was a major power in California's Republican Party. Ed Mills, vice president of Tuttle Enterprises, was the titular chairman of the state party, but Tuttle was the financial genius and guiding force. In 1964, he and Dart threw their support behind Goldwater for the Republican presidential nomination in the belief that the party had moved too close to the center and needed to be returned to its original principles. There was no subtlety in what that meant for these two aggressive businessmen. Neither was a movement conservative with strong views on social issues. Tuttle had even been considered a moderate in the Eisenhower years. What they wanted from government was quite simply a laissez-faire attitude toward business. Dart, with characteristic bluntness, later commented that he saw himself as a "big-issues guy . . . interested in the national economy and our defense ability, not all these crappy little issues like equal rights, or abortion or the Moral Majority or whatever."

In 1964, Tuttle and two other businessmen—A. C. "Cy" Rubel, chairman of Union Oil Co., and Henry Salvatori, an oil man who had founded Western Geophysical Co.—organized a thousand-dollar-a-plate dinner in Los Angeles to raise money for Goldwater. Left without a speaker at the last minute, Tuttle called Reagan and asked him to speak. His speech, called "A Time for Choosing," a variation on his standard GE address, was as much of a barn burner as his debut address at Eureka College. "After the speech we were swamped with requests from people who said these are the things Goldwater's been missing," Tuttle told Lou Cannon. "We decided we had to get the speech on television."

The only problem was that Goldwater's staff, notably campaign manager Denison Kitchel and adviser William Baroody Sr., were not enthusiastic about having Reagan as a high-profile spokesman for the campaign. In the fall of 1964, Goldwater was desperately trying to shed his image as an extremist, and his handlers feared having their candidate identified with a right-wing actor whose views had only recently included the privatization of Social Security. But the California contingent forced the Goldwaterites' hand by raising money for the half-hour NBC telecast themselves. After the speech was broadcast on October 27, 1964, Reagan was suddenly a national political star. Contributions for Goldwater surged, and Tuttle, Salvatori, and other Republican businessmen realized they had been tying their national ambitions to the wrong man, especially after Lyndon Johnson crushed Goldwater at the polls a few days later.

The Millionaire Backers, as the press in California called them, may have been too extremist for Barry Goldwater, but they became the nucleus of Reagan's "Kitchen Cabinet" as he made his move into politics. Besides Tuttle, Dart, Rubel, and Salvatori, there were the oil man Jack Wrather, Diners Club founder Alfred Bloomingdale, cattle rancher William Wilson, the publisher Walter Annenberg, and Charles Wick, the nursing home magnate. "They were rich, but, with the exception of Annenberg, not titans," wrote the journalist Sidney Blumenthal. "They were not founders of crucial enterprises like General Motors or IBM. If they had never existed, what well-known products would be missing? Tupperware, Duracell batteries, Lassie, TV Guide, and the Diners Club credit card. Without politics, final success would have eluded them."

The conclusion, then, is inescapable: the image of Reagan as a man who never wavered from the small-town values that he absorbed during a simpler, more wholesome period in American history is far off the mark. His values were actually quite malleable. He shifted his core beliefs depending on what he became convinced was in his own self-interest at the moment. He was a leftist until he felt duped by Hollywood communists and became an FBI informant. He was a committed labor leader until his own interests required self-serving deals with management. He was a New Dealer while the philosophy was benefiting him personally, but switched to Republicanism when the social welfare tab was coming out of his taxes. Since his mind disdained nuance and complexity, he could believe passionately in whatever one-dimensional viewpoint he held at any given time, and his boyish enthusiasm and disarming manners had a way of winning over doubters. The man who saw big business as an unalloyed evil and government as the savior of the people could believe the complete opposite a few years later without ever entertaining the possibility that the truth might lie somewhere in the middle.

Reagan on the campaign trail in 1980 was indeed a true believer—in a set of political ideas that vindicated his enmity toward government, accrued to his own personal wealth, and won him the admiration and financial backing of the Southern California country club set. The close-knit group of Sun Belt tycoons who bankrolled Reagan's rise in politics, the men who handpicked his appointees in Sacramento, donated millions to his presidential campaign, and helped vet the candidates for Washington cabinet positions—the men now feeding him his lines—were not gathered around him because they were enamored of his conservatism. They were not Burkean conservatives or acolytes of the John Birch Society. They had little interest in social issues like abortion, affirmative action, or school prayer. Most were not even particularly passionate in their anticommunism. They viewed Reagan quite simply as a potential liberator for the entrepreneurial class. And there were many more like them in other areas of the country, not the old-line manufacturers, the money men of Wall Street, or the managers of the Fortune 500 companies, all of whom had made their peace with the regulatory regime and the welfare state, but the rising class of entrepreneurs in the service sector, who wanted deep cuts in their taxes and government regulators out of the way. They were the ones pouring millions into Reagan's campaign coffers. They were the laughing hordes that stampeded into Washington for his inauguration. In their eyes, the Reagan Revolution would be their own.

CHAPTER 3

The Invasion

The banner of free enterprise began unfurling in offices throughout Washington even before Reagan took office, hoisted jauntily by the corporate leaders and conservative ideologues who descended on the capital like a conquering army. On the morning of the new president's inauguration, hundreds of corporate jets paralyzed the tarmac at National Airport, forcing the control tower to redirect incoming flights elsewhere. Limousines, which would become ubiquitous in the Reagan years, streamed into the city in a dazzling cavalcade of polished black steel. Police gave the privileged guests their own lanes on the Memorial and Fourteenth Street Bridges, but they still managed to form a gridlock on the streets of the capital, their limos double- and triple-parked outside every hotel in town. They were in a hurry to lay claim to their spoils. More than one newspaper commented on the unseemly spectacle of men in tuxedos and women in gowns fighting like drunken soccer fans for seats at the inaugural balls. Impatient to make her appearance at the Kennedy Center, Betsy Bloomingdale, California socialite and Reagan intimate, leaped from her limo in DuPont Circle and personally directed traffic with a mink stole wrapped around her shoulders.

Business leaders had spent the seventies funding conservative think tanks and manning embattled fortifications in the glass towers of K Street, fighting off what they saw as a tide of onerous taxation and government regulation. But now they were no longer carping at the gates of government. They *were* the government, and they would exert their new influence with an élan and defiance that would have been socially unacceptable just a few years before. One group of wealthy Indiana Republicans came to Washington aboard a private rail car that had once belonged to J. P. Morgan. When Henry Ford II was rejected in his efforts to buy up blocks of tickets, he threatened to pull back the three hundred limos he had promised to loan for the celebration, forcing the inaugural committee to back down and turn over the tickets. Texas millionaire John Bartlett was not so lucky. He paid $12,000 for six box seats at the Sheraton-Washington Hotel ball, only to fall victim to the disorganization that reigned at a number of the inaugural balls. When he briefly left the ballroom, he was denied readmission by the staff.

All in all, the scene was a far cry from Jimmy Carter's inauguration four years earlier, which had been titled the "Y'all Come People's Celebration." Humble folks were conspicuously absent at the $250-a-seat balls of the Reagan inaugural. It was a corporate celebration, written off as a business expense. To the surprise of the police, fewer than a thousand demonstrators showed up to disrupt the upper-class revelry. A lone protestor outside the Federal Trade Commission, wearing a red beret and a Communist Party pin, was accosted by a man in a three-piece business suit who ripped an upside-down American flag off his back.

Ostentation permeated the very air of Washington in a way it never had before—certainly not in the administration that had just been swept ignobly from the capital. Jimmy Carter had been a man of plebeian sensibilities. He discouraged luxurious living in the White House, doing much of his own housekeeping in the family quarters and carrying his own bags when he traveled. Cabinet members who ate lunch in the Oval office would be handed a bill before they left. Carter even mothballed the *Sequoia,* a presidential yacht that had been in service since the Hoover years. He felt the president had no business yachting while autoworkers in Detroit and steelworkers in Pittsburgh were losing their jobs. This frugality, a sort of Jed Clampett way of occupying the First Residence, set the tone in Washington. For Carter's inauguration, women wore modestly priced gowns and the president himself donned a $175 suit that he had personally bought off the rack a week earlier.

But now, Jimmy Carter was back home in Plains, Georgia, where he planned to live simply in a modest ranch house. And Ronald and Nancy Reagan, with the entourage of millionaires they brought with them to the White House, would send a far different message about material ostentation. As they treated their well-heeled guests to swordfish and chateaubriand at nine inaugural balls that cost corporate donors $11 million, Ron and Nancy were reassured by the press corps that they had a mandate to live more lavishly than the Carters. "A gala celebration of America's best and richest was just what many Americans wanted to see," cooed *Newsweek* magazine, "especially after the jug-band-and-blue-jeans tone of the Carter White House."

The glamorous First Couple did not disappoint. Nancy Reagan's inaugural wardrobe was valued at $25,000, including a $10,000 hand-beaded inaugural ball gown by Los Angeles designer James Galanos that took several women four weeks to embroider; a full-length mink coat by Maximilian, a New York furrier, valued at $8,000 to $12,000; and a $1,650 American alligator handbag by Judith Leiber. The new First Lady brought in two hairstylists, from New York and Los Angeles, and kept one on her presidential helicopter so she could arrive at each ball freshly coiffed. She was not alone in her extravagance. There were so many minks that one reporter described "hotel coat racks like giant furry beasts," so much partying that Ridgewells, the Washington caterer, estimated it served four hundred thousand hors d'oeuvres at fifty-six gatherings. "Ostentatious," growled Barry Goldwater when he was asked for his feeling about the celebration, which he thought sent the wrong message "at a time when most people can't hack it."

After a campaign in which he pledged to reduce the size of government and stop wasting taxpayers' money, one of the first things Reagan did on taking office was approve a $44.6-million renovation of the White House, the biggest such expenditure since the Truman administration. Nancy Reagan raised an additional $1 million in private funds to redecorate the Reagans' living quarters, some $250,000 of which was donated by oil executives and other wealthy businessmen. The oil contributions raised more than few eyebrows in Washington because the fund-raising effort had come just a month after Reagan had decontrolled oil prices, yielding billions of dollars to the oil industry. Senator William Proxmire called the oil company donations "as blatant a presidential conflict of interest as I can recall in the more than twenty years I've been in Congress."

Reagan did order a freeze on the redecoration of other federal offices. But the frugality that the new president was asking of government bureaucrats and ordinary Americans simply did not apply to the First Family. Months after the inauguration, Nancy Reagan's manicurist, Jessica Vartoughian, was still flying in from Los Angeles to do her nails at the White House. While attending the wedding of Prince Charles and Lady Diana Spencer in London, the First Lady brought along a hairstylist, a nurse, four hatboxes, eight ball gowns, and hundreds of thousands of dollars in jewelry loaned to her by Bulgari, the famed international jeweler. Shortly after Reagan took office, a group of businessmen even began raising $2.5 million to put the *Sequoia* back in the water, although the effort was eventually abandoned.

Nor did other top officials in the administration shy away from high living. Reagan's top officials could choose from any number of parties every night, most of them hosted by wealthy suitors and large corporations. Treasury Secretary Donald Regan attended twenty-eight social functions in a thirty-day period early in the administration. When Reagan officials gathered on the National Mall for a dinner party honoring Senator Paul Laxalt, who had run the new president's campaign, there were strolling musicians, silver candelabra, and trees strung with Christmas lights. Raymond Donovan, the wealthy New Jersey businessman and key Reagan fund-raiser, was so thrilled about being named Secretary of Labor that he hosted some three hundred guests, including David Stockman and Vice President George Bush, for a western-style barbecue on the lawn of his new $765,000 home.

The guests were treated to two bands, a mechanical bull, and huge open barbecue pits.

All this was done without a whit of self-recrimination. Charles Wick, the California nursing-home magnate who had been one of Reagan's closest advisers in his quest for the presidency, told the *New York Times* in late 1981 that the spectacle of wealthy lifestyles had always been a tonic for Americans struggling to make ends meet. "During the Depression, when people were selling apples and factories were still and guys were jumping out windows because they lost everything, people would go to the movies," he said. "They loved those glamour pictures showing people driving beautiful cars and women in beautiful gowns, showing that people were living the glamorous good life."

The style and attitudes of a president can have an enormous effect on a country. Kennedy's youth and cool style truly made the country feel as if the "torch had been passed to a new generation," as he said in his inaugural speech. Teddy Roosevelt accomplished little in the way of reform legislation in his first term, but his sermonizing about the evils of industrial trusts raised the public's indignation and gave enormous momentum to the Progressive movement. FDR's jauntiness filled a Depression-weary nation with courage and conviction that we could overcome our national woes. Reagan, too, inspired the country. He created the sense that we could restore our ebbing respect and power on the world stage. But he also transmitted a more pernicious message from his first days in office: that the blind pursuit of wealth was not tawdry or immoral but a supreme human virtue.

This exaltation of avarice was hardly a new concept. In his paeans to self-interest, Reagan borrowed heavily from his hero, Calvin Coolidge, who had presided over a similar period of laissez-faire enthusiasm in the 1920s. The sentiments could just as easily have been cribbed from Adam Smith's *The Wealth of Nations,* or from any of the apologias for bald capitalism that gave such repugnance to the Gilded Age. The message was deceptively simple: the market, unfettered by government regulation and taxation, created the most efficient allocation of a nation's resources. Free competition among entrepreneurs not only served the consumer by keeping prices in check but also created wealth for everyone. The theory had been belied as too simplistic by the realities of America's postwar affluence, which rested on a "mixed economy" combining free enterprise with the stimulus of government spending, particularly for defense. But Reagan's genius was in making an old theme sound revolutionary. In a nation weary from layoffs and galloping inflation, the new president found it easy to whip Americans into a frenzy of self-interest, especially if their avarice could be given the imprimatur of economics. Greed became a public virtue, and its impulses drove deep into the public psyche. For capitalists small and large, the creed was particularly liberating, its tenets excusing even the most predatory behavior. Within free-market economics there is a doctrine known as *perfect discrimination,* which holds that the maximum efficiency of the economy depends on sellers' always obtaining the highest possible prices for their products. In other words, every capitalist should, with impunity, operate like a motel chain or airline, changing prices daily in accordance with what can be squeezed out of the customer. Such free-market purism, the perfect rationalization for the gouger and the snake oil salesman, had been held in check since the Progressive era by public standards of civility. Now Reaganism was scattering those standards to the winds.

Ronald Reagan had freed the business classes from the public scorn that had never really ended after the Great Depression, and had been whipped up anew by the counterculture of the 1960s. By equating wealth with the American ethic of hard work, the sense that anyone could make it who was willing to sacrifice, Reagan had made material acquisition fashionable again. The new sensibility was perfectly enunciated by Bonnie Swearingen, the wife of John E. Swearingen, chairman of the Standard Oil Company of Indiana, while she was attending an inauguration ball at the Kennedy Center. As she sauntered through the ballroom wearing an emerald and diamond necklace and matching earrings, she told a reporter that she was proud to be displaying the fruits of her husband's hard work. "It's getting a little tiresome to always have to apologize for ourselves," she said. "If a little girl from Alabama whose father was a minister can appear in public wearing beautiful jewels and gowns, it should be a symbol to everyone that they can do it, too."

No one relished this new day more than the breed of businessmen who had been closest to Reagan during his rise in politics. These were not the executives of Wall Street and the Fortune 500 companies, the eastern stalwarts who for most of the century had held the reins of power in the Republican Party. They were the ranchers, oilmen, and developers of the West and the South whose fortunes had been made in the postwar period. They had not come to their riches through family ties or Ivy League educations or by slowly climbing the management ranks in major corporations. Most had built their businesses from the ground up in the booming communities of the Sun Belt. which left them with a raw notion of free enterprise that would not have been out of place in the Gilded Age. The wealthy families that had made up the eastern Republican establishment may have cherished their tradition of noblesse oblige, but this class of capitalists had little time for such altruism. They believed the best way to help the masses was to set an example of thrift and hard work, not to endow the arts and education or establish foundations for the poor. The general election campaign had been a holy crusade for this new class of self-made millionaires. No longer was the power base of the Republican Party going to be exclusively the golf courses and country clubs of Greenwich or Grosse Pointe. Sun Belt entrepreneurs, not the old-money industrialists of the East and the Midwest, would be the financial backbone of the Reagan campaign and a new force in GOP politics.

And as a new force, they would help develop a new weapon, one that would haunt the nation for years to come. To a degree that to this day has received little attention, Reagan's campaign effectively undid the campaign finance reform that had been put into place after the Watergate scandal. The campaign pioneered the use of "soft money" contributions to the Republican Party as a way to get around the $2,000 limit on contributions to candidates that was the bedrock of the post-Watergate reforms. This innovation, a blatant contravention of the effort by Congress to insulate American democracy from the illicit influence of wealthy donors, eventually paved the way for the fund-raising scandals of the 1990s and the widespread sense among the public that Washington was for sale. In the short term, it also opened the door for a direct corporate imprint on the Reagan Revolution.

The campaign accomplished this by ferreting out a loophole in campaign finance law. In 1979, Congress approved an amendment to federal election rules that allowed national political parties to transfer money to the states for campaign activities. At the time, the amendment was seen as an innocuous effort to promote more grassroots participation in presidential elections. State organizations would be allowed to use funds from the national parties for get-out-the-vote drives, telephone banks, campaign signs, and other election day activities. The idea was for regular people and grassroots organizations to have a role in choosing the nation's president. But the businessmen working for Ronald Reagan seized on the amendment as a way to get around the legal limits on contributions, setting up an operation to pour money into the states. Whereas Jimmy Carter's campaign used the amendment largely for its intended purpose—to promote "party building" at the grassroots level—the Reagan Republicans turned it into a colossal fund-raising effort.

The soft-money effort was run out of Republican National Committee headquarters by Ted Welch, a Nashville developer, and Robert Mosbacher, an oilman from Texas. Both had come to the campaign after backing other candidates in the primaries, Welch supporting Tennessee Senator Howard Baker and Mosbacher working to elect fellow Texan George H.W. Bush. But they could not have fit better into Reagan's team. They were carbon copies of the men who had nurtured Reagan's political career in California, brash, self-made businessmen unapologetic for their pursuit of wealth and for their efforts to create a government more sympathetic to private enterprise.

Welch had begun his business career selling Bibles and dictionaries door to door for Southwestern Publishing Company while attending the University of Tennessee on a football scholarship in the 1950s.

The same determination that enabled a five-foot-seven flyweight to survive on the football field paid off in business. He eventually saved enough to buy a share in Southwestern and, by middle age, was the owner of magazines, restaurant chains like Ruby Tuesday's, and vast holdings of real estate, including a half share in the Tower, a thirty-one-story office building in downtown Nashville. And like Justin Dart and Holmes Tuttle, with whom he joined forces in the effort to elect Ronald Reagan, Welch had a passion for raising money for Republican politicians. "Instead of playing golf, I raise money," he once said. He had been backing Republican politicians in his home state for nearly a decade when another Tennessean, Republican National Committee Chairman William Brock, made him the national party's finance chairman in 1977.

In the 1980 campaign, Mosbacher and Welch turned to friendly businessmen across the country and tapped them for contributions. Corporate money had been banned from federal elections for decades, but now donors could achieve the same result by giving money to local parties, which in many states had no such limitations. By election day, some $15 million had been raised for "grassroots" support of Ronald Reagan's candidacy. That was a paltry sum compared to the tens of millions of dollars that both Republicans and Democrats in future presidential elections raised in soft-money contributions from corporations. But Reagan was the pioneer. With the help of Welch and Mosbacher, he could take credit for undoing a sensible effort by a previous generation of Americans to remove the stain of legal bribery from national elections.

And the business interests that filled Reagan's campaign coffers got what they paid for. More than any president before him, Reagan reached into the boardrooms of America's corporations to fill top positions in his administration. Secretary of Defense Caspar Weinberger and Secretary of State George Schultz came from the Bechtel Corporation, an international construction company. Donald Regan, the chairman of Merrill Lynch who had long coveted a top position in Washington, hosted just enough cocktail fund-raisers on Wall Street to get the nod for secretary of the treasury. Raymond Donovan, the

New Jersey construction executive who headed up Reagan's fund-raising in New Jersey, became secretary of labor.

But it was in the government regulatory apparatus that Reagan's tutelage of business interests was the most egregious. In the vast majority of Washington's regulatory agencies, the new leaders were heads of industry—mostly from the Sun Belt—who came to Washington with barely concealed disdain for government. The people newly entrusted to prevent corporate lawbreaking were in many cases representative of the worst and most avaricious elements of their respective industries. Their mission was clear: reduce the number of regulations, slash the budgets, and weed out the most aggressive and effective staff members; in short, eviscerate the regulatory agencies that had been a thorn in their sides when they were in the private sector.

The federal regulatory apparatus would now be controlled by men like Robert Burford, a Colorado rancher who had repeatedly been cited by the U.S. Bureau of Land Management in the 1970s for illegally grazing his cattle on public lands and was openly defiant in his meetings with the agency's officials. Reagan appointed him director of his old nemesis, the Bureau of Land Management, giving him oversight of millions of acres of public land. In the Reagan years huge swaths of that public land would be opened for mining and free-cutting of timber.

Such conflicts of interest were the rule rather than the exception. Interior Secretary James Watt was president of the Mountain States Legal Foundation, which was funded to a large degree by mining, timber, and energy companies. John Crowell, assistant interior secretary for natural resources and the environment, charged with setting policy for the U.S. Forest Service, was a lawyer for major timber companies. C. W. McMillan, assistant agriculture secretary for marketing and inspection services, was the executive vice president of the National Cattlemen's Association. Richard Lyng, the undersecretary of agriculture, was president of the American Meat Institute, an industry group. Joseph Tribble, assistant energy secretary for conservation and renewable energy, worked for a Georgia pulp and paper company blamed for polluting a local river. Thorne Auchter, assistant secretary for occupational safety and health, worked in the family construction business in Jacksonville, Florida. Between July 1972 and November 1980, Auchter Company had forty-eight safety violations, six of them serious.

The list went on and on. The new ethos of the Reagan administration was exemplified by John Van de Water, whom Reagan nominated to become chairman of the National Labor Relations Board, notwithstanding his former presidency of the leading West Coast antiunion consulting firm. John R. Van de Water Associates had been advising companies how to thwart union organizing since the 1940s. At his confirmation hearing, an AFL-CIO secretary quoted from one of Van de Water's speeches to management: "Good faith bargaining simply means that you listen to the union's argument with yours. That's all that good faith bargaining is. You don't have to give one cent."

This new class of business leaders had a vision of corporate liberation and government subservience that had risen indigenously from the sands of the West and the marshes of Dixie. Even at the start of the 1980 Republican primaries, Sun Belt entrepreneurism was still a force independent of the more powerful business interests of Wall Street and the Fortune 500. The leaders of the traditional Republican establishment on the East Coast hardly greeted Reagan's election with elation. Most corporate CEOs and Wall Street executives backed former Texas governor John Connally or George H.W. Bush in the 1980 Republican primaries, seeing them as more reliable stewards of old-line Republicanism. These cautious business leaders were most interested in a balanced budget and the battle against inflation, and they worried, justifiably as it turned out, that Reagan's "voodoo economics" would fuel the mounting deficits. Moreover, Reagan had flip-flopped on the issue that was perhaps most important to them: the proposal for liberalized depreciation allowances for business. The stock market actually plummeted after Reagan's inaugural speech because, in the words of Robert Stovall, then vice president of Dean Witter Reynolds, "Reagan didn't say many of the things we expected about the economy and girding to fight inflation. What we got was recycled rhetoric."

What few on Wall Street fully understood in January 1981 was that Ronald Reagan was serious about getting government off the backs of big business and that, much to the dismay of the doctrinaire conservatives of the New Right, serving the interests of major corporations would be the hallmark of his administration. The self-made millionaires who had backed Ronald Reagan's rise in politics may have distrusted their more established counterparts in the East, but they had much in common. In the stately halls of the U.S. Chamber of Commerce, where the real economic power of the nation resided, highly paid lobbyists had been mobilizing for more than a decade for a remarkably similar vision of the economy. In the 1970s, the corporate presence in Washington had grown enormously. Thousands of lobbyists had taken up residence in the office buildings of K Street and other Washington thoroughfares to confront the burgeoning array of regulations emanating from the federal government. Their mission was to put a new luster on the tarnished image of big business.

Corporations had never really recovered the prestige they had enjoyed in the 1920s, a period when President Calvin Coolidge famously proclaimed, without fear of ridicule, that "the chief business of the American people is business." Such a sentiment would have provoked derisive editorials during the Great Depression and would have been impolitic even in the relatively conservative 1950s, a decade when the public eagerly read William H. Whyte Jr.'s *The Organization Man* and Sloan Wilson's *The Man in the Gray Flannel Suit,* books that cast a negative light on the materialism and cultural stasis that large corporations had brought to postwar America. Rage against the evils of conglomerates and multinational corporations reached an even higher pitch in the youth rebellion of the 1960s. Hollywood enshrined the image of the corporation as patently evil in films like *The China Syndrome, Network,* and *The Parallax View.* Still, even as it took this drubbing from the counterculture, big business spent little time worrying about its public image as long as profits kept soaring and no other nation could come close to challenging America's industrial supremacy.

But the 1970s shook the corporate man out of his complacency. A thicket of new health and safety and environmental regulations was emanating from the federal government at the same time that the Great Inflation began eating into profits and the producers of West Germany and Japan, recovered from wartime devastation, began competing with American business. Recognizing that their poor public image was weakening their clout in Washington, leaving the field open to the likes of Ralph Nader, the CEOs went on the counterattack. In 1972, they set up a Washington lobby known as the Business Roundtable, made up of the chief executives of some two hundred of the nation's biggest companies. Wealthy businessmen also began pouring millions of dollars into the coffers of conservative think tanks like the Heritage Foundation, the John M. Olin Foundation, the Hoover Institution, and the Manhattan Institute, which churned out many of the free-market ideas and rising conservative scholars that would later play major roles in the Reagan Revolution. No concept was dearer to the heart of this lobbying effort than the idea that the lack of competitiveness of major U.S. corporations was due to a shortage of capital to invest in new products and enterprises. "Capital formation" became the buzzword of the business lobby by the end of the 1970s, and its logic was pretty much swallowed whole by large swaths of the economics profession and the financial press, which treated it as received wisdom toward the end of the Carter years that the solution to the nation's lagging productivity lay somewhere in a mix of deregulation and business tax cuts.

Thus the East Coast business establishment and Reagan's Millionaire Backers wanted much the same thing from Washington, but they were separated by regional and cultural antagonism. Skepticism about Reagan's ability to lead the country was prevalent even among the small coterie in Washington that had been championing supply-side economics in the late 1970s, the most prominent among them Jack Kemp and David Stockman, then both congressmen; former *Wall Street Journal* editorial writer Jude Wanniski; and Arthur Laffer, the economist who had developed the so-called Laffer curve, which purported to show that corporate tax cuts would yield such a flurry of new investment that tax revenues would increase. In his memoirs, Stockman related his reaction when Kemp told him in 1979 that he was dropping his plans to run for president and throwing his support behind Reagan. Stockman felt Kemp had enlisted in a bizarre fraternity, "aligning himself with Jerry Falwell, the anti-gun control nuts, the Bible-thumping creationists, the anti-communist witch hunters, and the small-minded Hollywood millionaires to whom 'supply side' meant one more Mercedes."

But when Reagan became the front-runner for the nomination in early 1980, and the candidate speaking the loudest about tax reduction, he and the supply-siders would inevitably become political bedmates. In January 1980, Reagan granted an audience in his campaign headquarters at the Beverly Wilshire Hotel in Los Angeles to Kemp, Wanniski, and Laffer, the three high priests of supply-side. The three men, together with Stockman, had been lobbying for public acceptance of the philosophy for several years. A veritable debating society on tax policy arose in Kemp's office, where young supply-siders met and exchanged ideas, convinced that they were the vanguard of a revolutionary movement. They had even begun to make some headway with the GOP's old guard, which tended to value a balanced budget more than the idea of tax relief. Stockman and Kemp had enlisted fifty members of the House to support a package of deep tax cuts in early 1980, and the supply-siders were hoping that the election of a Republican president would improve the bill's chance of passage.

Their meeting with Reagan came during three days of policy briefings that the candidate's staff had organized so he could bone up on the issues. Wanniski remembered a classroomlike setting, with Reagan and Ed Meese, who was acting as moderator, sitting at a head table and the briefing participants seated at long tables at right angles on either side. Wanniski's initial impression of Reagan at the briefing confirmed everything that the supply-siders had feared. He found Reagan to be likable, even boyish. Told that his staff had neglected to order sandwiches for the session, a playful Reagan had said, "Who's on a diet around here?" But Wanniski was put off by the simplicity of the anecdotes that Reagan was spinning off in response to the briefing. Meese had to gently nudge him back to the issue at hand. The candidate seemed to be grasping only a small part of what was being told to him. "I was alarmed in the first two hours of discussion to think there was so little subtlety in his thinking," Wanniski wrote in a memo summarizing the briefing, "but after fifteen hours I realized what was going on: He was throwing off two-dimensional observations to invite debate."

Wanniski's conclusion was reminiscent of Jerzy Kosinki's novel *Being There,* in which powerful people mistakenly believe they are hearing brilliant metaphor in the childish utterances of Chance the Gardener. However, Wanniski had good reason for deluding himself about the profundity of Reagan's anecdotes, for the two men found they were soul mates on the issue of taxes. "He has the concept of economic growth . . . in his bones and thus finds himself completely comfortable with supply-side ideas," Wanniski wrote. Reagan shushed aides who tried to argue with the three supply-siders and began dragging out old stories about the government's unfair treatment of Hollywood actors in the war era. More important, John Sears, his campaign manager, had come to see the program as a way to align Reagan with the tax revolt that had begun with Proposition 13 in California and was spreading around the country. Almost from the day of that briefing, Ronald Reagan was an inveterate supply-sider, telling an interviewer in February 1980 that "an across the board reduction in tax rates, every time it has been tried, it has resulted in such an increase in prosperity . . . that even the government winds up with more revenue."

The supply-side briefing was a milestone in the Reagan Revolution. Reagan's embrace of the doctrine not only gave an academic veneer to his instinctive hatred of taxes and help set the stage for the yawning deficits that plagued his presidency but also enabled his administration, in the weeks after his inauguration, to overcome any remaining hesitation on the part of the nation's most powerful corporate leaders to support his economic program—support that would prove to be crucial in the successful battle with Tip O'Neill.

The job of lining up that support fell to a pit bull of a lobbyist named Wayne Valis. Valis was a bearded, fast-talking ball of energy who was fanatically committed to the cause of Reaganism and believed that any means necessary—even means that skirted the edge of the law—should be marshaled in the assault on the opposition. His maneuvering, well out of the public eye, would cement the alliance between Reagan and big business that proved so fateful for the country.

Valis was a native Virginian who was a loyal Democrat until he got to Rutgers University in the late 1960s and found himself repelled by the leftism of his professors. Combative by nature, he found himself getting up in his classes and arguing with his teachers. By the time he left college, his ideological transformation was complete: He was an active member of Young Americans for Freedom, a right-wing student group, and committed to a career of service to the Republican Party, beginning with work as a lobbyist in the Nixon and Ford administrations and later as a fellow with a conservative think tank, the American Enterprise Institute.

Valis was only in his late thirties when Elizabeth Dole, director of the White House Office of Public Liaison, hired him as a lobbyist at the beginning of Reagan's first term, but his reputation for political hardball was already established. In the previous months he had engaged in "negative research" for the campaign, assigned to dig out Jimmy Carter's liabilities so they could be exploited in Reagan's speeches and advertisements. It later turned out that he did that job a little too well. The White House admitted in 1983 that Valis had obtained access to materials the Carter campaign was using to prepare its candidate for a debate with Reagan. In a 1980 memo sent to David Gergen, who was later to become Reagan's director of communications, Valis said his notes were "based on a Carter debate staff brainstorming session" and that they came from "a source intimately connected to a Carter debate staff member." The disclosure blossomed into a miniscandal that prompted congressional and FBI investigations and was dubbed "Debategate" by the press.

But Valis was still a little-known figure when he threw himself into the effort to attract business support for Reagan. The day after Reagan's February 18, 1981, speech, in which he unveiled his proposal for deep tax and budget cuts, Valis assembled hundreds of corporate lobbyists in Room 450 of the Old Executive Office Building and exhorted them to put everything they had into the passage of the program. "Like the Confederacy, you have only won defensive victories," Valis told the lobbyists to thunderous applause. "That leads to defeat. If you will march with us this time, you will win offensive victories."

Over the next several months, Valis lined up dozens of meetings between corporate leaders and key figures in the administration, including Reagan. He also accepted a list from the U.S. Chamber of Commerce of Carter holdovers in the regulatory agencies that business considered nettlesome and dutifully turned it over to the administration's personnel office for action. Perhaps most important, he and Dole formed a de facto alliance with Charles Walker, the lobbyist for the U.S. Chamber of Commerce, to keep pressure on the administration to make sure the tax bill would contain gargantuan depreciation allowances sought by big business. "That was red meat for the corporate community," Valis recalled. "The combination of Reagan being serious about holding down spending and the tax provisions pulled them over to our side." David Stockman wrote later that he wanted to trim the depreciation allowance, which he projected would cost the taxpayers a mind-boggling $162 billion over five years, but he said Walker and other K Street lobbyists "would come at us like a battalion of tanks," with Dole and Valis applying pressure from within the administration. Walker, Stockman said, "got everything he wanted."

Valis was fond of boasting that he had lined up more than a thousand business organizations across the country to support Reagan's program, and he said the administration was not above using bare knuckles on those who would not play along. "Jim Baker would call me in and say, 'Do you have any laggards?' I would say, 'Well, GE has some issue with the Ex-Im banks. And it's their hot button.' He would say, 'You let them know that their Ex-Im problem could get unpleasant if they're not balls-out supporting Ronald Reagan.' My job was to look over all these corporate guys and make sure they were going pedal to the metal behind Ronald Reagan."

With Valis's prodding, the corporations threw their huge resources into the fight for Reagan's program. He said one reason that Tip O'Neill could not keep Democratic lawmakers from defecting was that in the days leading up to key votes on the budget and tax packages, the corporations lined up thousands of people to besiege members of Congress with telephone calls in support of the president. "I used to walk into the congressional offices like I was a regular citizen to make sure the phones were ringing off the hook," Valis said. "And they always were."

It was this synthesis of business interests—the cowboy boots and ten-gallon hats of the ranch wedded to the pinstripes and wingtips of Wall Street—that produced the essence of Reaganism. Everything else that was ostensibly part of Reagan's domestic agenda—ending handouts to the welfare queens, outlawing abortion, promoting school prayer, controlling crime, nurturing family values—became secondary issues whose value was mainly to divide the nation and distract attention from the coup d'état that the rich were staging in Washington. While some of the traditional goals of the conservative movement would be achieved over the next two decades, they were not the central focus of the Reagan White House. The real business of the administration—more than even the president himself was aware—was business. And the way to carry out that business was to implement a plan for the disembowelment of the public sector.

CHAPTER 4

Year Zero

The Reagan Revolution has rested on a fallacy—that somewhere in the American past shimmers a halcyon era when the masses lived happily and private enterprise flourished without interference from the dead hand of government. Ronald Reagan—nothing if not a dreamer, a man who made crucial decisions on the advice of an astrologer, who believed in extraterrestrials, who again and again confused Hollywood images with reality—tried to take America on a journey back to a Shangri-la that never existed. The Millionaire Backers, who knew that his presidency was just a money grab by the upper class, may have chuckled to themselves at how gullibly he bought into the lines he was reading. But Reagan was a true believer. His idea that America's greatness would be restored only if freed from the shackles of government unleashed one of the great philosophical misadventures of modern history. It may not have been as violent in its consequences as Pol Pot's Year Zero or Mao's Cultural Revolution, yet it brought seismic changes to American society, undermining our democracy, cheapening our culture, and reversing a seventy-year trend toward social progress. It was as insidious as any of the dystopian "isms" that convulsed the twentieth century, because it dimmed the fires of one of the world's great civilizations.

With his simple pledge to "get government off the backs of the American people," Ronald Reagan set in motion a tidal wave of deregulation and privatization that has transformed the nation. A long list of calamities that have befallen deregulated industries—two stock market crashes, the California energy crisis, the Enron scandal, the savings-and-loan bailout, the Northeast blackout, the rash of bankruptcies in the airline industry, and the subprime mortgage crisis, just to name a few—all arose from Reagan's misguided quest for free-market purism. All grew out of the evisceration of regulations that a more sensible generation of political leaders had put into place to keep market forces from making a shambles of our economy and culture. All enriched an elite of business interests at the expense of ordinary Americans, without achieving what was supposed to be the goal of deregulation: a general increase in the well-being of the nation.

At the same time, Reagan's tax cuts, trillion-dollar defense buildup, and sweeping budget cuts impoverished wide sectors of the government. His long-running diatribe against the inefficiency of government became a self-fulfilling prophecy. In the years following his presidency, many government agencies were so denuded of resources that they became the caricatures of ineffectiveness that Reagan had drawn in so many of his stump speeches. The nation was left with an Internal Revenue Service that virtually stopped auditing tax returns, an Environmental Protection Agency that turned a blind eye to polluters, a Federal Trade Commission that never took action against trade abuses, and a Federal Communications Commission that turned over the public airwaves to corporations.

For much of the twentieth century, when America was at the zenith of its power and influence, government was regarded—at least in the public utterances of our leaders, if not always in their actions—as a tool to achieve the betterment of the common man. The historian Richard Hofstadter could survey America at midcentury and proclaim the preceding five decades an Age of Reform, an epoch that had conquered the vast economic inequality and untold human misery that had marked the last three decades of the nineteenth century. Now the same government that achieved such reform is derided by conservatives as the "nanny state." Government is forced to stand aside as inequality once again becomes the standard-bearer in America, as incomes of working people stagnate, inner-city neighborhoods decay, multinational corporations divest from the nation, and our democracy is lashed and looted by the likes of Tom DeLay and Jack Abramoff, men who carry the water for powerful economic interests.

No one in a position of power bothers to examine the foundation of this stark turnabout in national affairs. No one asks anymore whether Reagan was right when he told us that government regulation and excessive spending on social programs were the source of our economic woes in the 1970s. For the Democratic Party, it's as if that battle was fought and lost, so we must accept Reagan's version of our economic history. What even so-called liberals forget is that Reaganism, to the degree that it was anything but a coup by the rich, was perpetrated not in the name of facts and analysis but in the name of ideology, an ideology that our most revered national leaders—Lincoln, Wilson, the Roosevelts, Truman, and Kennedy—had long ago regarded as obsolete and downright disastrous when allowed to guide national policy. Yet Reagan revived it, acting as if those lessons had never been learned.

The *ur*text of the Reagan Revolution was Adam Smith's *The Wealth of Nations,* the 1776 book that virtually founded the classical school of economics. Its thesis is familiar to any first-year economics student: Capitalism unfettered by government, guild, crown, or pulpit accrues to the greatest good for mankind. The self-regulating market creates the most efficient allocation of goods and services. Self-interest is the engine of capitalist production, and competition the guarantor of stable prices and wages.

Smith's philosophy has been transported virtually unaltered through the ages. It was the theoretical backdrop of the Gilded Age and the Roaring Twenties; its precepts were behind the writings of German émigré Friedrich A. Hayek, the seminal thinker of the postwar conservative movement; and it was the guiding light for Milton Friedman, George Gilder, and Jude Wanniski, the scholars with the greatest influence on the Reagan administration. Indeed, it has become an article of faith for the conservatives who have dominated

Washington in the post-Reagan era—the idea that government can only retard the creation of wealth and keep the nation from competing in the global economy. As Smith wrote of excessive taxation, they say of government: "a curse equal to the barrenness of the earth and the inclemency of the heavens."

Smith's formulation is ingenious in the abstract, but it bears little relation to the real workings of capitalism. Free enterprise never dwells for long in the state of "perfect competition" envisioned by Smith and his descendants. The picture of a vast constellation of entrepreneurs driving down prices and bidding up wages with their fierce competition is a pretty one indeed, but it is a fleeting image. What emerges from the fracas of competition tends to be a few large enterprises that quietly collude on prices and wages and make a mockery of the self-regulated market. In 1947, one of those periods in American history when the concentration of business was a political issue, a study by the Federal Trade Commission found that the 113 largest manufacturing corporations owned 46 percent of the property, plant, and equipment employed in manufacturing. The economist John Kenneth Galbraith noted in the early 1950s that the dominant manufacturers of key household goods had not changed in decades, prima facie evidence that the fierce competition envisioned in the laissez-faire model was absent from the American economy. "An economy where the typical industry is shared by a few firms," he wrote, "is awkwardly inconsistent with a theory of capitalism which requires that power to affect prices or wages or output or investment be impersonally governed by the reaction of the many."

It is also a misconception that government ever really stood aside and left markets to their own fates. More often it has fallen to heads of state and their ministers to be the handmaidens of the business class. In what is often regarded as the golden age of laissez-faire, the late eighteenth century in England, when the world first heard the roar of capitalist production, government was fanning the flames of commerce. The cotton manufacturers that made up England's leading export industry in that period depended on protectionist measures by the government. They saw to it that Parliament banned the importation of printed cotton and blocked the export of tools used in producing cotton goods. In 1800, Manchester cotton concerns even pressed for a prohibition on the export of yarn, even though they knew it would cut into their own revenues. By the 1830s, as the free-market dogma unleashed by Smith and David Ricardo reached a feverish pitch in England, it was the government that took the lead in the transition to a laissez-faire economy. Under pressure from manufacturers, Parliament amended the Poor Law in 1834 to withhold relief and create an industrial working class dependent on the emerging capitalists for sustenance. "There was nothing natural about laissez-faire; free markets could never have come into being merely by allowing things to take their course," Karl Polanyi wrote in his classic study of early capitalism, *The Great Transformation.*

> Just as cotton manufacturers—the leading free trade industry—were created by the help of protective tariffs, export bounties, and indirect wage subsidies, laissez-faire itself was enforced by the state. The [eighteen] thirties and forties saw not only an outburst of legislation repealing restrictive regulations, but also an enormous increase in the administrative functions of the state, which was now being endowed with a central bureaucracy able to fulfill the tasks set by the adherents of liberalism. . . . Laissez-faire was not a method to achieve a thing, it was the thing to be achieved.

In the United States, where Smith's creed was taken up with a vengeance by the nineteenth century, government funding, expertise, and guidance were present in important phases of the country's economic development. While fighting to keep the country together in the Civil War, Abraham Lincoln still found the resources to subsidize one of the greatest public works projects in U.S. history, the laying of the transcontinental railroad. The Union Pacific and Central Pacific Railroads, embarking on the mammoth project from either coast, one with Irish labor and the other Chinese, could not have tunneled through mountains, traversed canyons, and pushed Indians off their land without generous help from the federal government. Lincoln was personally committed to the project. When the Union Pacific was running short of money, he summoned Congressman Oakes Ames to his office on January 20, 1865, and asked him to oversee the government's bailout of the project. "Ames, you take hold of this," Lincoln said. "If the subsidies provided are not enough to build the road, ask double, and you shall have it."

By 1880, an Interior Department auditor found that Washington had given the railroads title to government lands valued at $391,804,610, a gift equivalent to $7.2 billion in 2004 dollars. The government also made loans to the railroads in that period totaling $64,623,512, or over a $1 billion in current dollars. It is true that Washington got back nearly double that sum in interest. And it was not always clean hands doling out the public's money to the railroads. The revelation that a host of Washington politicians received railroad stock through the Credit Mobilier of America became one of the biggest scandals of the nineteenth century. But the point is that the transcontinental railroad, the lifeline of so much of the nation's future commerce, could not have happened without the government. The Union Pacific and Central Pacific, the nation's two largest corporations in the mid-nineteenth century, owed their very existence to public largesse.

Examples of such public-private cooperation abound throughout American history. In 1942, deans at the University of Pennsylvania's Moore School scoffed at a proposal by two of the school's researchers, John Mauchly and J. Presper Eckert, for the construction of a mammoth electronic calculator that would be infinitely faster than the mechanical adding machines currently in use. The proposal would have gone nowhere had it not reached the ears of Herman Goldstine, a twenty-nine-year-old Army lieutenant who had been assigned to work with the Moore School in devising ways to improve calculations for the firing tables used to guide the trajectory of artillery shells, one of the most vexing problems facing the military in World War II. Goldstine believed that Mauchly and Eckert had the solution, and he convinced the Pentagon to fund the project. The result was the Electronic Numerical Integrator and Computer, or ENIAC, the world's first computer. It weighed thirty tons and took eighteen thousand vacuum tubes to do the work that a single microchip does today, but there would have been no Microsoft or Apple without this partnership between the government and the private sector.

Government tutelage also lay behind the aircraft industry and, in our own time, the Internet. This symbiosis between government and private enterprise has been so constant that it could almost be posited as a natural law, yet well into the twentieth century, it was treated by the economics profession as if it did not exist. Instead, the national mythology continued to celebrate the rugged captains of industry who thrust our society forward with the lathe, the locomotive, and the pile driver. It took the Depression—the ultimate repudiation of the idea of a self-regulating market—to make economists accept that government must have a place in their modeling.

The classical school of economics had considered a devastating depression and sustained 20 percent unemployment a theoretical impossibility. That was the famous conclusion of Jean Baptiste Say, a Frenchman who popularized Smith's theories on the European continent. Say's Law of Markets held that a downturn in consumption would always increase savings, and an increase in savings would spur investment and the production of goods. The production of goods would in itself create demand for the purchase of those goods, by placing income in the hands of workers, suppliers, and others involved in the production. To put it simply, supply creates its own demand. A key precept of Say's Law was that interest rates would have a natural tendency to fall to the level where investors would make use of available savings. Say's Law was virtually unchallenged in the economics profession for a century, until the 1930s proved it to be unsuited to the realities of modern capitalism.

The sustained darkness that fell over the U.S. economy—and the economies of much of the rest of the world—in the 1930s gave the lie to the notion of a self-correcting market. Unemployment levels reached 25 percent in 1932, with the gross national product off by almost a half from its peak level of 1929. The price of a bushel of wheat went from over a dollar at the peak to thirty-eight cents four years later. Samuel Eliot Morison, describing the torpor enveloping America, reported that "New York apartment houses offered five-year leases for one year's rent, entire Pullman trains rolled along without a single passenger, hotels and resorts like Miami Beach were empty." With consumption so abysmal, there should have been plentiful savings, and interest rates should have fallen to a level needed for those savings to flow into investment. In the eyes of the classical economist, the market economy should have righted itself, but no such correction materialized. The Great Depression lay over the country for a dozen years, until government spending for the war heated up the economy. Even as Adam Smith's theories lay mangled, many of the faithful pressed on. Andrew Mellon, Hoover's secretary of the treasury, warned the president that injecting government into the economy would disrupt a great social catharsis being provided by the Depression. "People will work harder, live a more moral life," he said. "Values will be adjusted, and enterprising people will pick up the wrecks from less competent people." Mellon was gasping the last breaths of Social Darwinism. Even a staunch free-marketeer like Hoover realized that laziness and ineptitude on the part of the lower orders was not behind the Depression and that only government could stave off the ruination of America. While unwilling to support direct relief, he signed a bill creating the Reconstruction Finance Corporation, designed to lend money to railroads, banks, agricultural agencies, and manufacturers.

A new era of government intervention in the economy was dawning. The economist who would cast such a giant shadow across the industrial democracies in the twentieth century was not Adam Smith or Jean Baptiste Say but John Maynard Keynes, who revolutionized economics by proposing that government come to the rescue when private investment was not doing its part. Keynes's *The General Theory of Employment, Interest and Money,* published in 1936, appeared propitiously at a time when the Great Depression was making a shambles of Smith's theories. Keynes delivered the finishing blow to Say's law by arguing—in a very receptive, depression-ravaged climate—that investment would not reliably flow from savings and that supply and demand could reach equilibrium at low levels of performance. Long-term unemployment and economic stagnation were not impossibilities but inevitable outcomes in a capitalist economy, unless some other dynamic came into play. That other dynamic was government. When the private sector failed to deliver spending on investment or consumption, government would fill the gap, stimulating the economy through monetary policy, direct expenditures, or tax cuts. Once the economy was back at its optimum performance, the infusion of government money would be scaled back, and any deficits incurred during that period would gradually disappear with the increased revenues.

With the New Deal as its proving ground, Keynesianism became the dominant school of thought among economists by the 1950s. It not only gave political cover to liberals who wanted to spend money on social welfare programs, but by promising full employment and economic growth, it was also largely accepted by Eisenhower and other probusiness Republicans. This was a heady time for American liberals. At no other time in the country's history had government policies been so attuned to the needs of the common man and woman. Even as a mood of conservatism settled over the country, marked by the voters' choice of Eisenhower over the liberal intellectual Adlai Stevenson, an activist government—a welfare state—was accepted as one of the key ingredients of our market economy.

Adam Smith's theories seemed to recede ever deeper into obscurity. Galbraith, who was one of Keynes's chief disciples in the United States, became famous in the 1950s for his theory of "countervailing powers." As his theory went, industry had become concentrated in such a small number of corporations that the competition celebrated by Smith had ceased to exist. The invisible hand of the market could not regulate prices and wages under the conditions of oligopoly, where the dominant players quietly conspired to keep prices artificially high and wages artificially low. So a system of countervailing powers evolved to keep the oligopoly from dictating the terms of commerce. Organized labor saw to it that workers were paid a living wage. Farmers banded into cooperatives to get fair prices for their goods. Chain stores like Sears & Roebuck had enough muscle with manufacturers to ensure that wholesale prices were held in check and passed on in the form of reasonable retail prices.

For Galbraith, the most important countervailing power was the government. It was the great referee that would not only guarantee the unemployed against destitution but also keep the great industrial trusts from running roughshod over small business. Galbraith wrote in the 1950s that "countervailing power has become in modern times perhaps the major domestic peacetime function of the federal government."

> Labor sought and received it in the protection and assistance which the Wagner Act provided to union organization. Farmers sought and received it in the form of federal price supports to their markets—a direct subsidy of market power. Unorganized workers have sought and received it in the form of minimum wage legislation. The bituminous-coal mines sought and received it in the Bituminous Coal Conservation Act of 1935 and the National Bituminous Coal Act of 1937. These measures, all designed to give a group a market power it did not have before, comprised the most important legislative acts of the New Deal.

This was the era of Jim Crow and McCarthyism, of bonfires of rock-and-roll records and outrage at the movement of Elvis Presley's pelvis, of CIA-backed coups in Guatemala and Iran, a time when the president was a former general and the secretary of defense was the former president of General Motors, Charles Wilson, the man who famously said that what was good for GM was "good for the country." And yet, in these conservative times, the average Republican accepted a level of state intervention that only the left wing of the Democratic Party supports today. Had Ronald Reagan attempted to turn his GE speech into a real political platform in the 1950s, he would have been a laughingstock. How could the upper or middle classes have complained about the mixed economy in the 1950s and 1960s when the

United States was enjoying the most stupendous economic growth and the highest standard of living ever known to mankind?

Part and parcel of this mixed economy was a growth in the regulation of business. The regulatory regime began in its modern form in 1887, when President Grover Cleveland created the Interstate Commerce Commission to keep the railroad monopolies from gouging farmers and manufacturers. It was the first federal agency to stand independent of the three branches of government, but it would hardly be the last. Washington's watchfulness of industry would grow in fits and starts over the next six decades. It began blocking undue concentration of industry in the Progressive era and eventually, in the years following the New Deal, helped restore the stability of business and prevent ruinous competition and deflation. By the end of World War II, independent regulatory commissions constituted a fourth branch of government. Entities like the Federal Communication Commission, the Securities and Exchange Commission, and the Federal Aviation Administration aimed at promoting fair competition and protecting the consumers' interests in an increasingly complex economy.

Conservatives are fond of deriding this tradition of reform, but no serious student of American history could draw any other conclusion but that it vastly enlarged the middle class and rescued millions from lives of misery. At the turn of the century, men, women, and children labored sixty to seventy hours a day in squalid factories for pay that was often less than five dollars a week. Deaths from industrial accidents were commonplace, with 1 out of every 399 railroad employees dying in the year 1901 alone. The exploitation of child labor was a national shame.

Writing of this period, the historian and literary critic Van Wyck Brooks lamented that European immigrants escaped the tyranny of their own countries only to be "utterly destroyed by American indifference. . . . No one either knew or cared when their babies were drowned in the stinking green water that lay about their wretched shacks, when their daughters were forced into prostitution, when their sons fell into boiling vats because the employers had provided no safety devices."

This was a time when the average income of American workers was $400 to $500 a year. It was also a time when Andrew Carnegie, just from the stock he held in his steel company, earned $23 million in 1900—without paying any income tax. His annual earnings from that stock averaged $10 million a year from 1896 to 1900.

A middle-class revolt against such injustices, fueled in part by the exposés of muckrakers like Upton Sinclair and Ida Tarbell, gave birth to the Progressive era and helped propagate a long-term trend toward greater state intervention in the economy. In the conception of the Progressives, the state would be a neutral ombudsman ensuring that vast agglomerations of wealth would not trample the interests of the common man and threaten democracy itself. "The state," wrote Richard Hofstadter, "must not be anti-business, nor even anti-big business: it must be severely neutral among all the special interests in society, subordinating each to the common interest and dealing out even-handed justice to all." It is a testament to the quality of leadership across the public and private sectors in the middle of the twentieth century that the nation achieved just such a detente between big capital and the working class. In the preceding decades, government programs and regulations, together with the attitudes they helped instill in businesses and the public, shortened the workweek, boosted wages, improved safety, took children off the factory floor, legalized unions, and propelled millions into the middle class—all while coaxing along big business as a partner in the reforms. Government, business, and labor working together, not always happily but with a degree of resignation, created what Frederick Lewis Allen called "the widest distribution of prosperity ever witnessed in the world." When Reagan's acolytes denigrate this partnership, they are mocking the economic democracy that made America one of history's great civilizations.

In the same way corporations grew used to bargaining with unions, they also came to accept government regulations, not only because they helped restore public confidence in business after the Depression, but also because restrictions on who could enter specific industries protected existing concerns and prevented destructive competition. Regulated monopolies, like utilities, guaranteed stable prices and wages and a fair rate of return for those allowed to enter key industries. Before the late 1970s, some two-thirds of the U.S. economy was regulated: electric power, telecommunications, aviation, radio and television, information technology, banking, stock brokerage, insurance, trucking, and busing were all subject to some form of government control. Relations between the independent commissions and the private sector were so cozy that by the 1960s consumer advocates were complaining that the agencies were the "captives" of the industries they were supposed to be regulating. Ralph Nader called for the outright abolishment of the Civil Aeronautics Board in 1975, so convinced was he of its alliance with the airline industry. Left-wing journalists Jack Newfield and Jeff Greenfield complained in their "Populist Manifesto" in 1972 that utilities regulation gave a windfall to politically connected business interests, at the expense of consumers: "Every time an American dials a telephone, or turns on a light switch, or cooks his dinner, or heats his home, the rich get richer and the poor get poorer."

Keynesianism, though it was mainly concerned with fiscal and monetary matters, emerged from the war as the triumphant symbol and theoretical underpinning of this state intervention. Government had fought the Depression to a draw and routed the Axis powers. It was doling out college money in the GI Bill and giving returning veterans relaxed credit to buy homes. The public sector was an undeniable hero in postwar America, and Keynes was its greatest advocate. Thanks to the propaganda of Reaganism, the Keynesian is now considered disreputable. But in the recent past he was celebrated as the bulwark of what Arthur Schlesinger Jr. called the "vital center," a guarantor against extremes of left and right. As it was practiced in this country, Keynesianism was never aimed at radically redistributing the nation's income. President Kennedy's embrace of the philosophy in 1962 led to a tax reduction that would yield 45 percent of its benefits to the wealthiest 12 percent of the nation's taxpayers. It pleased the corporate lobby but was scorned by Keynesian purists like Galbraith, who preferred to stimulate the economy though direct expenditures. Still, the acceptance of government spending as an important economic tool gave legitimacy to more significant forays into social welfare policy that would follow, like Johnson's Great Society and the generous spending on housing and food stamps under Richard Nixon, who publicly declared himself a Keynesian. Between rapacious capitalism and the evil empire of communism, America and the other Western democracies had found a third way. In 1965, a *Time* magazine cover declared, "We Are All Keynesians Now."

But the political winds can shift abruptly. All it would take in this case was a direct assault on the American way of life. On October 16, 1973, five Arabs and an Iranian gathered in the royal palace in Kuwait City for a historic meeting that would have dire economic consequences for the United States and other Western democracies. Outraged by Israel's invasion of Egypt and Syria ten days earlier, the start of the Six-Day War, Sheik Yamani of Saudi Arabia and five other leaders of the Organization of Petroleum Exporting Countries decided to flex their economic muscle. To punish the United States for its support of Israel, OPEC raised the price of a barrel of oil by 70 percent and the next day ordered a boycott on oil sales to America. "This is a moment for which I have been waiting a long time," Yamani told the assemblage. "The moment has come. We are masters of our own commodity."

The impact on the United States was immediate—and devastating. Oil prices, which had been $1.80 per barrel in 1970 and $2.90 in mid-1973, were at $11.65 by the beginning of 1974. Virtually overnight, gas-guzzling America was in the depths of the Great Inflation. Inflation rose ever higher into the double digits even as the nation's economy shrank, a previously unknown confluence of overheating and contraction that became known as *stagflation*. America's economy was in its most dire condition since the Depression, and policymakers were looking for someone to blame. Keynesianism, the most obvious scapegoat, was driven from the halls of the academy and from the forefront of economic policy. Along with it went much of the liberal consensus that had governed America for decades. Without that sustained period of inflation and the economic woes it visited on the country, Ronald Reagan would never have made it out of California.

Inflation was already on the rise before the oil shock. The first faint rumblings registered in 1966, when the consumer price index rose by 3 percent, not an alarming number by later standards, but enough to stir concern among policymakers. The economy in 1965 and 1966 was at a boiling point, still feeling the stimulative effects of the Kennedy-Johnson tax cut. Meanwhile, Johnson had begun pumping money into the programs of the Great Society. And 1965 was the first full year of the nation's commitment of ground troops to Vietnam, with a price tag of $6 billion. Economic growth was so strong—exceeding an annual rate of 7 percent in late 1965—that revenues still kept the federal budget in surplus. But on top of all this, business responded to the heady economic climate and war spending with an investment binge, plowing yet more money into the economy.

The annual spending on the Vietnam War kept escalating—reaching $20.6 billion by 1967—and neither Johnson nor Nixon had much stomach for attacking inflation with politically unpopular tax increases or budget cuts. Instead, Nixon responded with a series of moves that amounted to hitting the gas and putting on the brakes at the same time. He unveiled an economic package on August 15, 1971, that instituted short-term wage and price controls while offering tax deductions for individuals and corporations and other incentives for investment. At the same time, he announced that the United States would no longer observe the historic international monetary agreement reached at Bretton Woods, New Hampshire, in 1944, a pact that had set up a stable system of currency exchange rates tied to the dollar. The agreement had symbolized the global dominance of the United States in the postwar era. Now Nixon was essentially admitting that the U.S. economy was no longer stable enough for its currency to anchor the international system.

Even with U.S. prestige ebbing on the world stage, Nixon was not willing to battle inflation at the expense of economic growth, even in the short term. He knew too well the political hazards that come with an increase in joblessness, having narrowly lost a presidential election to Kennedy in 1960 while the Republicans were presiding over an economic downturn. To make sure he would not be running for reelection in 1972 at such a disadvantage, he had embarked on an expansionary strategy two years earlier that combined budget increases with a move by the chairman of the Federal Reserve, Arthur Burns, Nixon's longtime ally, to pump money into the economy. The strategy worked. The gross domestic product grew at a stunning rate of 9.8 percent in the second quarter of 1972, with a healthy pace of 5.3 percent for the year as a whole. But with spending on the Vietnam War still rising and the economy already near or at maximum capacity when he had begun the strategy, the inflationary impact was horrendous.

By the end of the third quarter in 1973, inflation was galloping at an annual rate of nearly 7.5 percent. Then OPEC began its embargo on oil shipments to protest U.S. support for Israel in the Six-Day War, quadrupling the price of oil and helping bring the annual inflation rate to nearly 9 percent in the fourth quarter and 11 percent for the entire year of 1974. Looking back in 1979 on Nixon's handling of the inflation crisis, his effort to ensure his reelection no matter the cost to the nation's well-being, the political commentator Michael Harrington saw malfeasance of the highest order: "The Watergate affair was shocking evidence of deceit and criminality in the highest office of the land—but this economic Watergate was, in terms of its consequences, even more momentous."

By the second half of the 1970s, it was easy to paint the Keynesian economist as a failure. All of the most important indicators of economic well-being in the United States were steaming in the wrong direction. For the period 1966 to 1970, inflation averaged 4.59 percent annually. From 1976 to 1980, that figure climbed to 9.68 percent. Average unemployment went from 3.9 percent in the first period to 6.8 percent in the latter. Annual productivity increases dropped from 1.66 percent—already anemic compared to those of previous years—to 0.33. The economic model that had served the country so well in the immediate postwar years seemed to be faltering.

Jimmy Carter bore the brunt of this economic torpor. While the nation experienced strong economic growth in the first three years of his presidency, skyrocketing inflation and continuing declines in productivity continued to bedevil America. And then came the second oil shock in 1979, after the shah of Iran's overthrow interrupted oil shipments. In 1980, Carter ran for reelection not only with U.S. hostages still imprisoned in Iran, but also with a shrinking GNP of –0.3 for the year and an inflation rate for the year of 12.5 percent. Whatever faults Carter may have had as a leader, his presidency had the bad luck to be sandwiched between two oil shocks while dealing with the inflationary legacy of the Vietnam War.

The economic pain of the Nixon and Carter years bolstered the fortunes of Adam Smith's modern-day disciples, who had been in the shadows for most of the postwar period but began to reemerge in the inflation-ravaged seventies. Their new champion was Milton Friedman, a Nobel Prize–winning economist in the University of Chicago's department of economics who became America's most respected conservative thinker in the 1960s and a major influence on the Reagan presidency. Friedman's philosophy, known as monetarism, was essentially a belief that a reduction of government and a slow and predictable growth in the money supply provided a solution to the nation's ills. It added up to the old idea that the market would take care of itself. But the fact that it was an old idea didn't matter. Friedman's cogent writings in favor of the theory and his years of networking with intellectuals left him in a perfect position to be the court economist when the House of Keynes had fallen. His theories more than any others would provide the intellectual framework for the decimation of American government.

Friedman did not arrive at his influence through his physical presence. He was balding and bespectacled and stood only five feet tall. With missionary zeal he advocated for the free market, believing that government interference in the economy was an abridgment of human freedom. And he was a genius at promoting his ideas. By the eve of Ronald Reagan's election as president, he not only had a Nobel Prize but his own public television show and a column in *Newsweek*.

When Friedman first began his crusade, his was a lonely voice. In the 1950s, the economics department at the University of Chicago was the last redoubt of laissez-faire economists. The nation had seen little but explosive, inflation-free growth since the New Deal and World War II had transformed government into a benevolent colossus. In the preface to a 1982 edition of *Capitalism and Freedom,* a concise statement of his philosophies, Friedman remembered the silence that greeted the original edition two decades earlier, when no mainstream newspaper was willing even to review the book: "Those of us who were deeply concerned about the danger to freedom and prosperity from the growth of government, from the triumph of welfare-state and Keynesian ideas, were a small beleaguered minority regarded as eccentrics by the great majority of our fellow intellectuals."

In the early 1960s, Friedman was proposing a radical restructuring of the U.S. government at a time when the nation's growth was the marvel of the world. Among the government programs that *Capitalism and Freedom* said had no place in a free and democratic society were farm price supports, tariffs, rent control, minimum wages and price controls, industry regulation, regulation of the public airwaves, Social Security, professional licensing, public housing, military conscription, national parks, postal services, and toll roads. In other words, Friedman would eviscerate the entire reform legacy of the Progressive era and the New Deal as well as some functions of government that had been present since the nation's founding.

But Friedman's most important economic precept—the one that will forever be next to his name in encyclopedias—was monetarism. As an extension of his free-market philosophy, Friedman believed that most failures of the U.S. economy in the twentieth century had been caused by the Federal Reserve's clumsy attempts to fine-tune the economy through monetary policy. Even before Keynes, the central bank had routinely dealt with sluggish economic growth by increasing the supply of money through either of two measures: a lowering of the discount rate in its lending to commercial banks or the purchase of government securities from banks and other financial institutions. Friedman claimed these moves may stimulate the economy in the short term, but cause inflation and retard economic growth in the long term. He believed the Fed should guarantee a slow and predictable rate of money growth, pegged to the average annual growth of the gross domestic product, about 3 to 5 percent a year. Such a strategy would occasionally entail some pain—especially when the system was first imposed—but would eventually result in healthy economic growth.

Friedman's system relied on an almost religious belief in the powers of the free market. He felt the effort by macroeconomists to deconstruct and manipulate a market system was doomed to failure. Efforts at collecting information and setting up abstract models would only make the economy more opaque. Better to accept the working of the unfettered market as an act of faith. The economy would settle on "natural" rates of unemployment and interest that would correct themselves if they strayed to undesirable levels. Friedman did not accept that the Depression had been caused by a failure of a market economy, but rather that the crash of 1929 and the ensuing decade of misery were due to bungling on the part of the Federal Reserve: "The fact is that the Great Depression, like most other periods of severe unemployment, was produced by government mismanagement rather than by any inherent instability of the private economy."

Barry Goldwater counted Friedman as an adviser and was the first major politician to adopt his theories, but the real debut of monetarism as national policy came when Richard Nixon embraced the concept at the start of his presidency. Nixon appointed Arthur Burns, who had once been Friedman's professor at Rutgers University, as the Federal Reserve chairman and named another monetarist, Paul McCracken, as the chairman of his Council of Economic Advisers. However, putting on the monetary brakes quickly retarded economic growth while failing to slow inflation, so Burns and the administration scrapped monetarism and embarked on an expansionist policy in early 1970. A year later, Nixon publicly proclaimed himself a Keynesian and instituted wage and price controls to counter inflation. The about-face embittered Friedman, who felt Nixon had absorbed the pain of a tight-money policy without waiting for the positive results.

But Friedman, after his 1976 Nobel Prize, had little trouble keeping his theories in the limelight as long as stagflation continued to gnaw at the U.S. economy. In 1979, Jimmy Carter's appointment to the chairmanship of the Federal Reserve, Paul Volcker, wrapped himself in the mantel of monetarism and set the central bank on a six-year regimen of tight money that would break the back of inflation but inflict such damage on the economy—especially manufacturing and agriculture—that it should have been as devastating to Friedman's standing as the Great Inflation was to Keynesianism. But the season of disgrace for monetarism had yet to unfold. Friedman's theories, unproven yet pleasing to those with an instinctive distaste for the redistributive policies of Keynesianism, would become part of the intellectual force behind Reagan's attack on government.

As Keynesianism fell, so, too, would the regulatory regime. A backlash against regulation had been growing throughout the 1970s, intensified by the complaints of business leaders that they were increasingly unable to raise capital and compete with overseas manufacturing because they were spending so much money coping with federal regulations. It was the first stirrings of the broad movement toward deregulation that continued to reshape our economy three decades later.

Business began souring on regulation as an increasingly activist government moved from so-called economic regulation—the promotion and protection of given industries—to "social regulation," designed to protect the health and safety of Americans. Between 1970 and 1974, Congress passed laws creating the Environmental Protection Agency, the Occupational Safety and Health Administration, the Consumer Product Safety Commission, the National Highway Traffic Safety Administration, and the Mine Safety and Health Administration, agencies that quickly became the bane of the corporate lobby, requiring their clients to spend millions of dollars to meet the new requirements of the federal government. The Code of Federal Regulations doubled from 1970 to 1980, from 54,000 to 100,000 pages.

When the U.S. economy was booming throughout the 1950s and 1960s, big business was content to let liberals toy with Keynesian policies and even tolerated economic regulations. But by the 1970s it was in an uglier mood. European and Japanese industries were recovering from the devastation of World War II and beginning to challenge the Americans in world markets. Inflation was raging in the 1970s and growth was uneven. All this was eating into business profits. The Watergate scandal produced a Democratic landslide in the 1974 congressional elections, raising fears among business leaders that a new round of regulations could be looming. "The danger had suddenly escalated," said Bryce Harlow, who was the senior Washington lobbyist for Procter & Gamble in that period. "We had to prevent business from being rolled up and put in the trash can by that Congress."

By the 1970s, what had once been a listless business lobby in Washington was bristling with conservative think tanks and pressure groups with the bankrolls of large corporations behind them. The Heritage Foundation, a conservative think tank founded in 1973, saw its budget increase from $1 million in 1976–1977 to $7.1 million in 1981–1982, thanks to funding from beer baron Joseph Coors, Pittsburgh industrialist Richard Mellon Scaife, Mobil Oil, Dow Chemical Company, and a host of other wealthy contributors. The American Enterprise Institute, the oldest of the major conservative think tanks, had a staff of 19 people and a budget of less than $1 million in 1970. Ten years later, it had a staff of 135 and a budget of more than $10 million. In the early 1980s, AEI's board included Richard B. Madden, chairman of the Potlatch Corporation; James Affleck, chairman and chief executive officer of American Cyanamid Company; Willard C. Butcher, chairman and chief executive officer of Chase Manhattan Bank; and Paul F. Oreffice, president and chief executive officer of Dow Chemical. To the ranks of traditional business lobbying groups like the National Association of Manufacturers and the U.S. Chamber of Commerce was added the Business Roundtable, which was founded in 1972 to curtail the influence of labor unions but ultimately broadened its mission to work for an overall reduction of government. Each of these organizations, and others like them, would later contribute policy ideas and staff to the Reagan administration.

It became a sacred mission for the new conservative lobby to prove that social regulation was sapping the energies and resources of

American free enterprise. In the late 1970s, Dow Chemical Company assembled a ten-person task force to do a study of the impact of government red tape on the company. It found that Dow had spent $147 million in a single year to comply with federal regulation. Of this total, $87 million was found to be "appropriate," $10 million "questionable," and $50 million "excessive." One of the most influential advocates of deregulation was Murray Weidenbaum, who became chairman of the Council of Economic Advisers under Reagan after founding the Center for the Study of American Business at Washington University in St. Louis, a conservative think tank that issued report after report blaming government regulation for curtailing business productivity. Weidenbaum personally authored a study for the Joint Economic Committee of Congress in 1978 estimating that regulations were costing the U.S. economy $102.7 billion annually.

Business groups seized on the estimate with glee. Amway Corporation bought newspaper advertisements, headlined "Regulatory Overkill," that trumpeted Weidenbaum's startling revelation: "The Center for the Study of American Business estimates government regulation costs a family of four more than $2,000 a year. . . . That's more than 10 percent of their income." The National Cotton Council, with an ad titled "Over-regulation could cost your family a home of your own," warned home buyers that they were "being eaten out of house and home by federal regulations. Many of them unreasonable. And all of them costing you money. As much as $130 billion a year or $2,000 per family." Weidenbaum's calculation was widely circulated in newspaper articles and congressional testimony. *Time* magazine called it "one of the most widely accepted estimates."

The estimate was based on a calculation of regulatory costs that Weidenbaum and an associate, Robert DeFina, had compiled for the year 1976. In doing so, they had relied on various sources, including—for the Occupational Safety and Hazard Administration costs—an annual survey of businesses conducted by McGraw-Hill. Their conclusion was that the regulatory cost for that year was $66.1 billion: $3.2 billion in public money for the operation of the regulatory agencies and $62.9 billion that businesses spent in compliance costs. To update numbers for the congressional committee in 1978, Weidenbaum extrapolated from the 1976 data, assuming a continuing twenty-to-one ratio of private to public costs. Even discounting for this slippery math, Weidenbaum's methodology had no shortage of critics. Mark Green, then head of Ralph Nader's Corporate Accountability Research Group, pointed out that Weidenbaum's estimate of $666 of added regulatory costs for every new car was based on a Bureau of Labor Statistics finding that the BLS later found to be invalid. A 1976 survey of automakers by the National Highway Traffic Safety Administration put the number at $250. In 1977, the Business Roundtable hired the Arthur Andersen accounting firm for a year-long study of forty-eight of the nation's largest companies and their dealings with the six most active federal regulatory agencies. The study, which the Roundtable later tried to downplay, found that regulations had cost the companies a combined total of $2.6 billion and added 1.1 percent to the cost of their products. A Library of Congress assessment of Weidenbaum's study cited "unresolved problems of double-counting and inaccurate addition" and noted that its tally of regulatory burdens included time spent filling out forms for federal contracts, loans, and subsidies. Julius W. Allen of the Congressional Research Service found "serious shortcomings and limitations" in the Weidenbaum study, which he said in some cases relied on data that were more than a decade old.

But the biggest criticism of Weidenbaum's study focused on his failure to consider the economic benefits of regulation. As Green put it, "His emphasis on costs and his neglect of benefits is about as sophisticated as attacking GM for costing shareholders $52 billion a year—and neglecting to mention that it also produces $55 billion a year in revenues."

While it is hard to put an economic value on a human life or an unpolluted beach, experts have made efforts to quantify the benefits of regulation. A 1979 University of Wyoming study sponsored by the Environmental Protection Agency found that air pollution annually cost the nation $5 billion to $16 billion in "mortality effects" and $36 billion in "morbidity effects," such as lost workdays in heavily polluted areas. Mark Green and Norman Waitzman, a graduate student at American University, wrote a 162-page study for the Corporate Accountability Research Group that looked at five federal agencies that Weidenbaum said had cost the economy $31.4 billion in a year—and found that the same agencies had yielded $36 billion in benefits.

Calculating the real costs and benefits of regulation may be impossible. There can be no doubting, however, that Weidenbaum's research—bought and paid for by corporations that poured money into his center—made no attempt to consider the benefits. And yet, with corporate money buying newspaper advertisements, issuing press releases, and contributing to politicians to support findings like those arrived at by Weidenbaum, the notion that regulations were a crushing burden on American business became received wisdom. A review of the Lexis-Nexis database of broadcast and print media items shows that between 1979 and 1990, the Center for the Study of American Business was mentioned 612 times. In the same period, the Corporate Accountability Research Group appeared only 42 times. So much for the "liberal media."

With the political winds blowing in their favor, companies found they could blame regulation for all of their competitive failures. U.S. automakers blamed environmental regulations for their competitive woes, not higher-quality Japanese cars with better fuel efficiency than Buicks and Cadillacs. Steel companies blamed clean-air and clean-water restrictions, not their failure to invest in modern equipment that would help them compete with overseas steel producers. When Anaconda Copper Company closed its main factory in Montana in 1980, costing fifteen hundred workers their jobs, executives blamed the cost of complying with environmental, health and workplace regulations. But others gave a different explanation: severe labor problems and decades of bad management that emphasized quick profits over investment in technology. "By the late 1970s, complaints of excessive regulation had become management's all-purpose copout," Susan and Martin Tolchin wrote early in the Reagan administration. Robert Reich, a Harvard University professor who would later become Bill Clinton's labor secretary, pointed out in 1983 that 48 percent of the $356 million that the U.S. steel industry spent on reducing pollution and improving worker safety in the 1970s was subsidized by state and local governments through industrial development bonds. And, he said, Japanese steel firms spent twice that amount for the same purposes in that period, while underpricing their U.S. competitors. "Regulatory rollbacks will not restore America's industrial edge," Reich wrote, "since regulations are demonstrably not responsible for American industry's competitive decline."

Perhaps the most authoritative assessment of whether government regulations were strangling U.S. industry came from the MIT Commission on Industrial Productivity. As noted earlier, the panel's exhaustive study of U.S. manufacturing, completed in 1986, was debated before congressional committees and widely accepted by corporate executives. The panel concluded that regulations had hindered the competitiveness of some individual industries, but that their overall negative impact on the U.S. economy had been negligible:

> The commission's sectoral studies revealed specific cases in which regulation had a serious impact on performance, but we did not detect a major effect across the board. . . . Although much environmental, health, and safety regulation was put in place in the 1970s, most economists estimate that this regulation was responsible for no more than 10 to 15 percent of the productivity slowdown during those years. During the 1980s regulation has not generally become more stringent, and the effect on productivity growth has diminished.

The panel also made reference to a survey of senior research-and-development officers of technology-intensive companies, less than a fourth of whom responded that government regulations had hindered their companies. "A somewhat larger number felt that the impact on the economy as a whole had been more important, but the problem was not regarded as an insurmountable barrier to U.S. competitiveness," the authors wrote.

But such reasoned analysis was drowned out by corporate propaganda, which created a groundswell of public indignation and influenced the media's treatment of the subject. The year before Reagan's election, all three major newsweeklies, *Newsweek, Time,* and *U.S. News and World Report,* ran cover stories that depicted excessive regulation as a drag on the economy. Under attack from the left, right, and center, regulatory agencies were on the defensive. Jimmy Carter, desperate to control inflation in the second-year of his presidency, decided to rein in the economic regulations that he felt were the most detrimental to the economy while strengthening the social regulations that he viewed as most vital to the health and safety of citizens. He deregulated airlines, trucking companies, and bus companies and began the deregulation of banking. In March 1978, he issued an executive order requiring government agencies to do an economic analysis before enacting any new regulations. He set up a Regulation Analysis Review Group headed by Charles L. Schultze, chairman of his Council of Economic Advisers, thus injecting an economist into a discipline that had previous been dominated by lawyers. Carter, a supposed populist, was buying into a program dictated by the nation's corporate elite.

The intellectual and political groundwork for an assault on the welfare state and the regulatory regime was solidly in place. Corporately funded think tanks had been turning out reams of studies to back up their claims that the bloated federal government, with its onerous tax rates and nettlesome regulations, was stifling America's competitiveness. The supply-siders—Laffer, Wanniski, Kemp, and Stockman—were agitating in Congress for an attack on the tax code. But more important, the American public was also increasingly receptive to a reordering of government, in no small part because of its increased tax burden. For much of the postwar era, the vast majority of American taxpayers had lived happily within a simplified tax code that did little to punish them for salary increases. As the Washington journalist Thomas Byrne Edsall described the tax code of the 1960s, "For 90 percent of the population, there were, in effect, three marginal tax rates: zero for the bottom fifth of the population, 20 percent for the nearly half of the population making from $2,700 to $7,000, and 22 percent for the next quarter of the population making from $7,000 to $11,000." The simplicity of the tax code meant that American families could sharply increase their income while staying within the same tax bracket. Only the people whose income placed them in the top 10 percent were subject to graduated marginal tax rates ranging from 26 to 91 percent. But the escalating inflation of the 1970s changed all that. Rising median incomes in the 1970s pushed many ordinary Americans into the tax brackets with graduated marginal rates, exposing them to the "bracket creep" that had once been a problem only for the rich. The results of inflation and real increases in income, Edsall wrote, were a "progressive rate system that was no longer separating the very rich from the majority of taxpayers but was impinging directly on the well-being of the working and middle classes [and created] a strong base of deep, anti-tax sentiments, sentiments seeping more and more into basic economic constituencies of the Democratic party."

Wide segments of the public were ready to listen to the growing antigovernment rhetoric. All that was needed was a popular champion—a role for which Ronald Reagan had been grooming himself for decades. Ever since he became convinced that the government took too much of his movie-star earnings to help pay the debt for World War II, ever since the federal government nearly indicted him for his conflicts of interest as president of the Screen Actors Guild, and ever since General Electric paid him to attack government, he had made the mockery of Washington his mission in life. Throughout the 1970s, both in his campaign speeches and in the commentaries that appeared on dozens of radio stations around the country, he busied himself denigrating the basic functions of the government he sought to lead. At one point he described government as "coming through the windows, underneath the door and down the chimney," as though it were a toxic gas or alien invader.

In the years leading up to his election as president, Reagan uttered scores of inaccurate statements about the federal government, some so outlandish that anyone could immediately recognize them as false. He once told an audience that the federal government operated nineteen thousand businesses when the real number of such "businesses"—like the Tennessee Valley Authority—was less than a thousand. He said in a radio address in 1979 that General Motors had to employ 20,000 people just to handle government paperwork; a company spokesman later responded that about 5,000 out of the company's 500,000 employees had assignments that included federal paperwork and that tax filings were among those duties. He was quoted in the *Washington Star* in March 1980 as saying that the Congressional Budget Office had come up with a list of forty-one items totaling $11 million in the federal budget that the agency had identified as unnecessary spending. The specificity with which he named the agency, the number of items, and the dollar amount was bizarre, since a CBO spokesman later said *the agency knew of no such list.* No one in the press ever called these fabrications for what they were: lies. The press just chalked it up to Reagan being Reagan. When he came up with a whopper in 1982 about England's once having executed people for gun possession, Press Secretary Larry Speakes suggested that the truth of his statements was beside the point. "Well, it's a good story, though," Speakes told a reporter. "It made the point, didn't it?"

Once Reagan became president, the evils of government became a handy excuse for anything that was wrong with the country. Responsible economists may debate whether the economic pain caused by the Federal Reserve Bank's tight-money policies under Paul Volcker was necessary to bring inflation under control. But none would deny that those policies were in part responsible for the severe unemployment of the 1980s, the worst since the Great Depression. And yet Ronald Reagan, in a major speech on government in May 1983, found a much simpler answer for unemployment: "Those who have for so long preached the benefits of bigger government should be asked to acknowledge that the economic conditions that led to recession and unemployment were created by years of growth in government and the climate of government expansion and interference."

In the same speech, Reagan came up with misleading poverty figures to back up his contention that Great Society programs begun in the 1960s had made poverty worse:

> As pointed out in a recent article by Charles Murray in the *Public Interest* magazine, the great expansion of government programs that took place under the aegis of the Great Society coincided with an end to economic progress for America's poor people. From 1949 until just before the Great Society got underway in 1964, the percentage of American families in poverty fell dramatically—from nearly 33 percent to only 18 percent. But by 1980, with the full impact of the Great Society's programs being felt, the trend had reversed itself, and there was an even higher proportion of people living in poverty than in 1969.

Reagan's statement not only contains an acknowledgment of the vast improvement in the lives of the poor in the post–New Deal era—a period of unprecedented government intervention in the economy—but it also omits some highly relevant elements in the poverty equation. As shown in Table 1, the rates of poverty for families began a steep decline in the aftermath of the Great Society, dropping from 17.4 percent in 1964 to 9.9 percent a decade later. That 43 percent decrease in the poverty rate improved the lives of more than twelve million families. The poverty level then stayed in the 10 percent range for the rest of the 1970s, until the 1979 oil shock once again undermined the economy. Reagan's comparing 1969 to 1980 was particularly disingenuous, because the former was a year of 3 percent economic growth and the latter a year of economic shrinkage. Any responsible economist knows the hazards in comparing the peak of one business cycle with the nadir of another. Of course, the biggest irony of Reagan's statement is that poverty rates continued to rise in the first three years of his presidency and would not fall back into the 10 percent range until 1999, the latter part of Bill Clinton's second term in office.

But it really didn't matter that so many of his claims were false. Reagan knew how to whip up a mob. He was speaking to an increasingly receptive audience. At a time when Americans were feeling the brunt of the poor economy and the new burden of taxation, Reagan was talking about "welfare queens" soaking up their tax dollars and

TABLE 1 Families Below the Poverty Line, 1963–2005 (Numbers in Thousands)

Year	*Families*	*Percentage*	*Year*	*Families*	*Percentage*
1963	31,498	17.9	1982	27,349	13.6
1964	30,912	17.4	1983	27,933	13.9
1965	28,358	15.8	1984	26,458	13.1
1966	23,809	13.1	1985	25,729	12.6
1967	22,771	12.5	1986	24,754	12.0
1968	20,695	11.3	1987	24,725	12.0
1969	19,175	10.4	1988	24,048	11.6
1970	20,330	10.9	1989	24,066	11.5
1971	20,405	10.8	1990	25,232	12.0
1972	19,577	10.3	1991	27,143	12.8
1973	18,299	9.7	1992	28,961	13.3
1974	18,817	9.9	1993	29,927	13.6
1977	19,505	10.2	1994	28,985	13.1
1975	20,789	10.9	1995	27,501	12.3
1976	19,632	10.3	1996	27,376	12.2
1977	19,505	10.2	1997	26,217	11.6
1978	19,062	10.0	1998	25,370	11.2
1979	19,964	10.2	1999	23,830	10.3
1980	22,601	11.5	2000	22,347	9.6
1981	24,850	12.5	2005	26,068	10.8

Source: U.S. Census Bureau, http://www.census.gov/hhes/www/poverty/histpov/hstpov2.html.

asking them if they were better off than they were four years earlier. You can bet they were listening. He had them convinced that he was going to rout the faceless bureaucrats who were squeezing the life out of the country. Of course, he spoke only in generalities, in saccharine sound bites that made his vision for the country seem benign, even heroic. He never mentioned selling national parks, ending nutrition programs for children, cutting development grants to struggling rural communities, gutting food stamps, or rolling back regulations key to the public's well-being.

The Reagan Revolution would implant a new order in America, one whose upheavals and vast inequalities were completely unnecessary, based on false assumptions about the inadequacy of the liberal consensus governing America. As any clear-eyed rendering of the recent past shows, Keynesianism should not have taken the blame for an inflationary scourge caused by extraordinary world events and the tactical missteps of Johnson and Nixon. The welfare state did not increase poverty. Taxes and government regulations did not put a drag on American productivity. Liberalism became the dreaded "L word" for reasons having more to do with demagoguery than reality, at least in the realm of economic policy. These truths somehow escaped Americans in the 1980 election and continue to escape them today, despite the ugly episodes that the retrenchment of government has produced in the last two decades.

CHAPTER 5

The Looting of America

One person not fooled by Reagan's fact-challenged fulminations about government was that legendary gadfly of the Senate, William Proxmire. Reagan's election, and the contempt for populism that it brought to the forefront of the nation, was an affront to all that Proxmire had stood for in public life. Here was a man *genuinely* interested in reducing government waste and *genuinely* dedicated to the interests of working people. In his two decades as a Democratic senator from Wisconsin, Proxmire had infuriated presidents and congressional leaders with his refusal to compromise his strong moral principles. He was reelected by his constituents five times without taking a dime in campaign contributions. He refused to accept reimbursement for travel expenses and was a fierce critic of wasteful government spending, particularly that lavished on the military. He did not miss a roll call vote in the Senate over more than twenty years, a record that still stands today.

Such rectitude did not fit easily into the new political order unfolding in Reagan's first term, and Proxmire could feel his power slipping away. The Republicans' new control of the Senate had cost him his chairmanship of the Committee on Banking, Housing, and Urban Affairs. More to the point, his way of thinking simply had little currency in the new era. On April 28, 1981, as he sat with his colleagues in

Room 5302 of the Senate Dirksen Office Building for the first several hearings on financial deregulation, he raised a lonely and prophetic voice against forces that were about to change America forever.

Seated among the witnesses opposite Proxmire was a man more representative of the new consensus in Washington, Donald T. Regan, secretary of the treasury. Regan's orientation was a far cry from Proxmire's stubborn fealty to the populist traditions of Wisconsin. Regan's views had been shaped in the boardroom of Merrill Lynch, where the quality of Washington leadership was measured not in its service to ordinary Americans but in the sustenance lent to the value of stocks and bonds. Regan had definite ideas about financial regulation. As chairman of Merrill Lynch, he had spent years trying to find a way around restrictions placed on banking, securities, and insurance firms after the Great Crash. Now, as he would make clear to the largely sympathetic group of senators, he was dedicated to getting rid of those regulations altogether.

First on his hit list was the McFadden Act, a 1927 law aimed at preserving community banking by restricting the ability of financial institutions to operate in more than one state. The law was all that stood in the way of national companies' swallowing up independently owned banks across the country. Regan was even more disdainful of the Banking Act of 1933, better known as the Glass-Steagall Act. The legislation had been enacted to break up the unethical collusion between banks and brokerage houses in the years preceding the Depression. Many depositors lost their life savings because commercial banks had invested money in stocks during the speculative frenzy leading up to the Great Crash. Some banks had engaged in a practice known as self-dealing—the loaning of money to hollow companies to make their books look attractive to investors. The bank was then repaid from the company's artificially inflated stock market capitalization. Glass-Steagall and other laws of this period removed inherent conflicts of interest by prohibiting investment banks, which underwrite and promote stocks, to be housed under the same roof as commercial banks and insurance companies, which have a fiduciary duty to wisely invest their clients' money.

But Regan felt such restrictions had been outmoded by the new realities of international finance. Under his chairmanship, Merrill Lynch had struck a blow against Glass-Steagall in 1977 by creating cash management accounts, money market funds that allowed account holders to write checks against their securities portfolio. *Forbes* hailed cash management accounts as one of the great financial innovations of the century. Others viewed them for what they were: a blatant attempt to circumvent Glass-Steagall. Walter Wriston, chairman of Citicorp, couldn't help but take a swipe at his Merrill Lynch counterpart as they sat on the dais together at a banking conference. "The future of banking in this country is already here," he told the audience, "and it's Merrill Lynch." Regan's only response was a broad grin.

Commercial banks cried foul when the cash management accounts were offered, but the U.S. Supreme Court allowed them to remain. That victory was not enough for Regan. The plan he was about to outline for the senators would not just modify banking regulation to accommodate the emergence of new financial instruments but throw out regulation altogether. "I have some very strong personal convictions about the need to reduce legal barriers that separate the activities of all financial institutions," he told the panel. He went on to endorse the elimination of all ceilings on interest rates and all controls on the types of loans provided by banks and other financial institutions. The Reagan administration's goal, he said, was to "allow all depository institutions to make the same type of loans in whatever amount they see fit."

Regan's blueprint would have enormous ramifications. Besides the huge changes it would bring to the contours of American commerce, it would lead to one financial crisis after another for the next quarter of a century, including the subprime mortgage crisis and the devastation in the financial sector that unfolded in the second half of 2008. But almost no one on the committee uttered a word of protest. The committee's new chairman, Jake Garn, a former insurance salesman from Utah whose campaign coffers were flush with donations from banking interests, was positively giddy about the Reagan administration's plan to free banking from government restrictions. "I think most of you know the entire time I have been on this committee, I have felt that the federal government has interfered far too much in the financial community," he said.

Although Regan and Garn insisted they were advocating for consumers, it fell to Proxmire to predict what sweeping banking deregulation really portended for the average American. With a dignity unaffected by the indifference etched in the faces of his colleagues, Proxmire explained that America's vast numbers of independently owned financial institutions—14,000 banks, 6,000 savings and loans, and 12,000 credit unions—made the country's financial system uniquely responsive to the needs of local communities. It preserved a semblance of democracy in the exercise of the nation's financial power.

> Most small businesses in the towns and cities of our country can find a local bank or other lender who has lived in the community all his life, who owns his bank, who knows the principal borrowers in the community by their first name, knows their character as well as their balance sheet, knows their wife and their kids and their dads and their mother, and the whole family. The owner, in turn, isn't owned or controlled by a New York firm or a San Francisco firm, and doesn't expect to move along to another part of the country in a couple of months or a couple of years. . . . And now we may be on the brink of changing that; with changes in McFadden-Douglas, Citibank might move into Oshkosh or Beaver Dam, Wisconsin, and with their vastly superior capital and advertising, they might persuade the local institutions to sell out to them. In the short run, no one gets hurt. Local owners of the financial institutions may even enjoy a handsome profit on the deals. *But the whole character of Oshkosh and Beaver Dam changes.*

If Proxmire's sermonizing sounds naive a quarter of a century later, almost as if it were dreamed up by Frank Capra, it is merely a testament to how dramatically the Reagan Revolution changed the terms of the debate. Before Reagan, politicians actually stood on the floor of the House and Senate and spoke idealistically about the needs of average Americans and the preservation of bucolic values. As it turned out, Proxmire's statement was eerily prophetic. The whole character of Oshkosh and Beaver Dam *was* about to change. Regan's plan for deregulation of the financial sector would take years to come to full fruition—what was left of Glass-Steagall would not finally be repealed until 1999—but the processes he and his Republican colleagues set in motion in 1981 were the genesis of so much that is wrong with the U.S. economy in the twenty-first century.

The Reagan administration's zest for financial deregulation was responsible for the boom-and-bust cataclysms of the 1980s and 1990s, the obscene inflation of executive compensation; the corporate scandals and stock market meltdown of 2000–2001; and innumerable crises in international finance, including the most devastating of them all: the subprime mortgage scandal. Deregulation corrupted financial institutions at the same time that it made them the lords of the world economy and allowed their proxies, people like Robert Rubin and Alan Greenspan, to dictate the policies of the federal government. History will marvel that these two standard-bearers of Reaganism—Greenspan and Rubin—were lionized as geniuses and visionaries at the very time they were steering the nation toward disaster.

Before delving into the two and half decades of thievery wrought by Reagan's financial deregulation, it is important to understand how insidiously his presidency injected its deregulatory agenda into virtually every sphere of government. Some of Reagan's biographers have noted that few statutes mandating deregulation were adopted during his time in office. It is true that Congress deregulated more industries during the presidencies of Jimmy Carter and Bill Clinton than it did in the Reagan-Bush years. But that hardly tells the whole story. Reagan achieved deregulation merely by ordering the bureaucracy to stop enforcing the regulations that already existed and by filling the government's ranks with people who had little inclination to interfere with the private sector. Why fight costly legislative battles when the same result could be achieved through executive inertia? Reagan changed the role of government from that of watchdog to lapdog without even bothering to consult the Congress. He also gave a potent political voice to the backlash against regulations, ensuring that the movement would continue to burgeon after he left office. If we suffer from tainted meat and untested drugs, if airlines are unsafe and drinking water polluted, if companies are free to bust their unions and inflate their earnings, if energy companies can create blackouts to gouge the ratepayers with impunity, we can thank Ronald Reagan.

The Reaganites went after regulatory agencies with relish, starving them of resources and staffing them with officials committed to their destruction. A few days after he took office, Reagan signed an executive order that put a sixty-day freeze on all new federal regulations, including many of the 119 regulations that Carter had approved in his final month. He also ordered that all future regulations pass muster with David Stockman's Office of Management and Budget. Ed Meese, Reagan's ideological gatekeeper, injected himself into the hiring of key regulatory officials to make sure they adhered to the administration's deregulatory goals. The scrutiny worked. Rather than follow tradition and fight for their agencies' budgets, the Reaganites actually appeared before congressional committees to ask that their funding be reduced. At the same time, the heads of many of the federal regulatory agencies met secretly with corporate leaders, while denying access to congressional staffers and consumer groups. In short order, the Environmental Protection Agency, the Occupational Safety and Hazard Administration, the Consumer Product Safety Commission, the Mine Safety and Health Administration, the Food and Drug Administration, and a host of other regulatory agencies gladly cut their staffs and curtailed their enforcement. "None of the lawyers I know can remember anything like the impact the election has had on the regulatory agencies," one lawyer who represented corporate clients said in March 1981. "They're offering me things I wouldn't have dared to ask for before."

OSHA was one of Reagan's favorite whipping boys, one that had been on his hit list even before he entered the White House. In 1978, he had called OSHA "one of the most pernicious of the watchdog agencies," adding later that "through such things as OSHA, the government is trying to minimize the ownership of private property in this country." A year later, he endorsed a bill calling for OSHA's abolition. Although he did not accomplish its abolition as president, he did drive a stake into its heart by appointing as its director Thorne Auchter, former head of a Florida construction company that had been the subject of numerous OSHA fines and citations. Between 1980 and 1986, OSHA's inspections of manufacturing concerns fell by 30 percent, and its fines dropped from $26 million to $13 million.

Reagan's deregulation was spearheaded by the Presidential Task Force on Regulatory Relief, chaired by Vice President George Bush but largely managed by James C. Miller III, who in the first months of the administration was the administrator of regulatory affairs within the Office of Management and Budget; Richard Williamson, assistant to the president for intergovernmental and regulatory affairs; and C. Boyden Gray, who was the task force's counsel. The three made it clear from the first days of Reagan's first term that the task force would be a tool of the business community. Bush sent thousands of letters to businesses, civic leaders, governors, and others urging them to report their worst regulatory horror stories and submit recommendations for reform. In a speech before the U.S. Chamber of Commerce on April 10, 1981, Gray told business leaders that they should feel free to go over the heads of regulatory agencies and take their concerns directly to the White House. "If you go to the agency first, don't be too pessimistic if they can't solve the problem there," he said. "That's what the task force is for."

Gray told the audience about a group of trade associations and corporate attorneys who had problems with a set of regulations and took up his invitation to get the White House involved. "We alerted the top people at the agency that there was a little hanky-panky going on at the bottom of the agency, and it was cleared up very rapidly. The system does work if you use it as a sort of appeal. You can act as a double check on the agency that you might encounter problems with."

But the White House's open-door policy did not extend to reporters, congressional investigators, and others who might want to know about its discussions with corporate leaders on the subject of regulatory relief. OMB was so resistant to inquiries from the Subcommittee on Oversight and Investigation of the House Committee on Energy and Commerce, chaired by John Dingell, the powerful Democratic congressman from Michigan, that it would submit data to the subcommittee only under subpoena. The agency at first claimed it kept no minutes or any other record of office visits by corporate representatives. Upon further prodding, OMB turned over a list of corporate leaders who had made appearances. According to one congressional staffer, it read "like a list of the Fortune 500." The subcommittee was able to document numerous instances in which the withdrawal of regulations closely followed the meetings. It also concluded that the involvement of the task force on any particular regulation was enough to freeze an agency's enforcement. But the subjects of the meetings revealed under the subpoena were described only in the broadest terms, and no minutes were made available. Even after being hauled before Dingell's committee, Miller and Gray refused to acknowledge killing any specific regulation, as the following excerpt from the June 1981 testimony illustrates. Miller is questioned by Democratic Senator Al Gore of Tennessee:

MR. GORE: You had a 20-minute meeting with the Chemical Manufacturers Association talking about regulatory relief a month before you asked to pull back the regulations on hazardous waste disposal, and you are telling me under oath that you did not even mention hazardous waste with the CMA?

MR. MILLER: I am telling you, to the best of my recollections, that topic did not come up.

MR. GORE: What about February 18, 1981? You met with the American Mining Congress and discussed "support for regulatory relief." Isn't it more likely that you discussed their support for the postponement of the Interior Department's rule on extraction of coals, which has now been postponed indefinitely?

MR. MILLER: I cannot recall that particular meeting.

It is easy, when dealing with the arcane details of government regulation, to forget that real people suffer when federal officials turn a blind eye to the excesses of corporations. After Reagan obtained drastic staff reductions in the Mine Safety and Health Administration, civil penalties dropped by 27 percent and the number of mine fatalities increased from 133 in 1980 to 153 in 1981, despite a three-month strike that year by the United Mine Workers. "We've lost direction. The morale of the inspector is destroyed," Hugh Smith, a federal mine inspector in Kentucky, complained in 1982. "It has never been put in writing that we shouldn't enforce the law, but our people know there's a change in attitude in Washington. You only have to watch the 6 o'clock news to know this."

Never was the immorality of the administration displayed more vividly than in a sad episode from the early 1980s, an all-but-forgotten tale of young lives lost and families shattered that by itself is enough to belie the benevolent, populist image of Ronald Reagan.

The story begins with the person of Jim J. Tozzi, an administration official who for decades has played an important behind-the-scenes role in undermining government, a man who at various times has managed to serve as government functionary and lobbyist for big business without ever changing his job description. Tozzi is the proverbial wolf in sheep's clothing. He has been the ultimate Washington insider, a disarming man quick to buy drinks or deliver a punch line at Capitol Hill receptions. A raconteur and former New Orleans jazz musician, he wears monogrammed cufflinks and once sold wine under his own label, Villa Tozzi. He is the kind of person even his political enemies find hard not to like. Rena Steinzor, a former scholar at the Center for Progressive Regulation, once called Tozzi her "favorite bad guy."

Tozzi has been known to kill time peering through a large telescope mounted in the window of a seventh-floor office overlooking Washington's DuPont Circle, the perfect metaphor for the watch he has long kept over federal agencies. Long before the cadres of Reagan deregulators descended on Washington, Tozzi was a one-man fifth column embedded in the bureaucracy. He has had a visceral distrust of federal regulators since he was hired in the secretary of the army's office in 1964 and entrusted with overseeing Army Corps of Engineers projects. His initial assignment was to monitor the flow of construction money, but he soon expanded his missions to reviewing—and challenging—the corps' regulations, making him something of a rarity at the time.

His pioneering work as a deregulator brought him to the attention of the Nixon White House, after its creation of the Environmental Protection Agency in 1970 provoked criticism from business groups. As Tozzi has told it, White House Chief of Staff H. R. Haldeman wanted someone placed in the Office of Management and Budget to keep a watch on the EPA's regulations: "Haldeman said, 'What did we let out of the box?' And at the time I was in the Office of the Secretary of the Army and Haldeman said, 'There's a nerd over at Army.'" So it was that Tozzi became chief of the environmental branch of OMB, where he put every proposed regulation under scrutiny and made sure that many never saw the light of day.

It was in this period that Tozzi became recognized by insiders as one of the most influential people in Washington, even though he was virtually unknown to the public. As one EPA official related in a 1982 interview, every proposed regulation had to be crafted in a way that would pass muster with Tozzi. "We would ask ourselves, 'What's our presidential strategy. What's our congressional strategy? What's our Tozzi strategy?'" the official said. There is little in the way of a paper trail to document the maneuvering of this seasoned Washington player, which is just the way he liked it. His derailment of proposed regulations was not described in internal memos or congressional testimony because most of it was accomplished through phone calls or face-to-face meetings with his innumerable contacts throughout the capital, as Tozzi himself has readily admitted. "I don't want to leave fingerprints," he once told the *Washington Post* in one of the few interviews he gave during his period in government.

Fingerprints is an apt term, for the episode that concerns us here was nothing less than a crime. After Reagan took office, Tozzi was named deputy administrator of the Office of Information and Regulatory Affairs, a division of OMB that Reagan, through executive order, gave sweeping powers to review all proposed federal regulations. Most of the regulations that passed through OIRA's maw would never be seen again. But few of the agency's actions were so irresponsible or would have such an immediate and devastating effect on human lives as one engineered by Tozzi during Reagan's second year in office. In June 1982, the Department of Health and Human Services proposed a regulation that aspirin bottles carry a label warning that consumption of the pain reliever could trigger Reye's syndrome in children suffering from chicken pox or influenza. Reye's syndrome is an often-fatal illness that attacks the brain, liver, and other organs, and physicians had noticed a link with aspirin consumption as early as the 1960s.

In proposing the regulation, HHS noted findings by the Food and Drug Administration that a "consensus of the scientific experts" supported evidence of a link between aspirin and Reye's syndrome and believed warning labels were justified. The FDA was supported by the federal Centers for Disease Control and Prevention and the American Academy of Pediatrics, the latter issuing a report citing a "high probability that the administration of aspirin contributes to the causation of Reye's syndrome."

Such a scientific consensus—especially when hundreds of children were developing Reye's syndrome every year, many after consuming aspirin—would have quickly resulted in regulation at any other time in the post–New Deal era. But Reagan had placed a concern for corporate profits ahead of the well-being of Americans, and the ideologues in OMB quickly moved against the regulation. The aspirin industry easily did away with the labeling proposal. In fact, Joseph White, president of the industry-funded Aspirin Foundation, found that all it took was a meeting with Tozzi in which he expressed the opinion of aspirin makers that the science was inconclusive. Tozzi, in turn, consulted an outside "scientific expert" and told the FDA, "You have not made your case."

With OMB holding the reins of power in regulatory matters, Health and Human Services Secretary Richard Schweiker withdrew the labeling proposal on November 18, 1982, saying the idea had been "premature." By then, the American Academy of Pediatrics had also backed off, after pressure from the Committee on the Care of Children, a group founded by the aspirin industry in response to the HHS proposal. Two members of the academy's committee on infectious disease resigned in protest, one speculating that the academy had caved in to industry pressure. It is not hard to imagine how such pressure was exerted. Harry Jennison, the academy's executive director, related years later that his group had planned in January 1982, months before the proposed HHS regulation, to warn pediatricians about aspirin in its monthly newsletter. Three hours before the newsletter went to press, three representatives of Schering-Plough Inc., maker of St. Joseph's Aspirin for Children, showed up at the academy's offices. "They wanted to make it very clear that if [the newsletter] went out, we would face a very serious lawsuit," Jennison said. The item was yanked from the newsletter.

Tozzi's version of these events has been curiously inconsistent. In 1987, he told the *Los Angeles Times* that he stood by his decision to kill the labeling plan. "Procedurally," he said, "it was the best decision I ever made." In 1993, he sounded a little less self-assured. "We don't know the other side of this," he told *Washington Monthly*. "We could end up with a whole generation of kids hooked on Tylenol because of that regulation." By the later 1990s, he was in full denial, insisting he had no role in the demise of the labeling initiative and that it was the about-face of the American Academy of Pediatrics that had caused HHS to withdraw the proposed regulation. This was a curious position for him to take, considering his statement of a few years earlier that stopping the regulation was "the best decision I ever made."

But it is easy to see why he went into retreat mode. By the 1990s, the grim fallout from "the best decision I ever made" had become abundantly clear. After the labeling of aspirin bottles was finally required in 1986, the number of Reye's syndrome cases reported in the United States had dropped from 555 in 1980 to only 36 the year after the labeling was required. In the ensuing years, the disease almost disappeared entirely. It was, of course, too late for the children who had died during the five years in which the Reagan administration blocked the labeling of aspirin bottles and impeded other steps by the HHS to warn parents of the dangers. In 1992, researchers at the National Academy of Sciences and the School of Public Health at the University of California–Berkeley completed a study that found that of the hundreds of children who died of Reye's syndrome in those five years,

1,470 could have been saved if aspirin bottles had been labeled. "These 1,470 deaths were especially tragic, because they were, typically, healthy children who never recovered from viral infection or chicken pox," wrote the the report's authors, Patricia Buffler and Devrea Lee Davis.

While Ronald Reagan was inciting audiences about the so-called excesses of the FDA—telling fantastic tales about drug companies sending truckloads of documents to Washington—1,470 children died because his administration did a favor for the aspirin giants. That tragedy alone should have been enough to tarnish Reagan's image forever. At the very least, it should have been the subject of an enduring scandal. But it was little more than a blip on the media's radar. A number of news organizations carried a brief Associated Press item about the Buffler-Davis study, but no major newspaper has since carried a single mention of the issue.

Those children were dead and buried long ago, forgotten by all except the families who suffered the loss. But the broader social and economic upheavals created by Reagan's deregulation agenda will haunt the nation for years to come. The blueprint for financial deregulation that the Reagan administration laid out in 1981 has been responsible for one crisis after another, eventually leading to the subprime mortgage scandal and the brink of a worldwide depression.

The first of those crises arising from Reagan's financial deregulation was the savings-and-loan disaster, which should have been a warning signal to America that its government was wildly off course. Its antecedents can be found in the 1970s, when thrifts were still important ingredients of community life in small towns across the country. The savings and loans were established in the nineteenth century solely for the purpose of providing home mortgages, and a combination of tradition and tight federal and state regulation ensured that they would remain community anchors—locally owned, bound to specific regions, conservative in their lending, and miserly in the interest they offered on deposits. Their board members tended to be pillars of the local business establishment.

But decades of stability for the thrifts was upset by soaring interest rates in the late 1970s, a product of the decision by Paul Volcker's Federal Reserve Board to combat inflation by drastically restricting the flow of currency. The skyrocketing rates were devastating to the thrifts on both sides of the balance sheet. Their loans were limited to fixed-rate mortgages, so high interest rates had little effect on their income. And federal regulations placed a cap on the amount of interest that thrifts and commercial banks could pay their depositors, limiting their ability to compete for capital. The result was a huge outflow of funds from savings and loans to money market funds, government securities, and other financial instruments that were allowed to pay interest at market rates.

By the beginning of the 1980s, an estimated two-thirds of the nation's thrifts were losing money, and thousands of them were virtually insolvent. Federal officials could have closed down the biggest losers at this point and paid off their depositors at a fraction of the hundreds of billions of dollars the bailout would cost a few years later. But this was the dawn of a new era in Washington, when the public interest would always take a backseat to corporate interests if money made its way to the right politicians. Desperate to stay in business, the thrifts showered campaign contributions on key members of the House and Senate banking committees, who were more than happy to do the bidding of the industry. Instead of a sensible plan for shoring up the savings-and-loan industry—perhaps with some relaxation of federal regulations—Congress dove headfirst into a reckless deregulation scheme that proved disastrous for the country.

The first leg of the scheme was the Depository Institutions Deregulation and Monetary Control Act of 1980, sponsored by Senator Alan Cranston and Representative Fernand St. Germain, both among the leading beneficiaries of the thrifts' campaign contributions. The bill created a six-year phaseout of interest rate ceilings on deposits in S&Ls and commercial banks. It also ended the S&Ls' long tradition as local institutions by lifting the restrictions that bound them to a specific geographic area. They would now be free to make mortgage loans anywhere in the country.

But those were not the most fateful elements of the bill. During a late-night revision of the House version, with only eleven other members present, St. Germain slipped in an amendment that would increase from $40,000 to $100,000 the amount of the deposits that would be insured by the Federal Savings and Loan Insurance Corporation, the industry's FDIC equivalent. Without so much as a hearing—"It took minutes. There was no debate," remembered Representative Henry Gonzalez—the full faith and credit of the federal government was now behind an industry gasping for air. Freed from dependence on the savings of people in their communities, thrifts could now attract deposits from corporations, pension funds, and credit unions—large institutional investors that would split their funds into parcels of $100,000, now fully insured by the federal government. The stage was set for a taxpayer-subsidized meltdown.

But it took the Reagan administration, with its fanatical commitment to deregulation, to turn what could have been a manageable government bailout into one of the nation's biggest national scandals since Teapot Dome.

With the prodding of Treasury Secretary Regan, Richard Pratt, Reagan's first chairman of the Federal Home Loan Bank Board, pushed legislation and regulatory changes that would attempt to rescue the thrift industry by turning it into a giant casino. With eight hundred thrifts eligible for closure by the federal government in 1982 because they did not meet net-worth requirements, Pratt approved accounting practices that let them inflate their worth and stay in business. He was also the key architect of the second plank of the upcoming crisis, the Garn-St. Germain Depository Institutions Act of 1982, which ended regulations restricting thrifts to mortgage loans. They could now lend money for whatever purpose they saw fit. With their reserves depleted by the escalating interest rates they were now forced to pay depositors, many thrifts gambled on risky but high-yielding investments just to stay afloat.

The recklessness of the Garn-St. Germain bill did not end there. The new law also allowed developers to own S&Ls and gave them such free rein in their lending practices that they could virtually loan funds to themselves, with no money down. Gone was the regulation requiring thrifts to have four hundred stockholders. They could now be owned by a single operator, however reckless or unscrupulous. Had their express purpose been to create the conditions for widespread fraud and financial disaster, Reagan's deregulation zealots could not have done a more complete job.

What was Reagan's attitude toward the Garn-St. Germain legislation? As he dragged his pen across the bottom of the bill, the president was in his usual fog of unreality. "All in all, I think we've hit the jackpot," he told the bought-and-paid-for legislators surrounding him. But not everyone in his administration was so gullible. "This was a failure of government," said William Seidman, who was then head of the Federal Deposit Insurance Corporation. "The Reagan administration turned these [S&L] people loose. I thought it was crazy."

Seidman would quickly be proven correct. Many of the failing thrifts were bought out by shady businessmen who dipped into what was left of their reserves and invested in all manner of harebrained schemes, like Michael Milken's junk bonds, a buffalo sperm bank, a kitty litter mine, and worthless real estate investments. The new S&L barons lived like kings, buying huge homes, yachts, and fancy automobiles with money that would have to be repaid by every American taxpayer.

The responsibility of the Reagan administration for the savings-and-loan debacle was not just in the legislative realm. This radical deregulation of the thrifts should have been accompanied by new vigilance on the part of watchdog agencies like the Federal Home Loan Bank Board. But the opposite happened. After Pratt quit in 1983 and went to work for Merrill Lynch, the thrift industry convinced Regan to replace him with one of their own, Edwin Gray, a former aide to Ed Meese who at the time of his bank-board appointment was an employee of a San Diego S&L owned by a major contributor to Reagan's campaign. Even Gray admitted later that he was intended to be a "patsy for the industry." But he turned out to have more spine than Regan intended and pushed for tighter regulation of brokered money entering the thrifts. He also fought Stockman's OMB for more bank examiners. He was unsuccessful on both counts, and Regan made him a pariah in the administration.

The thrifts used their influence with legislators and the administration to keep from being shut down, hopeful that the next risky investment—"one more roll of the dice," as Robert Kuttner put it—would put them in the black. Recognizing that the federal government's deposit insurance was nowhere near what it would take to rescue all the failing thrifts, regulators went along with what were essentially hundreds of individual Ponzi schemes. The game was allowed to continue through the election of George H.W. Bush. The S&Ls were not even mentioned in the 1988 campaign. But the scandal broke wide open in 1989. The consequences, as is now well known, were enormous: a $150-billion bailout paid by the taxpayers and an estimated hundreds of billions more in damage to the U.S. economy.

The looming crisis in the savings-and-loan industry in the 1980s was not enough to deter Congress and the White House from continuing its reckless quest for more financial deregulation. After all, the S&L mess worked out well for the new class of robber barons that emerged in the Reagan years. A small group of rich business types went on a spending spree, and the public picked up the $150-billion tab. Privatize the wealth and socialize the risk. That was the new ethos in the post-Reagan era.

Even as deregulation of the thrifts was spiraling toward disaster, the Reagan administration and its allies at the Federal Reserve and in the banking industry were working assiduously to do away with the Glass-Steagall Act—paving the way for scandals that would far surpass the savings-and-loan mess in their cost to the global economy. Regan drafted legislation in the summer of 1983 to repeal Glass-Steagall; the measure was approved in the Senate by a vote of eighty-nine to five—with Jake Garn leading the charge—but failed to get past the Democratic majority in the House. However, Ronald Reagan and his allies were not about to let democracy stand in the way of their goals. They had plenty of other means to achieve de facto deregulation when legislators would not bend to their will, and they began a slow dismantling of Glass-Steagall that would leave the law virtually toothless by the time it was officially repealed in 1999.

In the most effective of these nonlegislative initiatives, Reagan's appointees on the Federal Reserve Board mounted their own campaign against Glass-Steagall. In 1986, the board reinterpreted a key provision of the law, Section 20, so commercial banks could stray into investment banking as long as such activity did not yield more than 5 percent of a bank's gross revenues. A few months later, in the middle of 1987, the Fed bowed to pressure from Citicorp, J. P. Morgan, and Bankers Trust and agreed to allow large bank holding companies to engage in a wide range of underwriting activities, including commercial paper, municipal revenue bonds, and—most ominously—mortgage-backed securities. The Fed's chairman, Paul Volcker, who by this time was Carter's only remaining appointee on the board, opposed the move, arguing that the board had no legal authority to undermine Glass-Steagall. But he was outvoted by Reagan appointees.

Foes of Glass-Steagall won an even greater victory in August 1987, when Greenspan—Ayn Rand protégé and free-market purist—was appointed by Reagan as the Fed's chairman. He made little secret of his hostility to Glass-Steagall, which he believed was preventing U.S. banks from keeping up with their competitors in Europe and Asia. He enthusiastically supported another repeal bill that the Reagan administration, with the surprising sponsorship of Proxmire, put forth in 1988, a measure that once again passed the Senate but failed in the House. "One of the more attractive features of the Proxmire bill is that its near complete repeal of the Glass-Steagall Act allows for a market-driven evolution of financial services and products," Greenspan told a Chicago banking conference in May 1988.

The momentum for financial deregulation did not diminish one iota after Bill Clinton took office. He had pledged in his campaign to put people first and end the Reagan-Bush neglect of the public sector. But he ended up buying into the Reagan mantra of deregulation and continued efforts to undermine Glass-Steagall. He quickly developed a rapport with Greenspan, giving the free-market guru even more influence over White House policy than he had enjoyed in the Reagan-Bush years. And he made his chief economic adviser Robert Rubin, the former cochairman of Goldman Sachs and Company, a man who who saw the world through the prism of Wall Street. Rubin, who was head of the White House National Economic Council in Clinton's first term and treasury secretary in his second, became fast friends with Greenspan, the latter once joking that the longtime Democrat was the best Republican treasury secretary ever. Together, the two men ensured that Clinton stayed the course of Reaganism on economic matters, much to the chagrin of administration liberals like Labor Secretary Robert Reich and Joseph Stiglitz, chairman of the Council of Economic Advisers.

Greenspan continued the Fed's dismantling of Glass-Steagall. Two years after he became chairman, the board opened the door even wider for commercial banks to delve into securities, doubling the revenue limit from 5 to 10 percent. The board went further in 1996, raising the revenue limit to 25 percent, a gaping loophole that any commercial bank could exploit to move forcefully into investment banking and securities underwriting. About a year later, Bankers Trust became the first U.S. bank to own an investment banking concern, swallowing up Alex, Brown & Company.

Among the few elements of the original Glass-Steagall law that remained was its ban on banks' engaging in insurance underwriting, a restriction that powerful Wall Street interests, with the help of a $300-million lobbying effort—and not a little assistance from Greenspan and Rubin—would take care of soon enough. One of the companies paying the tab for the lobbying was the Travelers insurance giant, whose chairman, Sanford Weill, had been aggressively seeking to broaden the company's portfolio, narrowly failing in the summer of 1997 to acquire J. P. Morgan. Several months later, Travelers announced the $9-billion acquisition of the Salomon Brothers investment bank, which then merged with Travelers' Smith Barney, becoming Salomon Smith Barney.

Weill was just getting started. In February 1998, after a dinner with Citicorp chairman John Reed in Washington, he invited him back to his room at the Park Hyatt and proposed that the two companies merge. The new partners announced the deal on April 6, 1998, a $70-billion stock swap that was billed as the largest corporate merger in history. It combined the Salomon Smith Barney investment house with Citicorp, the parent of Citibank, creating the world's largest financial services concern. But the deal could not be completed with what was left of Glass-Steagall's restrictions standing in the way. Weill was essentially throwing down the gauntlet to Washington, forcing regulators and lawmakers to choose between repealing the law or blocking a gargantuan merger. Of course, the fix was in from the beginning. Weill met with Greenspan before announcing the merger, later telling the *Washington Post* that he had got a "positive response." Weill could also depend on Rubin, whom he had informed in advance. (According to one account, when Weill told Rubin he had some news, Rubin joked, "You're buying the government.")

In the fall of 1999, with the Clinton administration's backing and the enthusiastic support of Senator Phil Gramm, chairman of the Banking Committee, Congress approved the Financial Services Modernization Act, commonly known as the Gramm-Leach-Biley Act, which repealed Glass-Steagall. On the day his negotiators and Republican leaders reached an accord on the law, Clinton issued a statement predicting that consumers would be among the winners. "When this potentially historic agreement is finalized," he said, "it will strengthen the economy and help consumers, communities and businesses across America."

It certainly helped some people. Within days of Clinton's signing the repeal, Rubin announced he was leaving the government to become Weill's top lieutenant at Citicorp. Gramm also did pretty well for himself. The dismantling of Glass-Steagall allowed Swiss Bank UBS to acquire the Paine Weber brokerage house, and guess who ended up as the vice chairman of the new company's investment banking arm? In 2005 and 2006, Gramm and two other UBS lobbyists earned $750,000 in an effort to roll back state laws that curtailed predatory tactics in the mortgage-lending industry. By the spring of 2008, as UBS was writing off $37 billion in losses stemming from the mortgage crisis and threatening to shed eight thousand jobs, Gramm's role in no way made him a pariah in Republican circles. Instead, he was serving as co-chairman of John McCain's presidential campaign and was considered McCain's favorite for the post of treasury secretary.

The repeal of Glass-Steagall, the culmination of an effort that the Reagan administration had begun in its first months in office, did not turn out to be a boon for consumers or the economy, as Regan, Greenspan, Rubin, and Clinton had predicted. Joseph Stiglitz, the Nobel Prize–winning economist who had chaired Clinton's Council of Economic Advisers, wrote in 2003 that his was a lonely voice in the administration opposing the repeal of Glass-Steagall, and his concerns proved to be on the money. The best example was Enron, whose banks—including Citigroup and J. P. Morgan Chase—continued to loan money to the company even as its horrifying meltdown was well under way, perhaps concerned that an Enron bankruptcy would bring to light their own recklessness in lending their depositors' funds to the troubled firm.

It was no surprise that the conflicts of interest and sleazy behavior that Glass-Steagall was designed to prevent quickly reappeared once the law was shelved. The titans of finance knew they would, as did their patrons in Washington, but there were enormous sums of money to be made on Wall Street, and some of that wealth would be plowed into political campaign funds. The only people who were fooled by the propaganda—the claim that the law's repeal would benefit the consumers—were the consumers themselves, the average Americans whose tax dollars would fund the bailouts that inevitably followed the financial crises created by Reaganism.

Within two years after the repeal of Glass-Steagall, companies were inflating their earnings by billions of dollars. Brokers were happy to manipulate their analyses of these companies and lure in unsuspecting investors because millions of dollars in fees were flowing to their firms' investment-banking divisions. As Robert Sherrill wrote in *The Nation,* "Consider WorldCom's support by Citigroup (an octopus including Citibank, Travelers Insurance and Salomon Smith Barney brokerage). That octopus, which lent many millions to WorldCom and was lead underwriter of a $5 billion debt, kept touting WorldCom stock as a 'strong buy' almost to the day the company went under."

After the stock market crash of 2000–2001 eviscerated $8.5 trillion in market value, devastated retirement accounts, and cost hundreds of thousands of Americans their jobs, even the conservative press was wondering whether knocking down the barriers between investment banking, lending, and brokerage was a great idea. "Why We Had Glass-Steagall" was the headline in the *Wall Street Journal* on January 15, 2002. Or, as *The Economist* wondered, "Might J. P. Morgan and Citi have let their lending standards slip in order to win investment banking business from Enron? Was America wrong to scrap the laws that kept commercial and investment banking apart?"

And yet this was the dawn of the George W. Bush era, when the ethos of Reaganism was once again enshrined as holy writ, so the stock market implosion of the millennium would not give rise to new banking regulation. Instead, the financial press continued to deify Greenspan, Rubin, and Reagan, and the country plunged headlong into the subprime mortgage scandal. Without the repeal of Glass-Steagall and other aspects of financial deregulation in the post-Reagan era, the financial supermarkets like Citicorp and Merrill Lynch would never have been allowed to engage in the kind of reckless mortgage lending that set off such a historic economic crisis.

The antecedents of the subprime mortgage crisis clearly lay within the Reagan administration. When Richard Pratt, Reagan's first chairman of the Federal Home Loan Bank Board, drafted the Garn-St. Germain Depository Institutions Act of 1982, the bill included a provision, Title VIII, that enabled lenders for the first time to issue adjustable-rate mortgages and other exotic loans, such as those requiring interest-only payments for a period. The provision was aimed at helping rescue the savings-and-loan industry by allowing the thrifts to respond to the volatility in interest rates that prevailed in the early 1980s, but it would be precisely these types of loans that brought about foreclosures on hundreds of thousands of home mortgages beginning in 2007.

Even more significant for the future of the American economy was the decision by Reagan's appointees at the pre-Greenspan Federal Reserve in 1987 to allow large bank holding companies to handle the underwriting of mortgage-backed securities. This measure was one of several aspects of financial deregulation in the 1980s and afterward—including the repeal of Glass-Steagall—that promoted banks' headlong rush into the securitization of mortgages, with the dire results that now engulf our nation.

Securitization was part of the vision that Alan Greenspan and other Reagan offspring had for the world economy in the 1990s. The pool of funds flowing from debt instruments like credit cards, auto loans, and mortgages would be bundled into bonds and sold in the securities markets. Investors' dollars would open up vast new sources of capital for mortgages and other loans and spread the risk over a wider number of parties, making the financial sector more resilient. Spreading the risk would lower the cost of credit and make the dream of home ownership possible for legions of buyers whose credit histories might otherwise disqualify them.

But there were obvious dangers, which the people likely to make a bundle off securitization were happy to ignore. Since banks making the loans would be moving them off their books and into the securities markets, there was no incentive to worry about whether the notes could be repaid. Add to that a huge proliferation of unregulated lending institutions—which never could have existed under the government framework of the pre-Reagan era—and the advent of exotic new mortgage products like interest-only and adjustable-rate loans, and the result was a frenzy of mortgage lending with little in the way of income verification or other measures to assess credit-worthiness.

The dangers should have been obvious to anyone with a deep understanding of financial institutions. And yet Greenspan, in a number of speeches during his Fed chairmanship, extolled the emergence of new and exotic vehicles for allowing people to borrow money. "Innovation has brought about a multitude of new products, such as subprime loans and niche credit programs for immigrants," he noted approvingly in a 2005 speech. "The mortgage-backed security helped create a national and even an international market for mortgages, and market support for a wider variety of home mortgage loan products became commonplace."

But after this new and exotic world that so intrigued Greenspan turned into an international debacle, the maestro sought to dissociate himself from the mess. He told Leslie Stahl in a *60 Minutes* segment broadcast on September 16, 2007, that he had had no knowledge that so much of the collateralized debt being peddled in the securities markets was based on shoddy and irresponsible loans.

Stahl asked him why he hadn't spoken out if "you knew these practices were going on or maybe just suspected that there was something illegal or shady." Greenspan replied, "While I was aware a lot of these practices were going on, I had no notion of how significant they had become until very late. I didn't really get it until very late in 2005 and 2006."

But his effort to disown the consequences of his free-market extremism falls flat. Edward Gramlich, who was a Federal Reserve governor from 1997 to 2005, told the *Wall Street Journal* that he personally warned Greenspan about irresponsible mortgage lending around 2000 and suggested that bank examiners increase their scrutiny of consumer finance lenders acting as extensions of Fed-regulated bank holding companies. Gramlich, a Democrat appointed by Bill Clinton, said he never raised the issue with the full board because Greenspan felt such oversight was unworkable. "He was opposed to it, so I didn't really pursue it," he said.

In response to Gramlich's comments, Greenspan told the *Journal* that he did not remember the conversation but would have rejected such an idea—and still believed his reasoning was sound—because it would have been impractical for the Fed's examiners to monitor a multitude of small lending institutions. He said it could ultimately have undermined "the desired availability of subprime credits."

In March 2008, Greenspan finally conceded that more regulation of financial institutions could have staved off the subprime crisis, telling the *Washington Post* that "it was clearly a mistake" not to have bank examiners look more closely at lending but insisting that it was "very late in the game [that] we realized the size of the problem." At this point, he had regained his memory of Gramlich's warnings, although he claimed that Gramlich sent him a note before he died in the fall of 2007 that said he himself was not completely convinced in 2000 that more regulation would be necessary. Greenspan also leveled blame at borrowers for not converting their adjustable-rate mortgages to fixed-rates loans before they ran into trouble. "People who had taken out loans in June 2003 at adjustable rates could have converted those to long-term fixed-rate mortgages at a profit over the next 18 months. And people didn't. . . . They should have. I don't know frankly why they didn't."

Rather than point the finger at Main Street, perhaps Greenspan should have asked himself why he and his colleagues on the Federal Reserve Board had not moved to curtail the horrendous abuses in mortgage lending. Experts have pointed to a number of measures that were available to the Fed to stave off the crisis, including safeguards later put into place by Greenspan's successor, Ben Bernanke. "The Federal Reserve could have stopped this problem dead in its tracks," Martin Bakes, chief executive of the Center for Responsive Lending, a nonprofit watchdog group, told the *New York Times.* "If the Fed had done its job, we would not have had the abusive lending and we would not have a foreclosure crisis in virtually every community across America."

The answer to that question of why the Fed didn't act is ideology—the ideology that Adam Smith originated, Milton Friedman rejuvenated, Ronald Reagan made the new American consensus, and Alan Greenspan carried into the twenty-first century: the belief that the "invisible hand" of the market is never wrong. Most revealing in Greenspan's interview with the *Wall Street Journal* was his admission that he focused more on monetary issues than regulation because of his laissez-faire orientation and his philosophical differences with the laws passed by Congress. The man who in his youth sat raptly at the knee of his hero, the free-market purist Ayn Rand, who remained under her spell until the day she died, would not betray the cult, no matter what the cost.

And the cost has been enormous. By 2006, securitized mortgages—especially subprime mortgages, those issued to high-risk borrowers—had become a bulwark of the U.S. and international financial system.

The value of subprime mortgages in the United States increased from $190 billion in 2001 to $600 billion in 2006; in the same period, the proportion of subprime mortgages that became securitized jumped from 50 to 80 percent. When the bottom fell out of the U.S. housing market, not only were up to a million American households facing foreclosure, but a shudder swept through the world's financial system. Major financial institutions were left with billions of dollars in deregulated mortgage loans on their books. The nation's biggest banks and brokerage firms posted hundreds of billions of dollars in losses. Ironically, one of the biggest losers in the deregulation scheme that Donald Regan had helped launch in 1981 was his former company, Merrill Lynch, the nation's best-known brokerage firm. In late 2007, Merrill Lynch announced a write-off of $8.4 billion in failed credit and mortgage investments, while Citigroup swallowed similar losses of $5.9 billion.

Between June and November 2007, Merrill Lynch's stock value dropped by 36 percent and Citigroup's by 35 percent. In the same period, the dozen biggest Wall Street firms and the commercial banks with the largest investment arms—a list that included Bank of America, J. P. Morgan Chase, and Credit Suisse—lost more than $240 billion in market value. Merrill Lynch ended up being swallowed by Bank of America in a deal announced in September 2008. The once-venerable Lehman Brothers investment bank collapsed into bankruptcy. And Bear Stearns, an eighty-five-year-old company that had survived the Great Depression without laying off a single employee, was wiped off the map by the subprime mortgage crisis. Then came the near collapse of the global financial system and the $700-billion bailout package approved by Congress and the Bush administration. It was perhaps the ultimate irony that the president who positioned himself as the heir to Ronald Reagan had to resort to a huge government intervention in the economy to clean up the mess created by his hero's legacy. But it is probably too much for progressives to hope that the subprime mortgage crisis will drive free-market purists out of public life. The conglomerates that control the American media will make sure they never take the full blame for what they have wrought. In illustration, nothing could have been a greater repudiation of reckless deregulation than the California electricity crisis in 2000 and 2001. The California Public Utilities Commission and the Federal Energy Regulatory Commission issued reports containing voluminous evidence that the blackouts plaguing California in that period were the result of deregulated energy companies like Enron keeping their capacity off-line to drive up prices. As a *Wall Street Journal* headline put it September 2002, "As California Starved for Energy, U.S. Businesses Had a Feast." It was a spectacle of malfeasance that harked back to the corporate lawlessness of the Gilded Age, but the media quickly moved on, as did the public's outrage, especially with the likes of Dick Cheney arguing that the crisis had been caused not by deregulation but by too much regulation.

Through much of the 1990s, the mainstream media continued to buy into the claim of corporately funded think tanks that deregulation was an unalloyed victory for consumers. *Newsweek* proclaimed deregulation a success in 1997 in a shamefully slanted article that did not bother to quote anyone who might have had a dissenting opinion. "We have had enough experience with [deregulation] to draw some conclusions," wrote the article's author, Robert J. Samuelson. "And the main one is: it works." Samuelson based his entire article on a study by Robert Crandall of the Brookings Institution and Jerry Ellig of George Mason University, who had found that deregulation was saving consumers $40 billion to $60 billion a year. Samuelson's article addressed entirely what deregulation had allegedly saved consumers in prices, with no mention of the impact on jobs, wages, health and safety, and community values. But even those savings to the consumer were suspect: Samuelson mentioned parenthetically in the last paragraph of his story that the Crandall-Ellig study had been "funded by advocates of deregulation in the electric-utility industry."

Consider airlines, usually presented as one of the more successful experiments in deregulation. Even a liberal like Senator Edward Kennedy embraced airline deregulation as a way to reduce fares by increasing competition in the industry. The Airline Deregulation Act of 1978 allowed new companies to enter the airline business and removed controls on fares, routes, and aircraft size and configuration. In short order, a host of new airlines emerged in the 1980s and offered cut-rate fares. For a time, travelers could fly People's Express from New York to Boston for little more than the cost of a Greyhound trip. But that period of competition and price cutting was short-lived. Most of those upstart companies either went bankrupt because of ruinous price competition or were swallowed up by larger companies. Antitrust regulators in the Reagan administration turned a blind eye as the industry reconsolidated into a smaller and smaller number of players. Those that remained were able to use their size to undercut the prices of upstart competitors just long enough to drive them out of business.

Northwest Airlines was one of these survivors. It acquired Republic Airlines in 1987, enabling it to control more than three-quarters of the air traffic in Minneapolis–St. Paul, Detroit, and Memphis and overcome any potential competitors. In 1995, Spirit Airlines began offering low-cost flights in the Detroit-Philadelphia market, challenging Northwest's dominance. Spirit offered fares ranging from $49 to $139 and quickly grabbed a quarter of the market. But Northwest responded by matching Spirit's fares and dumping discount seats onto the market. After Spirit abandoned the route a year later, Northwest eliminated all of its own low-cost fares.

The two decades after deregulation saw the emergence of many other "fortress hubs," in which a single airline came to dominate a city's air travel through predatory competition. By 1998, Delta controlled 80 percent of the market in Atlanta, 94 percent in Cincinnati, and 77 percent in Salt Lake City. U.S. Airways controlled 92 percent of the market in Charlotte, North Carolina, and 90 percent in Pittsburgh. Continental had a 79 percent share at Houston Intercontinental, Trans World Airlines had 72 percent of the market in St. Louis, United Airlines had a 69 percent share in Denver, and American Airlines controlled 67 percent of the markets in both Dallas–Fort Worth and Miami. By the middle of 2001, four airlines controlled two-thirds of the domestic market, and five global alliances controlled three-quarters of international travel.

The consolidation was a windfall for the small number of companies left to dominate air travel; they saw record profits until the crisis brought on by the 9/11 terrorist attacks. But the result was not as much fun for passengers. Service deteriorated across the industry, with skyrocketing consumer complaints about delays, overcrowding, overbooking, and even the elimination of hot meals. Paul Hudson, a researcher for Ralph Nader's Aviation Consumer Action Project, found that air travel in the 1990s was slower than at any time since the 1940s for most flights less than a thousand miles, because of delays and connecting flights. Deregulation advocates continue to portray airline deregulation as a success. Clifford Winston of the Brookings Institution and Steven Morrison of Northeastern University found in one oft-cited study that average fares fell by 40 percent between 1976 and 2000 and that 27 percent of the decrease was due to deregulation. Their study was produced under the aegis of the AEI-Brookings Joint Center for Regulatory Studies, a corporate-funded think tank whose donors include U.S. Airways. Other studies have attributed the fare decreases not to deregulation but to technological innovation. Indeed, when fuel costs are removed from the equation, fares actually fell more rapidly before deregulation. Winston and Morrison acknowledged that fares had been falling since 1971. But even if we accept the 27 percent figure, which Winston and Morrison said saved consumers $20 billion annually, we still have to ask whether it was worth it. If someone can now pay $200 for a flight that would have cost $254, does that outweigh the other damage done to society, the airport delays and congestion, the endless mergers and bankruptcies, the airline employees who have seen their wages reduced, and the thousands who have lost their jobs as the industry consolidated?

By late 2005, four of the seven largest U.S. airlines, reeling from the fallout of the 9/11 terrorist attacks and high fuel prices, were under federal bankruptcy protection. After it filed for Chapter 11 in 2002, United Airlines laid off twenty-six thousand employees and—still ailing three years later—scrapped its workers' retirement plans, the largest pension default in U.S. history. Through it all, Alfred Kahn, who engineered airline deregulation as chairman of the Civil Aeronautics Board in the Carter administration, has insisted that he is proud of his creation. Asked to comment on the pending bankruptcies of Northwest and Delta in

September 2005, Kahn said, "This is the continued working out of the restructuring that deregulation promised and made inescapable."

In a Senate hearing two years earlier, Kahn said eroding service and delayed flights were also part of the grand scheme. "The problem with the previous system," he said, "was that it offered people good service at uniformly non-competitive high fares. A competitive market offers people options, including the option of crowded service, long lines, uncomfortable service, but at very, very low prices. And I'm proud of that. That was our intention."

And so it is in industry after industry in the post-Reagan era. Consumers are bought off with pennies—or led to believe they have saved money—while mergers cost thousands of people their jobs, wages plummet, service declines, and navigating American commerce becomes a daily affront to human dignity.

Any survey of the damage resulting from the deregulation of America is remiss without a word about the Reagan administration's moves toward removing all government controls over broadcasting, cable television, and telecommunications. Here we find the beginning of a movement that would pick the pockets of American consumers, penalize rural communities, and reduce radio and television to commercial drivel. The Telecommunications Act of 1996, a grand hoodwinking of the public that promised more competition and diversity in the media but instead wiped out whatever diversity was left, was the culmination of a process the Reagan administration set in motion in 1981.

Mark Fowler, Reagan's first chairman of the Federal Communications Commission, was the spiritual father of broadcast deregulation. He came into office with a profound disdain for the notion that television and radio airwaves were owned by the public, a concept that had been the cornerstone of communications law since 1934. He felt the airwaves should be the province of corporations, whose competition in the free market would be enough to serve the public interest. "It's time to move away from thinking of broadcasters as trustees and time to treat them the way that everyone else in this society does, that is, as a business," he said. "Television is just another appliance. It's a toaster with pictures." Fowler said he took it as an "article of faith that any successful businessman is meeting a public need." He was fond of cloaking himself in the mantle of Ronald Reagan, once boasting that he was "not the captive of any industry or industry in general. I am a captive of a philosophy of government we call Reaganism."

These were not just idle words. In Fowler's six-year tenure as chairman, the FCC reviewed or abolished 89 percent of the regulations governing broadcasting. By 1987, the commission had done away with the fairness doctrine, which required broadcast outlets to cover both sides of public issues; the provision that required broadcasters to allow public figures equal time to respond to attacks; the requirement that politicians be given airtime around elections; and the rule that stations keep a file of all their complaints from the public. Fowler also dropped the FCC's enforcement of misconduct on the part of broadcasting license holders.

But Fowler's most important contribution to the homogenization of news and entertainment was his success in liberalizing the multiple-ownership rule. Since 1953, the holdings of any one broadcaster had been limited to seven television stations, seven FM radio stations, and seven AM stations. Fowler managed to raise that number to twelve and did away with the rule that stations be held for three years before being sold. This reform was enough to set off a round of mergers in the broadcasting industry, including Capital Cities' acquisition of the American Broadcasting Corporation, the first sale of a major television network. Radio and television stations were soon being traded like any other commodity, making a mockery of their status as trustees of the nation's airwaves.

The Telecommunications Act of 1996, a sweeping deregulation of the communications, cable television, and telephone industries, was passed after furious lobbying and a blizzard of contributions to key members of Congress. According to the Center for Responsive Politics, the communications and electronic industries gave $23.7 million to congressional candidates in 1995–1996. The result was that a bill profoundly skewed toward powerful interests was passed with hardly any public debate. "I have never seen anything like the Telecommunications bill," one career lobbyist told journalist Robert McChesney. "The silence of public debate is deafening. A bill with such astonishing impact on all of us is not even being discussed."

Sponsors of the law estimated that deregulation of the cable and telephone industries would save consumers $550 billion over a decade—$333 billion in lower long-distance rates, $32 billion in lower local phone rates, and $78 billion in lower cable bills. Instead, cable rates went up by about 50 percent and local phone rates by more than 20 percent, according to a 2005 study by Common Cause.

Even more devastating for our culture and national discourse was the further evisceration of limits on multiple ownership of broadcast stations. Companies had been limited to owning forty radio stations; the law removed any limits, enabling a company like Clear Channel Communications to own twelve hundred stations around the country. The Common Cause study found that $700 million worth of buying and selling of radio stations occurred *the first week after the act became law.*

The act also did away with the limit of twelve television stations per company and boosted the national share of audience for one company from 25 to 35 percent. In the wake of this provision, the nation saw a frenzy of mergers in the broadcasting industry that left five companies—Viacom, Disney, News Corp, NBC, and AOL–Time Warner—in control of 75 percent of prime-time viewing.

Higher telephone and cable TV rates, vastly increased concentration of the media, the death of local radio, the homogenization and dumbing down of programming, less broadcast coverage of news—all these emerged from the movement begun by Ronald Reagan, the man they called the Great Communicator.

CHAPTER 6

Merger Mania

When John Shad, chairman of the Securities and Exchange Commission, flew from Washington to New York in June 1984 for a speech before the New York Financial Writers Association on the issue of corporate takeovers, he was the last man anyone would expect to commit an act of political heresy. It was, after all, no secret how the former vice chairman of E. F. Hutton got the nod for his appointment. While most Wall Street executives initially backed George H.W. Bush or John Connally in the 1980 Republican primaries, Shad was an early Reagan supporter and the head of his New York State finance committee. As a reward for his financial and political loyalty, he became the first senior executive of a securities firm in fifty years to head the SEC, the proverbial fox guarding the chicken coop. Shad believed fervently in Reagan's view of laissez-faire government, and he moved quickly and aggressively to strip away securities regulations that he believed were gumming up market efficiency and curtailing the formation of capital.

After thirty-one years on Wall Street, Shad was used to viewing the SEC as an adversary, and that attitude colored his relations with the staff. He defied convention and actually requested that Congress cut his funding and personnel. The people he really respected were men he had left behind on Wall Street, and like them, he saw corporate consolidation as a beautiful thing, a quick path to riches for the deserving few. Shad was hardly a man who would bring anything in the way of real regulation to the securities industry. As *The Economist* magazine put it shortly after his appointment: "Mr. Shad will rock no corporate boats."

Delivering speeches was never one of Shad's strengths. While he was forceful, even intimidating, with his staff at a conference table, he was awkward before a larger group. Balding, overweight, and stoop-shouldered, with a double chin and the ears of a chimpanzee, he was an unimpressive sight testifying in a mumble before congressional committees. But as he stepped behind a dais at the Sheraton Centre Hotel in Manhattan, Shad had a message to deliver that he knew was going to electrify his audience—and provoke outrage among ideologues in the Reagan administration. For Shad's views on corporate takeovers had been evolving. He had long defended corporate consolidation as an important engine of capital formation, despite abundant evidence that the rash of mergers and acquisition in the 1980s was just shuffling around America's corporate entities and diverting money and energy badly needed for new investment. He was not moved by the plight of employees and communities left behind when acquired companies shuttered their operations and left town for no reason other than to provide a bonanza for arbitrageurs, investment bankers, and takeover lawyers on Wall Street. The people cashing in on merger mania were Shad's kind of people. At E. F. Hutton, he had been head of mergers and acquisitions, a headstrong, chain-smoking workaholic who lived for the next merger deal. He was the prime mover in the 1977 takeover of the *Kansas City Star* by Capital Cities Communications, a deal that had cost dozens of employees their jobs and finished off the paper's decades-long reputation for journalistic excellence. His natural sympathies were with corporate raiders.

But now even some of Shad's closest confidants on Wall Street were beginning to see things spiraling out of control. People like takeover lawyer Martin Lipton, who had made millions advising companies on their mergers, and former SEC commissioner A. A. Sommer felt the amount of capital being poured into acquisitions and the colossal debt being taken on by corporations were posing a grave danger to the nation's economic well-being. Shad had begun to quietly back proposals in Congress for laws to prevent the most obvious abuses growing out of the merger craze. But neither Reagan nor his cabinet had taken any position on the proposed laws, and members of the press had been clamoring to hear the administration's view on the subject. Now Shad was going public with an appeal for Washington to put on the brakes. When he circulated advance copies of the speech, entitled "The Leveraging of America," to staff members at the SEC, the free-market ideologues within the commission were in open rebellion. Gregg Jarrell, a politically ambitious SEC economist, a graduate of the University of Chicago and a disciple of free-market guru Milton Friedman, made no secret of his disgust. "B.S.," he wrote in the margins of his draft. "You've got no evidence." Another Chicago School zealot, SEC commissioner Charles Cox, appealed to Shad not to make the speech.

But Shad, nothing if not stubborn, delivered it anyway. He told the dumbfounded financial writers that companies burdened with takeover debt would have little left to spend on new investment and might even be forced into bankruptcy if the economy soured. He even went so far as to acknowledge that the management of many acquired firms was not weak or inefficient, disputing what had been the prime rationalization for supporting hostile takeovers—that they were benefiting shareholders by displacing ineffective executives. "In today's corporate world, Darwin's survival of the fittest has become acquire or be acquired," he said. "The more leveraged takeovers and buyouts today, the more bankruptcies tomorrow." Shad was so proud of the speech, and so convinced of its import, that he had his legal assistant distribute copies to chief executives of all the Fortune 500 companies in the country.

Shad's speech sent alarm bells ringing. Donald Regan and free-market purists in the SEC, the Office of Management and Budget, and the Council on Economic Advisers moved decisively to bring him back into the fold. The White House made sure the 1985 Economic Report to the President included a chapter, written by free-market economist Joseph Grundfest, that lauded corporate takeovers as a benefit to the economy. In case the SEC commissioners had missed it, Douglas Ginsburg, then head of OMB's regulatory section and later an unsuccessful Supreme Court nominee, met with them in May 1985 and told them the administration favored a hands-off approach to takeovers. Later that year, Ginsburg and Jarrell helped arrange the appointment of Grundfest as an SEC commissioner, tipping the board's balance even further toward free-market orthodoxy. Chastised by the administration, Shad never again expressed any public misgivings about the takeover craze, and the SEC backed away from its regulatory proposals, announcing that market conditions had mitigated the worst abuses in the takeover wars to a degree where no action was necessary to stop greenmail, golden parachutes, and junk bonds. Without SEC or administrative backing, the legislative proposals died. For opponents of hostile takeovers, it was a missed opportunity. Congress never again—even after the speculative bubble burst in the stock market crash of 1987—made a serious attempt at meaningful legislation to regulate hostile takeovers. Nor did the government take any other steps to slow the pace of mergers and find more productive uses for American capital.

Whatever else Ronald Reagan may come to stand for in history books, he is likely to be remembered as the forefather of the corporate scandals that marred the last years of the American Century and carried into the millennium. The evisceration of business ethics and the widening fissures of inequality spreading across the economy are the direct outgrowth of forces Reagan set in motion in his first term.

Reagan's fingerprints can be found all over the so-called merger mania of the 1980s and 1990s, giving him clear responsibility for the sweeping social and economic changes that corporate buyouts have left in their wake. The feverish scramble for acquisitions, besides discouraging badly needed investment in U.S. industry, was the driving force behind the overheated stock speculation and unseemly corporate behavior that led to a crisis of public confidence in business. The merger frenzy produced much that is disquieting about America: the loss of job security, mounting corporate debt, the increasing trivialization of the media, overnight fortunes for some and stagnating wages for others. And yet this element of Reagan's legacy, admittedly not the sexiest aspect of Reagan's life and times, has been virtually ignored by biographers and in the journalistic retrospectives of his presidency.

A trend toward mergers had been gathering strength throughout the 1970s, but Reagan's policies opened the floodgates and made mergers and acquisitions—and the relatively new phenomenon of the hostile takeover—a central feature of American commerce. Between 1980 and 1986, the number of mergers increased threefold, from 1,565 to 4,323. The value of those deals grew even more prodigiously, from $33 billion in 1980 to more than $204 billion in 1986. Virtually no sector of our economy—banks, automakers, steel companies, television networks, movie studios, oil companies—was left untouched by mergers over the next two decades, most of which, according to the most reliable studies, have yielded new corporate entities with lower profits, devalued market shares, and reduced workforces. (The trend even touched the company so dear to Reagan, MCA, which was acquired by a Japanese company in 1990.) This reshuffling of corporate ownership, which continued unabated until a recession began in 2001, injected a new sense of insecurity into workplaces, communities, and households while arguably yielding little of value to anyone but an elite of investors, bankers, lawyers, and arbitrageurs.

Reagan's embrace of mergers was no small victory for the nation's corporate titans. For much of the twentieth century, consolidation of big business had been a touchstone of popular discontent. Beginning in the Populist and Progressive eras and for decades afterward, many mainstream politicians, academics, and journalists had regarded industrial trusts as the enemy of competition and small-scale property ownership, as potent a threat to the American way of life as state-sponsored socialism. And the criticism did not come just from the left. Two of the intellectual fathers of the postwar conservative movement, Richard Weaver and Friedrich A. Hayek, regarded monopoly as an evil comparable to socialism. In his influential 1944 book, *The Road to Serfdom,* Hayek had written that "the movement towards totalitarianism comes from the two great vested interests: organized capital and organized labor. Probably the greatest menace of all is the fact that the policies of these two most powerful groups point in the same direction." Indeed, the Federal Trade Commission under Richard Nixon, after what was then an unprecedented rash of mergers, warned in a 1969 study that we were on our way to becoming a nation of "a few hundred business suzerainties under whose influence a multitude of small, weak, quasi-independent corporations will be permitted a subsidiary and supplemental role."

Such sentiments were swept out of Washington in the 1980s. Relief from government regulation was one of a handful of core beliefs that really mattered to Reagan and his business supporters, and anything that stood in the way of the natural consolidation of the nation's productive forces was a barrier to be removed. Reagan and his aides made it clear that antitrust enforcement would be virtually abandoned and consolidation of American business encouraged. "Bigness doesn't necessarily mean badness," William French Smith, Reagan's old friend from California and his appointee as attorney general, told reporters, turning the old trust-busting sentiment on its head.

The new administration moved with alacrity to sweep antitrust sentiment from Washington. At the top of the agenda was the neutering of the Federal Trade Commission and the Justice Department's Antitrust Division, the two government agencies that had traditionally served as a check on unsound mergers. William Baxter, a lawyer appointed to head the Antitrust Division, not only ordered a virtual freeze on most antitrust suits; he also pledged to review twelve hundred old consent decrees and to intervene on the side of defendants in some private antitrust suits. For the chairmanship of the FTC Reagan chose James Miller III, a deeply conservative economist who had directed deregulation matters on his transition team. Even though the FTC had been a quiescent agency for much of its seventy years, its very existence was an affront to free-market conservatives, and Miller made it clear he was there to destroy whatever powers it still had. At his first meeting with the full staff, Miller walked into the FTC's hearing room with a pair of red devil's horns strapped to his head. Intended as a joke, it was met with a stony silence from a staff worried about its future. "It was almost like he was taunting us," said Albert

Foer, a former FTC official who was in the room at the time. "I don't think he really cared whether we thought it was funny or not."

With Baxter and Miller leading the charge for the shrinkage of their own agencies, both the FTC and the Antitrust Division were saddled with deep budget and manpower cuts early in the administration, and their activities dwindled. Mergers that virtually every administration of the previous four decades would have challenged as a matter of course were given the green light. Of the 10,723 mergers that came to the attention of the Justice Department between 1981 and 1987, the Antitrust Division challenged only 26 in court. The FTC was even less active, filing only seventeen administrative complaints in the same period.

The huge corporate tax cuts in Reagan's first term also fueled the merger wave. Business leaders had been complaining for more than a decade that a shortage of capital was one of the factors preventing U.S. industry from retooling factories and fostering the kind of innovation needed to compete with the Japanese and other overseas industrialists. Supply-side theorists predicted that Reagan's tax cuts, which included deep cuts in depreciation allowances, would spur a new round of business investment. But while it seems to have been forgotten by a current generation of conservative politicians—most notably President George W. Bush—the plan to use tax cuts to spur new investment was a failure. Rather than build cars, forge steel, or build new airplane factories, industrialists used their tax windfall to generate quick paper profits by buying up other companies. The tax cuts—combined with vastly increased military spending—also yielded record-breaking budget deficits that drove up interest rates and actually produced a credit crunch, discouraging new investment.

Americans' investment in productive capacity, which had already been lagging behind that of nations like West Germany and Japan, actually declined during the Reagan years. As noted earlier, Harvard economist Benjamin Friedman has found that the portion of national income invested in plant and equipment had been well over 3 percent in each of the three decades that preceded Reagan's election but averaged only 2.3 percent during Reagan's years in the White

House. In none of the years that Reagan was in office did the rate exceed 3 percent.

Reagan's alma mater, General Electric, was one of the biggest corporate beneficiaries of the 1981 tax cuts. In the first three years of the Reagan administration, the company paid no income tax. In fact, it was given tax rebates during that period totaling $283 million, despite pretax profits of more than $6.5 billion. Citizens for Tax Justice, a liberal advocacy group in Washington, estimated that the 1981 tax law yielded well in excess of $1 billion for the company over a half-decade. But none of this amount was funneled into new investment or jobs for Americans. Instead, the company shed fifty thousand jobs in the early 1980s through layoffs, attrition, and the selling off of subsidiaries. At the same time, the tax windfall helped General Electric pay for a welter of corporate acquisitions. Among the companies GE acquired in that period were Utah Construction, RCA, and NBC.

But it was not just corporate tax cuts and lax antitrust enforcement that drove the frenzy of mergers. One of the policies that redounds the most to the discredit of the Reagan administration is the calculated inertia of the Securities and Exchange Commission, which turned a blind eye to the unsavory practices and passion for deal making on Wall Street that far more than any rational business considerations fueled the frenzy of mergers. The rash of hostile takeovers in the 1980s, along with the unseemly tactics of corporate raiders, arbitrageurs, investment bankers, and Wall Street lawyers, is still regarded by many as an epoch of greed unlike anything the nation had seen since the Gilded Age. No episode in American history could have been more insulting to the notion that corporations could be good citizens and contributors to the common well-being of the nation. In the 1980s, the corporate wealth of the United States became stakes in a grand casino. And the SEC, which had abundant power to put the brakes on the most destructive deal making, stood by and watched the frenzy. The ideologues of the Reagan administration maintained the SEC's inactivity even amid howls of protest from the public, pressure for action by Democratic leaders in Congress, and even protests from nationally known financial leaders like Felix Rohatyn and Lee Iacocca.

The 1970s had been a stellar period for the SEC, a quasi-judicial agency governed by four commissioners. It had earned a reputation for what the *New York Times* called "vigorous, nonpartisan independence" in its enforcement of the nation's securities laws, a track record due in large part to the rectitude of the agency's enforcement chief, Stanley Sporkin. A Republican who rose to his position during the Nixon administration, Sporkin had a reputation for prosecuting the abuses of corporations regardless of the executives' political ties. Some of the targets of his investigations were businessmen with close ties to Democratic and Republican presidents. It was on Sporkin's advice in 1972 that William Casey, then the SEC's chairman, rebuffed pressure from the Nixon administration to ease up on the investigation of the financier Robert Vesco. Under Sporkin's leadership in the mid-1970s, the commission helped expose the existence of slush funds that hundreds of corporations maintained to bribe foreign government officials, a scandal that led to passage of the Foreign Corrupt Practices Act in 1977.

Sporkin's aggressiveness led to complaints by Wall Street executives that he was too zealous in trying to promote his brand of morality in the securities industry, and their complaints found a sympathetic ear in the Carter administration at a time when Washington was increasingly buying into the notion that excessive regulation was putting a drag on capital formation. Harold Williams, Carter's appointee as SEC chairman, moved decisively to clip Sporkin's wings. He sharply curtailed corporate investigations and joined the chorus advocating deregulation of the securities industry. The Foreign Corrupt Practices Act was rarely used during his tenure. But this relative inertia was not enough for the Reagan administration. A three-hundred-page report issued by the Reagan transition team in December 1980, while praising the commission as one of the "best government agencies," recommended that its budget be reduced by 30 percent and that the enforcement division staff be reduced from two hundred people to fifty. It also criticized Sporkin's investigate zeal and recommended that he and other department heads be replaced because of their "philosophical incompatibility." Sporkin left the agency shortly after Reagan took office.

John Shad made every effort to transform the culture of the SEC into one more accommodating to business. During his seven-year tenure, Shad was in constant contact with his former colleagues on Wall Street, giving them unprecedented access to the SEC. He forced his staff to attend lectures by corporate chieftains like Johnson & Johnson chairman James Burke and even swashbuckling investors like Warren Buffett. He even broke an unwritten rule that commissioners' meetings were to be confidential and restricted to the agency's staff. In early 1983, as the SEC was locked in a dispute with the mammoth Aetna Life and Casualty Co. over its bookkeeping practices, Shad invited Aetna's chief executive, John Filer, and Wall Street takeover lawyer Joe Flom to a commissioners' meeting to argue their case. The commission voted against Aetna, but the image of Flom sitting in a commissioner's chair appalled some in the agency. "It was improper," John Evans, then a Republican SEC commissioner, told the *Washington Post.* "I don't see any reason just because it was Joe Flom to let them in—perhaps even more so because it was him." David Schwiesow, an SEC staff attorney who attended the meeting, called it "the oddest thing I ever saw."

With the gutting of antitrust enforcement, the slashing of corporate taxes, and the new permissiveness at the SEC, all the pieces were in place for an unprecedented consolidation of big business. Corporate executives seeking to expand through mergers and acquisitions wasted little time in taking the measure of the new administration. Just a few months after Reagan came into office, the Justice Department and FTC sat by idly as DuPont, Seagram, and Mobil engaged in a high-stakes battle to acquire Conoco, the nation's ninth largest oil concern. Conoco's executives, dreading a hostile takeover by Seagram or Mobil, went with DuPont as a "white knight," agreeing to a $7.57-billion merger. Not only did the size of the deal break all records; it signaled a willingness by the Reagan administration to approve mergers that would have been blocked even by previous Republican regimes. The implications of the deal were not lost on Reagan's Democratic opponents, like Senators Edward Kennedy of Massachusetts and Howard

Metzenbaum of Ohio. "Every corporate boardroom and every lawyer representing a corporation in this country is saying, 'If ever we're going to move now is the time,'" Metzenbaum said. "William Baxter has the wrong perspective, and he ought to go back to reading his law books."

True to Metzenbaum's prophecy, the deals got bigger, costlier to employees and small shareholders, and further and further afield from what had once been considered business ethics. In early 1982, the public looked on in puzzlement as four huge companies—Bendix Corporation, Martin Marietta, United Technologies, and Allied Corporation—engaged in a bloody and Byzantine battle to control each other. The skirmish originated in the boardroom of Bendix, a Michigan company that manufactured aerospace and automotive products. The company's chairman, William Agee, launched a $1.5-billion takeover bid for aerospace competitor Martin Marietta. Martin Marietta responded with a $1.5-billion counteroffer to take over Bendix, a move that as the decade wore on would become known as a Pac-Man defense, the goal being to swallow the other player before he swallowed you. The war might have stalemated, but new combatants entered the fray. United Technologies joined up with Martin Marietta to shore up its bid for Bendix, and a fourth company—Allied Corporation—teamed up with Bendix in its bid to swallow Martin Marietta.

In the end, Martin Marietta escaped the takeover attempt, and Allied Corporation ended up acquiring Bendix. But it was hardly a defeat for Agee, the man who had started what Lee Iacocca called a "three ring circus." Before Allied took over, the Bendix board granted Agee a $4.1-million severance, paid for by the company's shareholders. Thus was the public introduced to the odious concept of the golden parachute, part of the new ethos of greed permeating Wall Street and corporate America in the 1980s.

The Congressional Joint Economic Committee later calculated that $5.6 billion in credit—being supplied by twenty-eight major American banks and eleven foreign banks—was tied up in the takeover battle, which the committee found to be highly destructive at a time of high interest rates and economic recession. "Millions of ordinary Americans are not amused by this spectacular misuse of their savings by the corporate world and the banking system," said Democratic representative Henry Reuss, the committee's chairman.

Between 1982 and 1988, more than ten thousand mergers and acquisitions took place in the United States, affecting enterprises that together had in excess of $1 trillion in capital. The mergers swept America's best-known companies into a complex web of ownership that was well beyond the ability of the average consumer to comprehend. Most of the deals were financed with junk bonds and other borrowed funds. The "leveraged buyout," in which the acquirer buys the company almost entirely with borrowed funds and then repays the loan out of the acquired company's assets, became the cornerstone of the hostile takeover movement in the 1980s. In many cases, banks were supplying up to 90 percent of the funds, forcing the new corporate entity to focus on quick profits after the merger rather than the type of long-term investment that yields innovation and real financial stability. A disturbing proportion of these debt-sodden deals made no business sense other than to provide wads of cash to the small group of people shuffling the cards. In some cases, a series of mergers would put together an unwieldy corporate amalgam that would then be purchased by a corporate raider and sold off in parts, with the lives and careers of employees tossed about like packages in the shipping bay. A typical series of transactions that demonstrated the absurdity of the era was neatly summarized in 1989 by the economics professors Walter Adams and James W. Brock:

> In 1983, Esmark, marketer of Swift meats, Butterball turkeys, Playtex products, and STP oil treatments, spent $1 billion to acquire Norton Simon, producer of Hunt's tomato products, Wesson oil, Reddi-wip, Orville Redenbacher's popcorn, Johnny Walker scotch, the Avis car rental service, and Max Factor cosmetics. The next year, Esmark-Norton Simon was acquired by Beatrice Foods, maker of La Choy, Rosarita, Tropicana fruit drinks, Jolly Rancher candies, Milk Duds, Air Stream motor homes, Samsonite luggage, Stiffel lamps,

> and Culligan water softeners. Two years later, in 1986, Beatrice-Norton Simon-Esmark (which now ranked as the nation's 26th largest industrial concern) was bought out by Kohlberg Kravis Roberts in a $6.2 billion deal. And for what purpose? To sell off the various Beatrice-Norton Simon-Esmark divisions that had just been consolidated!

Corporate raiders and arbitrageurs, like Ivan Boesky, T. Boone Pickens, and Carl Icahn, became the new robber barons, preying on companies whose stock had been devalued by the straitened economy and scrappy overseas competition, so that they were ripe for takeovers. These predators would snatch up controlling interests in the companies and use them as gambling chips, flipping them for quick profits or even selling them off piece by piece, like buying a car and selling it for parts. Often companies would repel the takeover threat by buying back their stock from raiders at grossly inflated prices, a process that became known as *greenmail,* as odious and costly to the shareholders as the golden parachute. Icahn was fond of writing articles that claimed he was benefiting the economy by dislodging inefficient management and restoring corporate ownership to the shareholders. But no one was fooled. His goal, like that of other raiders, was quick and enormous profits. The predators of Wall Street walked away with huge fortunes acquired through pain to employees and communities as plants closed and many of the less successful buyouts ended in corporate bankruptcy.

Reagan's abandonment of antitrust enforcement, his corporate tax cuts, and his neutering of securities regulation only helped accelerate big business's growing reluctance to invest in America. By the 1970s, most economists were in agreement that what the country needed to emerge from its economic torpor was a boost in its sagging productivity, which would come about principally through improvements in technology and investments in new plant and equipment. But a new timidity, uncharacteristic of the nation that had spawned the likes of Henry Ford and Andrew Carnegie, had settled over American industry. Rather than sink capital into new factories and products that could compete with overseas industrialists, American business leaders preferred "paper entrepreneurism," the illusion of profitability through accounting, tax avoidance, financial management, mergers and acquisitions, and litigation. "It does not create new wealth," complained the economist Robert Reich in the early 1980s. "It merely rearranges industrial assets. And it has hastened our collective decline." The trend had been growing in American business since the conglomerate building of the 1960s, but Reagan's policies gave paper entrepreneurism an enormous impetus.

Proponents of Reagan policies argued that mergers and acquisitions displaced inefficient management and created wealth by enhancing shareholder value in the acquired companies. But all this deal making was largely benefiting a small group of players on Wall Street, institutional investors, and savvy corporate executives. They might be making a killing by selling their stock for the highest bids by raiders or arbitrageurs. But small shareholders, small employers, and communities—that is to say, the part of America that Reagan often professed to care about—were the losers.

Even some of the outward benefits of the 1980s mergers were illusory. Stock market gains for the newly merged companies were frequently short term, and shareholders often saw their investments suffer. After DuPont paid $7.8 billion for Conoco, DuPont's stock dipped by 40 percent the following year. T. Boone Pickens's company, Mesa Petroleum, began acquiring stock in Gulf in October 1983, a bid that drove the value of Gulf stock from 41 to 80 per share by March 1984, when Chevron acquired Gulf—including Mesa's shares—in a record-breaking consolidation valued at $13.2 billion. The deal was a windfall for the biggest players in the game. Mesa and its partners made $760 million on the deal, and Pickens picked up an $18.6-million bonus. Investment bankers who worked on the deal charged $65 million in fees. But where did the money come from? Chevron raised nearly $11 billion from bankers and other lenders. It was therefore Chevron's borrowed funds that enriched Pickens and his partners. Meanwhile, shares of Chevron stock plummeted from 40 to 31 after the acquisition. A number of studies during that period documented long-term stock losses by the majority of merged companies. Even many of the people making the most money on the mergers began to question whether many of them made economic sense. "My experience," the takeover lawyer Martin Lipton said in 1985, "tells me that many hostile takeovers and 'white knight' takeovers have turned out to be unsuccessful for the acquirers."

A rising chorus of economists, journalists, businessmen, and others began to protest the takeover craze. Felix Rohatyn, then a senior partner at Lazard Freres & Company, which had helped orchestrate a rash of consolidation in the 1960s and was making a bonanza of fees in the latest rash of takeovers, saw a vast difference between the 1980s and the earlier period. He felt that the 1960s trend toward consolidation had helped create business efficiency and diversification of industries, whereas the 1980s were all about fees and short-term killings on the stock and futures markets for a handful of parties. "All this frenzy might be good for investment bankers now, but it's not good for the country or investment bankers in the long run," he said. Business, he warned, "is killing the goose that laid the golden egg."

Many economists worried that the huge amounts banks were loaning to finance acquisitions were crowding out credit that might have been extended for new investment. Stephen Brobeck, former executive director of the Consumer Federation of America, voiced such concern in 1983 testimony before a congressional committee. "In 1981, $30 billion to $38 billion of all consideration paid [for mergers] was lent by U.S. banks. As important, at least $70 billion was tied up in merger-related loan commitments from these institutions. Legally obligated to honor these commitments, banks could only respond to the Fed's tight-money policy by raising rates." Others worried about the moral flavor of the men at the helm of America's great corporations, and thus at the helm of the economy. The chief executive officer of a major corporation, if he or she is not concerned about employees or communities, at the very least has a fiduciary duty to shareholders. But the advent of golden parachutes and greenmail, coupled with the record salaries and bonuses that corporate board members were voting themselves, raised the question of whether they were motivated by anything but self-interest. As former SEC chairman Williams put it in 1985, "The whole idea of corporate accounting to shareholders is being washed down the drain."

Examples of that betrayal were not hard to find. Less than four months before the Charter Company filed for bankruptcy in April 1984, its top five officers voted themselves bonuses of $250,000 each. Auto executives collected tens of millions of dollars in bonuses at the same time they were citing weak car sales and exacting billions in wage concessions from their workers. In the Reagan years, corporate leaders were crossing lines that a few years before would have been unthinkable. A 1984 article in the *New York Times,* entitled "The Age of Me-First Management," almost seems quaint in the age of Enron, but it perfectly captured the moral revulsion aroused by the budding era of greed. "It doesn't take a revolutionary to figure out that something is amiss in American business today," the article said in its lead paragraph, "that a 'me-first, grab-what-you can' extravagance increasingly appears to be cropping up among the nation's top executives. It shows itself in the disproportionate salaries and bonuses paid to so many corporate chiefs; in the unseemly scrambling over the assets of great corporations; the multi-million severance payments awarded even to CEOs who fail and drive their companies into the ground."

The revulsion was even greater at the ground level, in the households and communities that were suddenly cast adrift in a new and heartless economy. Before Bendix chairman Agee escaped with his $4.1-million golden parachute, the damage to people swept up in his effort to take over Martin Marietta was incalculable. "The human toll was vast," said Berl Falbaum, a manager of news and public affairs for Bendix who lost his job after Allied finally succeeded in taking over Bendix. "Careers were ruined, normal job paths were completely disrupted, people were forced to delay normal things like buying homes. On the business side, everybody was working on the merger. Productivity fell dramatically." Once the merger was complete, Allied cut deeply into Bendix's headquarters in Southfield, Michigan, laying off three hundred people in "redundant" positions. To understand the human cost exacted by the merger fever that began in the Reagan years, multiply that three hundred by hundreds of thousands. The Association of Outplacement Consulting Firms estimated in 1984 that twenty thousand managers would be dismissed as a result of mergers in that year alone.

Opinion polls have shown that America's trust of corporations dwindled during this period. And yet this disapproval of the trends sweeping across the country never was laid at the door of Ronald Reagan, who remained as popular as ever. Besides his instituting of policies that encouraged takeover fever, Reagan's words from the bully pulpit, his apotheosis of greed, influenced the behavior of corporate executives. They were able to justify their methods by merely adopting the Reagan creed that self-interest was in the interest of the common good. In the words of the late James Tobin, a Nobel Prize–winning economics professor at Yale, "The undiluted pursuit of personal gain is more accelerated in society as a result of the conservative ideological revolution. It affects the way businessmen and everybody else looks at what they're doing." The public somehow was not seeing that while Reagan had not invented mergers or callous behavior on the part of corporate executives, he lent enormous impetus to their most avaricious impulses. When it came to corporate greed, the Great Communicator was also the Great Enabler.

Even as public disapproval mounted over the hostile-takeover movement, the Reagan administration resolutely blocked any efforts to stop it. In 1984, Representatives Timothy Wirth and John Dingell mustered widespread Democratic support for a bill that would temper the worst elements of the takeover craze. One element of their bill would have required shareholder approval before publicly held companies could submit to greenmail and buy back their stock from a raider at a premium. The bill would also have taken the advantage of secrecy away from raiders by requiring that they make an immediate public disclosure when they had obtained 5 percent of a company's stock. But after the White House chastised Shad and influenced the SEC to withdraw its support, the legislation went nowhere.

Unlike the conglomeration trend of the 1960s, which petered out as the decade came to a close, the merger wave that began in Reagan's first term, having become a durable feature of American commerce, continued its furious pace after he left office. The 1990s surpassed even the previous decade in the number of deals, with hostile takeovers replaced to a large degree by friendly mergers of companies looking to be bigger players in the global economy. Each year of the 1990s set a new record in the numbers and values of deals. Mobil purchased Exxon, creating the world's largest company without a peep from antitrust regulators. Worldcom Incorporated swallowed MCI, becoming the largest telecommunications company. The rash of megamergers among media companies has been particularly worrisome to consumer advocates, raising the specter of a future in which the nation's artistic output—publishing, television, radio, filmmaking, print journalism—will be in the hands of a small number of large companies. General Electric swallowed NBC. Disney swept up ABC. Time Inc. merged with Warner Brothers, forming a company that later ate up CNN. The nightmare vision of media concentration seemed to have arrived when Viacom purchased CBS in 1999. Among the far-flung properties of the two companies were MTV, Nickelodeon, Showtime, Paramount Pictures, Blockbuster, Simon & Schuster, and Infinity Broadcasting, with its 160 radio stations. But even this colossus was dwarfed by AOL's acquisition of Time Warner in 2000, which created the world's largest media company.

In each of these mergers, the investment community was assured that the combinations made business sense. The joining of huge corporate forces would create synergy, efficiency, and greater profits. The big media, increasingly owned by corporate conglomerates, gave the stamp of approval to the acquisitions, rarely taking the view of consumers. But the real forces behind the megamergers—and the ultimate consequences—became clear when the stock market began tumbling in 2000 and sleazy corporate accounting methods became public. What became obvious was that major firms were acquiring company after company not because of synergy or efficiency but because they could boost the value of their market shares by using the mergers and shoddy accounting practices to create the illusion of greater earnings.

The predatory actions of the corporate raiders that the Reagan administration encouraged in the 1980s had made earnings and market share the central concern of nervous corporate executives. Any responsible economist knows that corporate earnings are not a reliable measure of a company's health and that investing in the future sometimes means sacrificing short-term profits. But in the "market for corporate control," low quarterly earnings are irrationally and shortsightedly seen as a sign of weak management that should be shunned by investors or even ousted in a takeover. So company executives in the 1990s resorted to a quick and easy way to maintain market share: by acquiring other companies. Each of the acquisitions enabled the acquirer to create the illusion of increased earnings, which inflated market share and yielded new capital for the next acquisition.

But after the stock market bubble burst, these towers of speculation and accounting chicanery came tumbling down. The falling stock market revealed the inherent instability of huge companies hastily put together by mergers. A study commissioned by the *Wall Street Journal* in the summer of 2002 found that the stocks of the fifty biggest corporate acquirers had fallen three times as much as the Dow Jones Industrial Average. Tyco International, which acquired seven hundred companies in three years in a bid to become the new General Electric, saw its stock plummet by more than 60 percent over a three-month period. The fortunes of Worldcom fell even more dramatically. Bernard Ebbers, Worldcom's former president and CEO, had made it clear from the start that what mattered to him was investors, not customers. "Our goal is not to capture market share or be global," he told *Business Week* in the late 1990s. "Our goal is to be the No. 1 stock on Wall Street." So Worldcom swallowed seventy-five companies over a five-year period, including the $37-billion acquisition of MCI. But when the falling stock market made further acquisitions impossible, the company's inflated earnings turned into huge losses. WorldCom's shares plummeted by 95 percent between 2000 and 2002. Ebbers, who had borrowed millions from his own company to buy stock, owed the firm $366 million when he resigned in disgrace in the spring of 2002.

In varying degrees, the same fate awaited hundreds of other major companies. Many of them, like AT&T Corp., found themselves frantically selling off companies they had acquired in the booming 1990s. As is now well known, the merger of AOL and Time Warner was a spectacular failure. On the day the merger was announced, the combined market capitalization of the two companies soared from $222 billion to $318 billion. Unfortunately, the succeeding two years brought nothing but plummeting income and shares. By the end of January 2003, the media giant's market capitalization stood at $62 billion, and it was paralyzed by huge losses and $26 billion in debt.

No spectacle, of course, was a more potent symbol of the irrationality that Reagan did so much to create than the collapse of Enron, the Houston-based energy firm that was the nation's seventh largest company before billions of dollars of its stock disappeared. Enron's mind-boggling betrayal of employees and shareholders and its unseemly manipulation of power prices in the midst of California's electricity crisis should in itself have been enough to forever repudiate Reaganism.

Where was the Securities and Exchange Commission while this free-for-all on Wall Street was reshaping the corporate map? Where were the Federal Energy Regulatory Commission, the Federal Trade Commission, the Justice Department Antitrust Division, and a host of other federal regulatory agencies whose job it is to protect citizens from corporate thievery? They were fulfilling the promise of Reagan and his Millionaire Backers. They were letting the market work its magic.

CHAPTER 7

The Effluvia of Commerce

Ronald Reagan completed the mission that his Millionaire Backers laid out for him all those years ago in California—the infusion of commercial values into virtually every sphere of American life. Big corporations now have a sway over our culture that would have appalled Adam Smith or Calvin Coolidge, perhaps even Ronald Reagan himself were he alive and capable of a lucidity that frequently eluded him.

The effluvia of commerce greet us everywhere we turn. Corporate logos and advertisements bellow at us though our televisions and computers, over our telephone lines, in the piles of junk mail on our doorsteps, in the classroom and the textbook, on the scoreboard, in the names given to our public arenas, in the sponsorship of cultural events, in line at the post office and the supermarket, in elevators, at gas pumps, in the doctor's waiting room, on the jetliner, in the museum cafeteria, on the labels of our clothing, in the very ringing in our ears as we lie in bed at night.

The huge corporate amalgams that have emerged from the frenzy of mergers since the early 1980s are now very much our masters. They are the arbiters of our tastes and leisure, our relationships, even our thoughts. Large corporations figured out long ago that their growth depended not only on the manufacture of goods and services but also on the manufacture of desire. Few were as honest as Charles Kettering, director of General Motors' research labs in the 1920s, who called it "the organized creation of dissatisfaction." Since Kettering's time, the creation of dissatisfaction has made many advances. With the explosion of information and the proliferation of media, commercial messages are constantly bombarding our senses, pulsating like strobe lights in our consciousness.

Ronald Reagan, the Great Enabler, ushered in a disturbing new order by clearing away barriers to the final conquering of the human soul by the corporation. John Kenneth Galbraith, in his influential 1952 book *American Capitalism,* referred to the labor movement and government as "countervailing powers" that prevented big business and commercial values from running roughshod over the nation. He could easily have listed ethics, or community values, as another countervailing power. Before the late 1970s, school boards would never have let corporations advertise on video monitors in our classrooms, and never could there have been a publicly owned arena named Tommy Hilfiger at Jones Beach Theater. A company called Space Marketing would not have had the audacity to float a serious proposal for a mile-wide billboard orbiting above the earth's atmosphere. It would have violated accepted standards of civility. Ronald Reagan not only stripped away government and helped decimate the labor movement; he also contributed mightily to the erosion of community standards. At the hands of Reagan and his acolytes, barriers that once shielded venerated cultural and civic institutions from commercialism have crumbled as dramatically as the Berlin Wall. Corporate hucksterism now seeps into the classroom, the pulpit, the medical clinic, the nonprofit sector, amateur athletics, jurisprudence, even the naming of important cultural landmarks.

Some of the consequences of Reaganism have reached the level of absurdity. There has been an explosion of school-based marketing since the Reagan years. Schoolchildren are confronted with commercial messages in their cafeterias, school assemblies, athletic facilities, and curricula. Corporations sponsor school stadiums, gymnasiums, education programs, even entire school buildings. And their influence on the school day and educational programming is growing every year. A generation ago, only a science fiction writer could have imagined Jared Fogle, the mascot of the Subway fast-food chain, invited into schools to lecture children on obesity (his secret to losing weight: a diet limited to two Subway sandwiches a day); or children learning about nutrition from curricular materials supplied by Hershey's Chocolate and McDonald's; or classroom lessons on the Alaska oil spill sponsored by Exxon; or a Proctor & Gamble environmental curriculum that describes disposable diapers as good for the earth. When a Georgia school hosted a "Coke Appreciation Day," a student who wore a Pepsi T-shirt was suspended, until his parents complained. It sounds like *Brave New World.* But this is not some horrid futuristic vision; this is American public education today.

How did we get here? In 1983, Terrence Bell, Reagan's first secretary of education, commissioned a study of America's schools entitled *A Nation at Risk.* Proclaiming that America's schools were faced with a "rising tide of mediocrity," the report cautioned that our failures in the classroom threatened our ability to compete in the global economy. And of course, the Reagan administration's prescription for solving the problem was more corporate involvement in the schools. With the media and educational establishment accepting the report as gospel, corporate leaders pounded home the message that the private sector could rescue failing schools from bumbling bureaucrats. School-business partnerships—found in only 17 percent of the nation's schools in 1984—were in place in 51 percent of schools by the 1989–1990 school year, according to a study by the National Association of Partners in Education. Another study, by the Center for the Analysis of Commercialism in Education, found that media citations of commercial activities in schools had increased by 395 percent between 1990 and 2000, with the biggest emphasis on sponsorship of programs and activities.

With Reagan cutting school aid and local tax-cutting fever spreading across the country in the 1980s, schools increasingly turned to corporations for financial help, entering into lucrative contracts with soft-drink producers and accepting donations of equipment and educational materials. Few parents or school boards seemed to care that in exchange for the gifts, schools often agreed to give advertisers access to a captive audience of schoolchildren. The best-known example of such marketing was provided by Channel One, a twelve-minute television news program now seen by more than 40 percent of the nation's teenagers every day. Developed in 1990 by Whittle Communications, Channel One offers schools a television set for each classroom, two VCRs, and a satellite link in exchange for an agreement that the program be shown daily to every student, with two minutes of commercials. A former Reagan administration official, Chester Finn, was a key adviser to Whittle, and the first President Bush chose as his education secretary a Channel One investor, Lamar Alexander, later a U.S. senator.

Reagan was not calibrating his policies on the arc of public opinion. From the time of the Gilded Age, Americans have had a healthy suspicion of big business, and polls in the 1970s and 1980s showed that distrust intensifying. Professors Thomas Ferguson and Joel Rogers, in an exhaustive review of polling data published in the *Atlantic Monthly* in the mid-1980s, reported that "public skepticism toward business, and support for government regulation of it, actually increased on several dimensions during the 1970s." They found that from 1969 to 1979, the percentage of Americans who believed that there was "too much power concentrated in the hands of a few large companies for the good of the nation" increased from 61 to 79 percent, and that the share of those thinking that business was making "too much profit" went from 38 to 51 percent. Perhaps most surprising, from 1971 to 1979, the percentage who believed that "government should put limits on the profits companies can make" sharply increased, from 33 to 60 percent. Other polls found that Americans had grown disenchanted with materialism and our consumer society. One such survey, conducted by Chivas Regal and released just before Reagan left office, found that "three quarters of the working public would like to see a return to a simpler society with less emphasis on material wealth."

But Reagan acted as if the 1980 election, in which he gained only 50.7 percent of the ballots cast, in the lowest voter turnout in thirty-two years, gave him a mandate to grant big business an unprecedented entrée into the lives of Americans. It was not just the tax cuts and deregulation that gave corporations new power. The administration adopted a series of policies that received little attention at the time but served the express purpose of giving corporate America a much larger sway over our culture. At the same time, he gave his imprimatur to the sweeping away of traditions that had once served as a check on the behavior of corporate executives, Hollywood production companies, music labels, publishing houses, architects, developers, rock stars, and other cultural leaders, in an unspoken social contract that kept them from plunging headfirst into crass commercialism.

The ethos of Reaganism contributed mightily to what thinking people find so distasteful about modern America: the explosion of advertising, the rise of "infomercials," product placement in films, the takeover of health care by for-profit HMOs, the commercialization of schools, the slow creep of advertising into public broadcasting, the selling of naming rights for public landmarks, and many other corporate encroachments on the public and nonprofit sectors. In the post-Reagan era, we have become a culture that worships business. The number of financial publications has exploded in the last two decades, while those devoted to culture and politics have struggled to survive. Even while steeped in scandal, corporate CEOs are treated like rock stars, their autobiographies topping the best seller lists and their compensation soaring into the stratosphere, whether or not they perform for their companies.

Bald commercialism has even affected people who were once heroes of the counterculture. Musicians and artists have forged alliances with corporations that would have been unimaginable in the pre-Reagan era. Artists ranging from Eric Clapton and David Bowie to Tina Turner and Ray Charles performed for Pepsi commercials in the 1980s. The Rolling Stones agreed to the first corporate-sponsored rock tour in 1997, with Mick Jagger and Sheryl Crow, the opening act, appearing onstage with clothes from Tommy Hilfiger's new "Rock 'n' Roll collection." For the supposed bad boys of rock, whose 1960s hit "Satisfaction" satirized conspicuous consumption, it was an abject bow to corporate greed.

The new empowerment of corporations has cost us huge chunks of our lives. Americans now work more hours on average than our counterparts in any other developed nation, for reasons closely linked to the Reagan Revolution: the stagnation of middle-class wages and the insecurity of corporate employment. In a world where the next round of corporate downsizing is always just around the corner—as CEOs seek to impress Wall Street with their ruthlessness—it becomes a matter of survival for employees to stay at their desks as long as their coworkers. When we are not working, we are shopping, drawn by the vastly expanded forms of credit engendered by the post-Reagan deregulation of the financial sector. But woe to those who make too much use of the credit dangled before us by deregulated financial institutions. In the final indignity for this new generation of debt junkies, President George W. Bush signed legislation in 2005 that weakened citizens' ability to clear their debts through bankruptcy, a blatant giveaway to banks and credit card companies.

These noxious elements of contemporary American culture have no popular constituency; they were slid past Americans distracted by wedge issues like race, welfare, crime, and abortion. They were very much part of the Reaganites' vision for the future. Most were stated goals of Reagan's administration, while others were inevitable consequences ignored by corporate leaders hungry for more profit. As a case in point, the Reagan administration, as will be shown below, took very purposeful steps to eliminate fee-for-service in medicine and place the nation's health care in the hands of for-profit HMOs. Fast-forward to 2006, and ten hospitals in the Los Angeles area are under criminal investigation for discharging ailing homeless people onto the streets in violation of the law, a practice that officials say is happening throughout the country. In one case, Bellflower Hospital, part of Kaiser Permanente, the nation's largest HMO, was charged with dumping a gravely ill and demented sixty-three-year-old woman into a crime-ridden area of Skid Row in Los Angeles. She was found wandering the streets in her hospital gown and slippers.

The genius of Reagan and his handlers was that these visions were never enunciated in such dystopian terms. In Reagan's speeches, the plan for corporate hegemony was always hidden behind paeans to the good old-fashioned inventiveness and entrepreneurial instincts of Americans, as if we were still a nation of artisans and small-scale capitalists, not the epicenter of a global oligopoly where corporations have no real allegiance to any single country. Cyrill Siewert, the chief financial officer at the Colgate-Palmolive Company, summed up the Reagan era in 1989 when he described his company's lack of devotion to the country that was showering it with tax breaks: "The United States does not have an automatic call on our resources. There is no mindset that puts this country first."

It would be naive to think that the dictates of commerce ever played anything but a predominant role in the shaping of our culture. Long before shopping was a national pastime or television shows were created to promote action figures, the corporations that Thorstein Veblen called the "master instruments of civilization" were shaping people's lives. The settlement of most of the nation followed the pathways of business. A corporation lays a railroad bed or builds a factory, and a community emerges around it. Henry Ford offers five dollars a day in his auto plant, and thousands of southern black field workers migrate to Detroit. Our very identities as citizens have always been determined largely by whether we are factory workers, miners, bankers, or college professors.

Capitalism took hold in England at the end of the eighteenth century only by laying waste to a feudal economic and cultural order that had prevailed for centuries. The trading classes, as Karl Polanyi wrote in his classic study of nascent English capitalism, "had no organ to sense the dangers involved in . . . the destruction of family life, the devastation of neighborhoods, the denudation of forests, the pollution of rivers, the deterioration of craft standards, the disruption of folkways, and the general degradation of existence including housing and arts, as well as the innumerable forms of private and public life that do not affect profits." No less an eminence than Edmund Wilson was held in thrall by the majesty of passages in Karl Marx's *Das Kapital* that described the cultural devastation wreaked by the emergence of capitalism. "It is a vision which fascinates and appalls us, which strikes us with a kind of awe," Wilson wrote of capitalism sweeping away the feudal order,

> wrecking it and overspreading it: accelerating, reorganizing, reassembling, in ever more ingenious complexity, ever more formidable proportions; breaking out of the old boundaries of nations; sending out the tracks and cranes of its commerce across countries and oceans and continents and bringing the people of distant cultures, at diverse stages of civilization, into its system, as it lays hold on the destinies of races, knocks new shapes out of their bodies and their minds, their personalities and their aspirations, without their really grasping what has happened to them. . . . There is also a human principle at work—"those passions which are," as Marx says, "at once the most violent, the basest and the most abominable of which the human breast is capable: the furies of personal interest."

So capitalism, for all the benefits it has bestowed on humankind, has always been relentless in its upending of society. The phenomenon that concerns us here—the saturation of our society with commercial messages and the corporate manipulation of our very thought processes—took on new forms in the twentieth century. The blandishments of business reached ever deeper into our lives as the advertising and public relations industries became more ubiquitous and honed their techniques in influencing human behavior. In the nineteenth century, when the challenge of market capitalism was to increase production, advertising could afford to be a staid vehicle for conveying information about a product, with wordy advertisements printed in agate. But by the 1920s, machine production techniques had advanced so rapidly that supply threatened to overwhelm demand. For capitalism to survive, business would have to manufacture not only commodities but also the consumer's desire to purchase those commodities. "Unless he could be persuaded to buy and buy lavishly, the whole stream of six-cylinder cars, super-heterodynes, cigarettes, rouge compacts and electric ice-boxes would be dammed at the outlet," wrote Frederick Lewis Allen. The modern imperative of advertising came to the fore, with all its implications for the tenor of society.

As always, the forward march of commerce would mean knocking down barriers of taste. Publishers of newspapers and periodicals in the nineteenth century would have considered full-page advertisements an abomination. In the 1870s, *Harper's* politely refused an offer by the Howe Sewing Machine Company to pay eighteen thousand dollars for the back cover of the magazine. "Advertising was considered an embarrassment—the retarded child, the wastrel relative, the unruly servant kept backstairs and never allowed into the front parlor," wrote Stephen Fox in his history of the advertising industry. Those seeking to buy ads were often companies offering bogus patent medicines, and publications that accepted them looked financially shaky and risked their credit rating.

However, such delicacy in matters of aesthetics would gradually erode with the expanding demand for advertising space. One study found that the average display advertisement in the *Boston Evening Transcript* and the *New York Tribune* in the 1860s was about four column inches. It was four times that size in 1918, and full-page ads became common in national magazines. By 1912, most of the mass-circulation magazines that had been publishing the corporate exposés of muckrakers like Lincoln Steffens and Ida Tarbell began to move away from such articles, in part because business threatened to withhold advertisements.

The advent of radio, and eventually television, only made commercial messages more ubiquitous. Freed from the limitations of written text, advertisers could now reach children and the illiterate portion of adult Americans, still significant in the 1920s. No longer could one just put down the newspaper or turn the page; the commercial message was ambient, immutable. Not just the person whose eyes were on the page was the audience, but entire families. For the people whose interests were threatened by radio—namely, the print media—broadcast advertising was a threat to the sanctity of home and hearth. "The family circle is not a public place," the trade publication *Printer's*

Ink huffed in April 1922, "and advertising has no business intruding there unless it is invited." Many stations at first only mentioned sponsors at the beginning and end of programs, but those barriers soon fell. Broadcasting became as much about advertising as it was about programming.

More than anything else, the explosion in advertising in the United States resulted from remarkable increases in capitalist production, which grew by an unprecedented 7 percent a year between 1922 and 1927. The advertising industry recognized by the 1920s that creating demand for the output of the ever expanding American capitalist machine meant more than just connecting citizens with their natural demand for products and services. That demand had to be fabricated in ways just as ingenious as the manufacturing itself. The goal of advertisements became to associate products with youth, health, beauty, affluence, and sophistication. "Reach for a Lucky instead of a sweet" was aimed at associating smoking with good health. And because these advertisements were now beaming nationwide, across areas rural and urban, the message had to be extremely general to avoid offending any segment of the audience. Advertisers began absorbing the lessons of psychology and social science in the ways to influence mass behavior and break down consumer resistance. "The making of one general will out of a multitude of general wishes," wrote Walter Lippmann, ". . . consists essentially in the use of symbols which assemble emotions after they have been detached from their ideas. . . . The process, therefore, by which general opinions are brought to cooperation consists of an intensification of feeling and a degradation of significance."

The impact that this commercial inundation was having on society and the American character became a prime area of study for writers and intellectuals after World War II, and for good reason. As the historian Edward M. Potter noted in 1954, advertising had taken its place alongside schools and religion as a prime "instrument of social control" and "guide to human behavior" and yet—unlike those other two sacred institutions—had no socially responsible goals, only the nurturing of more consumers. He calculated that $6.54 million was spent on advertising in the United States in 1951, about $199 per family, compared with about $5.01 million, or $152 per household, spent on primary and secondary education two years earlier.

Along with the greatest prosperity ever known to mankind, America in the 1950s had brought about a stultifying conformity to values that bore the unmistakable imprint of corporate America. The era begot research by psychologists and sociologists like Erich Fromm, C. Wright Mills, Hans Gerth, and T. W. Adorno into the role that an external culture plays in shaping the personality, with the implication that ambient commercialism might be rewiring the human brain, especially the brain of a child. The father, Mills and Gerth wrote, "may not be the primary authority, but rather the replica of the power relations of society," while Adorno theorized that "broad changes in social conditions and institutions will have a direct bearing upon the kinds of personalities that develop within a society." Those broad changes, of course, were larger than just commercial advertising. William H. Whyte famously conceived of the "organization man," regimented by his membership in the corporation. And David Riesman, in his book *The Lonely Crowd,* observed a new personality type, the "other-directed man," who took his cues from the crowd and the mass media, whereas the "inner-directed man" of the nineteenth century had lived with unchanging values nurtured by family and religion. Bearing the brunt of all this commercial manipulation was the child. "Even before American children learn the language of the primer and the schoolroom," wrote Max Lerner in the 1950s, "they mimic the language of the commercials on TV, and of the world of comic little Disneylike men and animated packages that accompany the commercials."

In the 1960s, of course, academia was in open rebellion against the coercion of consumer society, and an entire generation of college leftists was enthralled by Herbert Marcuse, the German émigré whose *One-Dimensional Man* updated Marxist theories for postwar America. In Marcuse's eyes, real human freedom had been extinguished by the need to conform to a panoply of cultural experiences—customs and mores, modes of leisure, literature, fashion—necessary to sustain capitalist production and consumption. "For 'totalitarian' is not only a terroristic political coordination of society," Marcuse wrote, "but also a non-terroristic economic-technical coordination which operates through the manipulation of needs by vested interests. . . . Not only a specific form of government or party rule makes for totalitarianism, but also a specific system of production and distribution which may well be compatible with 'pluralism' of parties, newspapers, 'countervailing powers,' etc."

But if corporate America sometimes seemed to have succeeded in making the country in its own image through much of the twentieth century, there is also another story, that of government, nonprofit institutions, and even some corporate leaders themselves making sporadic attempts to prevent commercialism from distorting the American character. The Progressive era and the New Deal, besides giving rise to more regulation of business and the legalization of labor organizing, sought to enhance the aesthetic sensibilities of Americans and protect them from the acids of bald commerce. Walter Lippmann, in a 1914 essay that derided the carping of socialists about the intrinsic evil of capitalism, nonetheless acknowledged "in everyday life a widespread rebellion against the profit motive." He noted approvingly that the "craftsman" and the "statesman" were resisting the "profiteer": "Endowment, subsidy, state aid, endless varieties of consumers' and producers' co-operatives; public enterprise—they have been devised to save the theater, to save science and invention, education and journalism, the market basket and public utilities from the life-sapping direction of the commercialist."

Much of the reform effort in the Progressive era emanated not from "reds" and "anarchists" but from the professional classes, the lawyers, merchants, petty capitalists, and newspapers editors who in the small towns and cities of America had once been community pillars, "as though they were clergymen," in the words of Henry Adams, "and each profession were a church." Since the end of the Civil War, their influence had been eclipsed by the rise of huge corporations and millionaire businessmen, whom they saw as having little regard for community and no refinement in cultural matters. The Progressive era gave rise not only to the muckraking journalists but also to a bevy of "realist" novelists, like Jack London, Theodore Dreiser, and Upton Sinclair, who chronicled the rapacious effects of big business or the plight of the poor. College professors, social scientists, and other intellectuals, who had become highly specialized by the turn of the century and felt ignored and humiliated by the corporate class, also joined in the reform movement. As the historian Richard Hofstadter pointed out, the most prominent social scientists of the period were marked by their opposition to the plutocracy: Thorstein Veblen in economics; Lester Ward, the founder of sociology; John Dewey in philosophy; and the political scientist Charles A. Beard, whose opposition to the "vested interests" extended to a famous 1913 treatise, *An Economic Interpretation of the Constitution of the United States,* which argued that the Founding Fathers had rigged the government to keep the lower orders in their place.

Writing in 1903 in *McClure's,* one of the muckraking magazines, Ray Stannard Baker raised fears that big labor and big business were joining in a cabal to run roughshod over the culture and traditions of the common man: "The unorganized public, where will it come in? The professional man, the lecturer, the writer, the artist, the farmer, the salaried government employee, and all the host of men who are not engaged in the actual production or delivery of necessary material things, how will they fare?" The Progressive impulse derived some of its impetus from the very top, from the presidencies of Theodore Roosevelt and Woodrow Wilson, with their concerns for the preservation of community and the dignity of the common man. But William Allen White, in his 1910 book *The Old Order Changeth,* posited that all of this agitation for reform was also bubbling up from a New Citizen, who had a "divinely planted instinct" against the corporate men steamrolling across the country.

The Progressive movement had enough momentum that its reform spirit survived the probusiness epoch of the 1920s and was reborn in the New Deal, whose architects were not shy about using the powers of government and regulation to keep our cultural life and small-town traditions from wilting. Franklin Roosevelt lent support to a back-to-the-land movement whose adherents viewed American self-sufficiency as a bulwark against the stifling uniformity of mass production. FDR may not have bought wholly into the movement's plans for a mass exodus from the cities, but fearing the persistence of urban employment, his administration inserted $25 million into the National Industrial Recovery Act for the creation of subsistence homesteads. M. L. Wilson, the chief of the Subsistence Homestead Division, part of the Department of the Interior, viewed a revival of husbandry as a salutary revolt "against the crass materialism and the shallowness of the Jazz Age." His idea of Utopia was the Mormon village in Utah, with its neat homesteads equipped with modern power and plumbing but still remote from the metropolis.

Eleanor Roosevelt directed some of the subsistence homestead funding to subsidize small handicraft production. The idea occurred to her as she toured an impoverished Quaker community near Morgantown, West Virginia, where the local inhabitants had staved off destitution by establishing small handicraft mills. With her prodding, the government set up a community in nearby Reedsville in 1933 that was designed to subsist on farming and small handicraft factories. Renaming the town Arthurdale, the government bought land for fifty homes, each on two to five acres of land and equipped with insulation and indoor plumbing, still a rarity in many poor rural communities in the Depression. Instead of giving back their wages to a company store, the inhabitants bought groceries at the Arthurdale Cooperative Store. The Interior Department set up dozens of other subsistence communities in the next several years in places like Granger, Iowa; Dayton, Ohio; and Hightstown, New Jersey, where Jewish needle workers set up a village around gardening and a clothing factory. The communities came under fierce attack by conservatives in Congress, who viewed them as experiments in socialism and blasted the high cost of such settlements. Indeed, some of the communities had been based on false assumptions about local markets and ended up failing. Arthurdale was defunded and fully turned over to private hands during the war effort in the early 1940s, but it remained a viable community. FDR, in an address at the Arthurdale High School graduation in 1938, said the money spent on building the community made just as much sense as the subsidies lavished on big business. The expense, he told the graduates, "we justifiably charge off as the inevitable cost of all progress—just as we have in the past charged off the huge government share in the development costs of the railroads, the cables, the airplanes, and the hundreds of millions in dollars in improved highways that have made the automobile possible."

Even more antithetical to the corporate view of America was the Works Progress Administration and its efforts to fund cultural activities that were not supported by the private sector. Launched as part of Roosevelt's Second New Deal in 1935, the WPA created cultural programs that at their peak employed forty thousand artists, writers, musicians, and theater workers. The inventions of the phonograph, the radio, and motion pictures had idled tens of thousands of musicians and other live performers. Playhouses were closing in droves as the sales of movie tickets skyrocketed. The Loew's chain, which had thirty-six live theaters offering productions forty to fifty weeks a year before 1930, had only three in business by 1934. Even worse was the plight of many painters, sculptors, and other artists, who had always lived hand to mouth but teetered on the brink of destitution in the Depression. The WPA gave them employment in states and cities across the country. Artists were dispatched to paint murals and erect sculptures in public buildings. By the end of the decade, the Artists Project had adorned hospitals, schools, post offices, and other public places with 2,500 murals, 18,000 pieces of sculpture, and 108,000 easel paintings. Musicians employed by the Federal Music Project were giving five thousand performances a week in orchestras, chamber and choral groups, opera companies, and other performance units across the country. More than twelve hundred plays were produced in thirty-one states by the Federal Theater Project, and the Federal Writers Project employed more than six thousand writers who turned out eight hundred works by 1941, including the famed American Guide Series, an encyclopedic rendering of life in all fifty states and many big cities that are still in print today. Among the writers put to work by the WPA were Ralph Ellison, Richard Wright, Studs Terkel, John Cheever, Saul Bellow, Margaret Walker, Arna Bontemps, and Zora Neale Hurston.

While Roosevelt tried to work hand in hand with corporate leaders, many of the New Deal programs could not help but clash with big business and its conservative patrons in Congress. The administration pursued a new Pure Food and Drug bill to eliminate false advertisements, mislabeling, and unsafe products in the food and drug industries. To drum up support for the bill, the FDA put on a public exhibition of adulterated foods and toxic medicines. The purveyors of these products had induced people to paralyze themselves by using mislabeled rat poison to remove unwanted hair, burn their insides by treating obesity with dinitrophenol, or attempt to cure cancer by drinking a mix of ammonia, turpentine, and eggs. The exhibition showed a picture of a woman who had blinded herself with eyelash dye. Labeled the "Chamber of Horrors" by the press, the exhibit enraged businessmen, who viewed the legislation as an infringement on consumer choice.

But the WPA programs and the subsistence homesteads were in a sense even more subversive because, as M. L. Wilson told Interior Secretary Harold Ickes, they were "laying the basis for a new type of civilization in America." In an address to Congress in January 1935, FDR lamented that the programs of his first term had not "weeded out the over-privileged" nor "effectively lifted up the underprivileged." He told the legislators he had a mandate from the people to "forswear that conception of the acquisition of wealth which, through excessive profits, creates undue private power over private affairs and, to our misfortune, over public affairs as well."

Such language horrified the vested interests of the nation, who eventually put a stop to the WPA's cultural programs. In July 1938, J. Parnell Thomas, a red-baiting Republican congressman from New York, goaded the House Committee to Investigate Un-American Activities to begin a probe of the WPA theater and writers' projects, which he said were "hotbeds of Communists" and "one more link in the vast and unparalleled New Deal propaganda network." The six-week investigation was widely covered in the press, and by 1939, in part because of the bad publicity created by HUAC, all the cultural projects had lost their funding and been disbanded.

In reality, neither the Progressives nor the New Dealers aimed to turn over the nation to the communists. The Progressives were drawn from the ranks of often conservative professional classes who merely wanted an elite more responsible than the avaricious businessmen who seemed to be controlling the country. The New Deal, through its myriad regulations and government interventions in the economy, sought to prevent business from driving the nation into periodic scourges of deflation and unemployment, and at the same time to stimulate culture that might otherwise be eviscerated if all American endeavors were driven by the profit motive.

Such efforts, largely dormant in the decade and a half after World War II, would flower again in the cultural rebellion of the 1960s. A new back-to-the-land movement would send young people into the countryside, where they formed communes and food cooperatives. Abbie Hoffman halted trading by tossing handfuls of money onto the floor of the New York Stock Exchange, and the image of the corporate executive reached perhaps its lowest level since the Great Depression. Some of the impetus would again come from government, such as the wave of social regulations in the 1970s and the Johnson administration's creation of the National Endowments of the Arts and Humanities in 1965. But more of the efforts came from an anticorporate ethos that flowered within the culture itself and seemed to portend a renewal of civic spirit and corporate retrenchment.

It was this long and venerable tradition of putting a check on corporate domination—decidedly conservative in the ways it sought to preserve American folkways—that was upended by the Reagan Revolution. Reagan saw to it that bald commerce would once again trample on much of aesthetic and cultural value in American life, thrusting aside the poets, the artists, the activists for the poor, those who dreamed of a better and pristine society.

One of those dreamers thrust aside was a woman named Peggy Charren. Charren led a group of Massachusetts housewives in an extraordinary exercise in citizen democracy in the 1970s that prompted the first significant government limitations on television advertising.

In large part because of her efforts, even the Nixon appointees on the Federal Communications Commission accepted the logic that the commercialism flowing from television sets had the potential to warp the minds of young children. But her movement, already wounded by the corporate lobby in the late 1970s, withered and died as soon as Reagan came to power. Virtually all of the reforms that Charren and legions of supporters around the country had worked so hard for years to wrest from the government were undone in a matter of months. The story of Charren's aborted crusade is another sad emblem of the America that Reaganism left behind.

Charren's group, Action for Children's Television, or ACT, was founded in 1968 in her living room in Newton Center, Massachusetts, where she and three other housewives, their careers on hold for a few years while their children were in school, decided over coffee that something had to be done about the shortage of high-quality television programming for kids. The only other groups focusing on the issue in those days were right-wing organizations interested in censoring television. Charren was not of this ilk. She had been raised in a progressive middle-class household in Manhattan in the 1930s and 1940s, when her parents, a wholesale furrier and his wife, subscribed to left-leaning newspapers like *In Fact* and *P.M.* and imbued their children with a social ethic. Their daughter came to adulthood a purist in matters of free speech and had no interest in censoring the content of kids' programs, even if some were too violent for her tastes. Instead, she approached the children's television issue from the standpoint that programming for young people should be edifying and inspirational. She was a lover of children's books who had spent years setting up book fairs for Boston-area school districts. "We had school libraries with wonderful books for children," Charren said. "I thought, gee whiz, why can't children's television be like a good children's library? I was focusing on what was missing in children's television, not so much on what was there."

But with children's television inundated with advertisements for toys, sugary cereals, and vitamins, ACT inevitably ended up fighting against commercialism. The group's first target was the Boston television station WHDH, which broadcast *Romper Room,* a locally produced franchise of a national show that depicted teachers instructing children in a nursery school setting. This was a nursery school with a difference: its teachers pushed commercial products, including a *Romper Room* line of toys, throughout the show. "The program was full of sales pitches," Charren said. Under pressure from the mothers, the station agreed to reduce the host's role in hawking products.

ACT was just getting started. In 1970, Charren and the other mothers each spent fifteen dollars for a bus ticket to Washington to meet with commissioners of the Federal Communications Commission. To their surprise, six of the seven commissioners sat down with them, and chairman Dean Birch, a conservative Nixon appointee with a disposition to confront television executives—who he thought were treating the president too harshly in their news programs—lent a particularly sympathetic ear to the mothers' complaints about commercials aimed at children. "He took off his jacket and rolled up his sleeves and said, 'I think this is something we should pay attention to,'" Charren said. "We went home thinking that democracy does work." Within days, the FCC had put forth a notice of proposed rule making that would limit the duration of ads on children's shows.

The spirit of reform, at least in the way the commissioners viewed the issue of children's television, had been quietly percolating in the FCC for more than a decade. In the act that founded the agency in 1934, it was given the power to withdraw the license of any broadcasting station whose program lineup was not upholding the public interest. The airwaves, after all, were owned by the public, entrusted only by revocable license to private interests. In 1974, the FCC issued a policy statement making clear that the offering of quality programming for children was part of a television station's obligations in promoting the public interest: "We believe . . . that the broadcaster's public service obligation includes a responsibility to provide diversified programming designed to meet the varied needs and interests of the child audience. . . . In this regard, educational or informational programming for children is of particular importance." Newton Minow, whom Kennedy appointed as FCC chairman in 1961, engendered a widespread public debate about children's programming, becoming famous for his description of television as a "vast wasteland." While the 1974 policy statement was mainly aimed at programming, the FCC had also begun paying stricter attention to the extent of television advertising. In 1969, ABC tried to push the boundaries of federal regulations by broadcasting a cartoon called *Hot Wheels,* essentially a thirty-minute advertisement—or what Charren would later dub a "program-length commercial"—for the miniature toy cars manufactured by Mattel. One of the toy giant's competitors, Topper, filed a complaint with the FCC, which ordered *Hot Wheels* taken off the air after finding that the show violated the law by exceeding the time allotted for advertisements. "We find this pattern disturbing," the FCC said in its ruling. ". . . for [it] subordinates programming in the interest of the public to programming in the interest of salability."

With the prodding of Charren and the other organizations, the agency would go even further. Its 1974 policy statement required broadcasters within two years to make a meaningful effort to provide television programming for children and to end the most abusive practices in the use of commercials. Commercials on kids' programs would be limited to 12 minutes per hour on weekdays and 9.5 minutes on weekends, and no longer would program hosts be allowed to pitch products. A study by the FCC's Children's Television Task Force, aimed at determining whether self-regulation by broadcasters had been successful, found in 1979 that most stations had complied with the commercial limitations but that many had flouted the guidelines calling for new children's programming. The study found that licensees were carrying an average of 2.6 hours of "instructional" programs per week, down from 2.8 hours four years earlier.

But the government, and the National Association of Broadcasters, was steadily moving in the direction of making commercials less ubiquitous in the lives of children. By the late 1970s, ACT was awash in private donations, most notably from the John and Mary R. Markle Foundation, and boasted a membership of twenty thousand, a staff of twelve to fifteen people, and a budget of up to a half-million dollars.

It also had new allies like the Center for Science in the Public Interest, which joined ACT in 1978 in petitioning the Federal Trade Commission for an outright ban on commercials aimed at young children. The FTC was empowered to regulate deceptive advertising, and the two advocacy groups argued that nothing could be more deceptive than commercials aimed at children too young to differentiate them from regular programming.

Charren and her allies were approaching the FTC at exactly the right time. The agency had entered a period of activism under Carter's appointee as its chairman, Michael Pertschuk, a consumer advocate who was instinctively drawn to the logic of limiting television commercials aimed at young audiences. The FTC issued notice of a proposed rule in 1978 that would eliminate all television advertising directed to children too young to understand they were being subjected to a sales pitch. The measure also would have banned the advertising of sugared products to children eight to eleven. At the same time, the commission assigned its staff to conduct an exhaustive study of the impact that commercial advertising had on the developing mind. The effort, led by commission staff member Tracy Westen, was truly monumental in scope, encompassing sixty thousand pages of documents from the world's leading experts in health, children's psychology, and nutrition and more than six thousand pages of oral testimony.

The findings painted a disturbing picture of a nation addicted to television. On average, preschool children watched thirty-three hours of television a week, or a third of their waking hours. Adults watched four hours a day, the equivalent of ten years of around-the-clock viewing by the age of sixty-five. More to the point, kids watched twenty thousand television commercials a year—seven thousand of them for sugared products—and the youngest among them clearly did not understand what they were seeing. Leading psychologists concluded that children ages three, four, and five thought that television characters were real beings living inside the television set, and when Tony the Tiger told them to eat Frosted Flakes, he was as real as all the rest. The evidence also showed that half of children by age two had gum disease and at least one decayed tooth, and by age eighteen the average child had fourteen decayed teeth. Half of the fifteen-year-olds had never been to a dentist.

Despite the weight of such evidence, drafting regulations to deal with the problem would not have been easy. Because there was such a shortage of programming for young children, most of them were watching programs that also attracted older children not included in the ban. The solution, as Westen later suggested, would have been stricter FCC rules requiring stations to create children's shows without advertising as a public service. But the staffs of the FTC and the FCC never had a chance to explore such ideas. Alarmed by the prospect of losing revenues from children's advertising, a broad coalition of corporate interests—cereal and candy manufacturers, broadcasting companies, toy makers, even tobacco companies—began a major lobbying effort against the proposals. Looking back on that era, Westen believes the staff tried to achieve too much with one package of regulation and ended up alienating too wide a section of interests. Charren said Pertschuk did not help matters by delivering a speech that endorsed the proposed rules before they had even been the subject of hearings. "I don't know where his head was, but he came on like gangbusters," said Charren, who otherwise admires Pertschuk. "You can't do that if you are the chairman of a commission. You have to have hearings. You can't make up your mind in advance."

Pertschuk ultimately recused himself from voting on the issue, but that concession did not decrease the backlash against the commission, in an era when deregulation was quickly becoming the watchword of policymakers in Washington. Under pressure from powerful lobbyists, Congress first blocked passage of the FTC's budget and then passed legislation stripping the agency of its power to regulate children's advertising.

As discouraging as this was for the growing coalition of children's advocates, which included the American Academy of Pediatrics, the National Congress of Parents and Teachers, the Consumers Union, and the Child Welfare League, far worse was to come. With the inauguration of Ronald Reagan, any notion of protecting children from irresponsible television advertising was driven out of Washington. Not only did the FTC kill its investigation of children's television in 1981, but none of the data collected during the three years of fact finding were ever published. Worse, Mark Fowler, the free-market ideologue whom Reagan tapped to head the FCC, threw out the agency's guidelines for children's television in December 1983, removing any limitation on the duration and character of commercials in children's programming. Reagan administration officials justified the move by saying that broadcasters should be allowed to offer the programs and commercials that consumers demanded without interference from the government. "If people wanted [the shows] to be better, they would be better," said John Kamp, a senior attorney in the FCC's Mass Media Bureau under Reagan. Or as Fowler put it, "The marketplace will take care of children."

All that Charren and her thousands of members had worked toward since the late 1960s was undone in less than two years. Broadcasters reacted, even before Fowler lifted the guidelines, by jettisoning the low-rated educational children's programming it had developed in the 1970s. CBS fired twenty people working on children's programming and scrapped the show *30 Minutes.* CBS killed the Emmy-winning shows *Animals, Animals, Animals* and *Kids Are People Too,* and NBC got rid of the prime-time children's specials on *Project Peacock.* An FCC study found that between 1979 and 1983, the average time per week that commercial television stations devoted to children's programming dropped from 11.3 to 4.4 hours, and there was no longer a single children's series shown in the after-school period on any network. Children's programming was again relegated to the Saturday morning ghetto with its depressing miasma of toy and cereal ads, now completely unregulated. Even more disturbing, the deregulation opened the door for the program-length commercial, the very phenomenon that the FCC had so forcefully regulated just a decade earlier. Shows created specifically to promote action figures like GI Joe or Pokémon became standard fare on Saturday mornings.

The *Washington Post* cheered the demise of the FTC's rule-making proceeding with a 1981 editorial entitled "Farewell to the National

Nanny." It suggested that Washington had "better things to do than play national nanny, monitoring what children see and hear on TV," a role the paper said should be the job of parents "acting individually and collectively against the products that are so advertised." One wonders if the editorial writer would be so glib about the current state of children's television. Young people are deluged with advertisements for McDonald's and other fattening foods at a time when obesity and diabetes have become national epidemics. Quality programming for children is virtually missing from commercial broadcast and cable stations.

The notion that children's programming should be consistent with the public interest, once a bedrock principle of the FCC, is now no longer even on the table. "If you watch most television aimed at children," Tracy Westen said in a 2005 speech at Loyola University in Los Angeles, "I doubt you would conclude that the advertising and the programming is there for the benefit of the child. It's clearly there for the benefit of the sponsors. So you have one set of institutions that are designed to nurture and help children as they grow older, and we have another completely different institution that's designed to sell them products and to inculcate them into lifetime purchasing habits."

It was not just children's television sacrificed on the altar of the free market. With Reagan's election, the long struggle between civic and commercial values took a decided turn toward the latter. The Reagan administration moved across a dizzying number of fronts to empower large corporations and insinuate commercialism into previously sacrosanct areas of American life. This was the explicit goal of a series of blue-ribbon panels set up in Reagan's first term. Most prominent was the President's Private Sector Survey on Cost Control, ostensibly intended to harness the wisdom of business executives in finding ways the government could reduce expenses. Chaired by J. Peter Grace, chief of W. R. Grace & Company, the survey was overseen by a 150-member executive committee made up of CEOs from many of the nation's largest companies. The choice of Grace as chairman was questionable from the start. Public Citizen, Ralph Nader's consumer lobbying group, found that W. R. Grace had paid no net federal income tax on $684.1 million in profits between 1981 and 1983 and that either the company or its subsidiaries had been investigated for environmental contamination of at least thirty sites in the previous decade. It was unknown at the time that W. R. Grace would spend $8 million in 1986 to settle a lawsuit accusing it and another company of causing the pollution in two wells in Woburn, Massachusetts, that had led to the leukemia deaths of five children and an adult, litigation made famous in the film and best-selling book *A Civil Action.*

Then seventy years old, a small, portly man with a slight lisp, Grace made no secret from the start of where his politics lay. He told an audience around the time of his appointment that New York City's nine hundred thousand Puerto Ricans were "all on food stamps," and one of his first acts as chairman of the survey was to circulate a four-page memo to commission members claiming that the media's coddling of feminism and homosexuality was one reason "traditional family values have suffered such an erosion." Not surprisingly, Grace's panel was contemptuous of the media and tried to operate in total secrecy. At the beginning, it resisted an effort by the General Accounting Office, the investigative arm of Congress, to obtain a list of its one thousand members. It may have been afraid Congress would find out that scores of its top members had been given assignments to cut costs in government agencies that regulated their very industries, a blatant conflict of interest.

The GAO and the Congressional Budget Office later found—and even the White House acknowledged—that the commission report, which claimed it could save the government $424 billion over three years, was riddled with inaccuracies and vastly overstated potential savings. Public Citizen's report aptly summed up the commission's work: "The implicit philosophy of the commission's report is that if American corporations were free of various federally mandated environmental, health and safety regulations, they could operate in a more cost-effective and publicly responsible manner. But Grace's own company's environmental and workplace record illustrates the pitfalls of weakening or abandoning such laws."

The Grace Commission, as it became known, failed to have a lasting effect on government. More insidious, even though it gained less attention, was the President's Task Force on Private Sector Initiatives. It was this panel, derided by economic conservatives as having not achieved enough, that played a vital role in delivering the nation's nonprofit sector into the clutches of corporate interests and leaving us a country where almost no major social or cultural endeavors fail to have a commercial imprint. The task force was headed by C. William Verity Jr., the chairman of Armco Inc., then the nation's fifth largest steel company, a man who kept on his desk a small card bearing a passage from Ayn Rand's *Atlas Shrugged,* the bible of free-market purism. It was Verity's job to put the arm on major corporations to increase their charitable contributions, to prove that the nation could survive with the draconian cuts in social programs that Reagan had in mind for the country.

From his days as the governor of California, Reagan had been harping on the idea that sustaining the poor and healing the sick should be the responsibility of private interests, not the government. He was fond of dragging out a quote from Tocqueville's *Democracy in America* to prove his point: "Wherever at the head of some new undertaking, you see the government in France or a man of rank in England, in the United States you will be sure to find an association. The people wield immense influence over their magistrates and often carry their desires into execution without intermediaries." What he never told the audience was that the America that Tocqueville visited in 1831 and 1832 had a population of a little more than twelve million people, less than that of today's New York metropolitan area, most of it subsisting in small rural communities where volunteerism could make a difference. The idea that volunteerism alone could solve the social problems of a modern postindustrial nation was an absurdity, as most Reagan administration officials were well aware.

Reagan's first round of proposed budgets cuts for social programs amounted to more than $128 billion. Charities themselves stood to lose $45 billion in federal funding over a three-year period, according to an Urban Institute study. In 1980, the entirety of corporate philanthropy totaled only $2.5 billion. When pressed by a reporter, Verity admitted that even if he was successful in convincing businesses to quadruple their contributions, "it is unrealistic to expect us to fill what is not just a gap, but a chasm."

Still the campaign moved forward, a useful fiction to give the administration political cover for the gutting of food stamps, public housing, health care, and other social programs. And of course, nonprofit institutions, many of which were on the brink of insolvency because of the federal budget cuts, had no choice but go along with the ruse, and they lined up to press corporate America for handouts. Halfway through Reagan's first year in office, major corporations reported a dramatic increase in appeals from antipoverty groups, cultural institutions, universities, and other nonprofit groups. "We've been deluged with thousands of requests, a 100 percent increase in the first quarter of this year," Mary Hall, vice president of Weyerhaeuser Company in Tacoma, Washington, said in 1981.

Corporations did fork over more money, the amount growing from $2.5 billion in 1981 to $3 billion in 1983, but little of it ended up going to the poor. Instead, it flowed to universities, museums, and art exhibits. In fact, the amount of money donated for health and human services actually declined between 1979 and 1983. As an analyst of corporate philanthropy told the *New York Times,* "Higher education and the arts are visible, uncontroversial and closely linked with the class interests of those giving out the money. But what can a homeless hungry person do for a corporation? He doesn't work at the company, he doesn't buy its products and his good will won't do the corporation much good. That's the real reason why most corporate money doesn't go to poor people."

Increasingly, nonprofit institutions, particularly those acting as the custodians of our culture, began to see corporations as partners, and corporate values bled into their activities. Commercialism and corporate advertising became a standard accoutrement of cultural events. By the end of the 1980s, art exhibitions, musical concerts, theater productions, and amateur athletic events were increasingly accompanied by corporate sponsorship, with the prominent display of logos and other commercial messages. Barriers began to crumble. The values of the Reagan administration made it socially acceptable for corporate executives and board members of cultural institutions, even those not losing federal funding, to see their destinies as intertwined. Who in previous decades ever would have imagined that the Whitney Museum of American Art would open branch museums on the property of Fortune 500 companies? First there was the Whitney branch that opened in 1983 inside the new world headquarters of Philip Morris at Park Avenue and Forty-second Street in Manhattan. One of the nation's most venerable art institutions, famous for showcasing the work of abstract expressionist artists who attacked the commercial values of America, was now fully partnered with a company most noted for its sales of cigarettes and beer. Next, in 1986, came a new Whitney branch four times larger than its Philip Morris site, this one in the Equitable Life Assurance Society on Seventh Avenue. One need not even ask whether the Whitney would exhibit any art likely to shock its corporate partners or their customers. "What does it mean then for American art when the most important museum of American art not only weds itself to corporate institutions, but celebrates the union?" Michael Brenson, a *New York Times* art critic, wrote shortly after the Equitable branch opened. "The issue is not ideological purity. Nor is it corporations. It is the ability of a museum to maintain its clarity of purpose and broad understanding of art. . . . To prove itself worthy of public trust, a museum's ongoing struggle for independence and purpose has to be unmistakable."

Such sentiments became anachronistic in the post-Reagan era, a period in which no institution or endeavor is too sacred to be spared commercial manipulation. Even the visit of Pope John Paul II to the Americas in 1999 was backed by what the *Washington Post* called "an All-Star roster of corporate sponsors." PepsiCo, the prime sponsor, heralded the event by selling potato chips with the Pope's picture on each bag. Before long, corporations were no longer content with piggybacking on events sponsored by nonprofits and began fielding their own events. In 1999, Altoids, the "Curiously Strong Mint" owned by Philip Morris, spent $250,000 putting together a traveling exhibit of emerging artists and dubbed it the "Curiously Strong Collection."

Reagan bore direct responsibility for the corruption of the nonprofit sector, now so intertwined with for-profit affiliates and suffused with commercial values that its mission of serving the poor, providing health care, or upholding our culture is often hopelessly compromised. Many spheres of American life that by tradition had been painstakingly shielded from commercial manipulation would increasingly be subject to the caprice of the marketplace. Desperate for funding in the wake of Reagan's deep budget cuts, major nonprofit institutions across the country answered the siren call of the corporation. In the Darwinian struggle for survival that followed the Reagan administration's budget cuts, a huge number of nonprofits closed their doors, and too many of those that remained inevitably absorbed the private-sector values of their new sponsors, often at the expense of their core mission.

Large nonprofits are now often indistinguishable from for-profit corporations, with huge executive salaries, sprawling office complexes, and high-priced lobbyists. Many of their operations are wedded to for-profit affiliates, and yet they are still exempt from taxes. An exhaustive study by the *Philadelphia Inquirer* in 1993 found that the nation's nonprofit hospitals devoted only 6 percent of their expenditures to caring for the poor, while diverting hundreds of million of dollars into commercial affiliates like hotels, restaurants, health spas, laundries, marinas, and parking garages. The newspaper also found that many directors and executives of nonprofits sit on the boards of companies that do business with the nonprofits.

With the new corporate bent of many nonprofits and the rapid growth of investor-owned hospitals in the post-Reagan era, huge amounts of resources are diverted to pay for layer upon layer of administrators. Between 1970 and 1998, the number of hospital administrators increased by 2,348 percent—with most of the increase after 1985—while the number of physicians grew by 250 percent. Charity care in hospitals has declined dramatically, even as beds go unfilled and medical equipment and personnel sit idle. A 2001 study found that 350,000 hospital beds, or one-third of the nation's total, are empty on an average day, while millions of people are denied charity care.

Much of this intermingling of for-profit and nonprofit activities has grossly violated federal tax law, but Reagan ensured that the Internal Revenue Service would turn a blind eye. In 1980, the IRS examined 23,807 tax-exempt organizations. In 1988, the last year of the Reagan administration, that number had dropped by more than half, to 11,907, even as the number of nonprofits soared. By 1993, the IRS was examining less than 1 percent of the estimated 450,000 institutions claiming nonprofit status.

The Reagan administration's devastation of nonprofit medical care is hardly limited to hospital management. An even greater disservice to the American public grew out of the administration's promotion of for-profit health maintenance organizations. In 1982, the Reagan administration announced that it was ending all funding for traditional fee-for-service medical providers and launching a major campaign to promote investment in HMOs. Membership in HMOs had grown from 3.5 million in 1970 to 11.5 million in 1981, and the administration predicted that it would surpass 30 million by 1990. Reagan officials made it clear that they wanted the nonprofit HMOs, which had been the largest share of the industry, to convert to for-profit status. Managers of nonprofit HMOs, many of them hospital administrators, did not fit in with the Reaganites' plan for a health care industry dominated by the private sector. "They were more concerned with doing a social good than with producing a return on investment," Anthony R. Masso of the Department of Health and Human Services said of the nonprofit HMOs in 1982. "They were not well suited to manage the organizations when they became multimillion-dollar enterprises." In other words, they cared more about people than profit, making them pariahs in the eyes of the Reagan administration. In 1985, three-quarters of HMO members were in nonprofit plans, a percentage that dropped to one-third by 1999. Executives of HMOs that converted to for-profit status were often rewarded with bonuses and stock options.

Few Americans appear happy with Reagan's vision of a for-profit health care industry. Proponents of HMOs predicted that turning over medical care to the private sector would give patients more choice of physicians and better service at lower prices. But none of these predictions have come to pass. In 2001, nearly half of Americans worked for companies that gave them the choice of only one HMO, and in many cases they were limited to physicians within that HMO's network. Physicians have become the virtual employees of for-profit companies that reward them for avoiding expensive procedures and the treatment of seriously ill patients. HMOs have no incentive to provide quality service to ill patients, lest they attract more of them and be left with higher expenses—and lower profits—than their competitors. A study by Physicians for a National Health Program, founded by two faculty members at Harvard Medical School, found that for-profit HMOs scored worse than nonprofits on all fourteen quality indicators reported to a national commission that monitored managed care. Other studies have found that for-profits had higher death rates than nonprofits, with the disparity larger for poor or ill patients. In other words, if you are affluent and healthy, you may not have noticed the deleterious consequences arising from the HMO revolution.

But physicians have noticed. Survey after survey has found that doctors, by an overwhelming majority, believe HMOs have forced them into unethical behavior and caused them to spend less time with patients. A survey of medical school deans found widespread concern that managed care was hampering medical research as competition and profit seeking in the industry reduced professional collegiality. With their income depleted by the phaseout of fee for service, many physicians have taken to selling medical products in their offices, a patently unethical practice. Can patients really be sure they need that topical cream the doctor is prescribing if he or she is making a profit from selling it?

Patients are not likely to hear any of these complaints from their doctors, since doctors are often barred under HMO contracts from speaking up. One of the founders of Physicians for a National Health Program, David Himmelstein, caused a stir in the profession when he wrote an editorial for the *New England Journal of Medicine* that included language from his contract with U.S. Healthcare, a for-profit HMO: "Physician shall agree not to take any action or make any communication which undermines or could undermine the confidence of enrollees, their employers, their unions, or the public in . . . the quality of U.S. Healthcare coverage. Physician shall keep the Proprietary Information *and this Agreement* strictly confidential" (emphasis added). The message was clear: Even upon concluding that an HMO's refusal to fund a medical procedure would jeopardize the life of a patient, the physician is bound by contract to keep his or her mouth shut. After the journal article was published, U.S. Healthcare terminated Himmelstein's contract. Only a *Time* magazine article and accompanying public outrage prompted U.S. Healthcare to reinstate Himmelstein.

Commercialism has also corrupted other venerable institutions. Advertising by attorneys, once considered unethical, is now commonplace. Reagan's sharp reductions in aid to higher education and his willingness to give corporations entrance into new areas of American life accelerated the influence of private enterprise on colleges and universities. By the 1990s, many major technical schools, like MIT, CalTech, and Penn State, were spending more on research than on teaching, while collecting millions of dollars for work done under contract with commercial companies. Many individual professors have also entered into consulting contracts with private industry. These arrangements allow corporations to exert enormous influence on the research conducted in universities, usually more concerned with marketability than societal benefit.

No institution has been safe from the reach of corporations in the post-Reagan era, no area of our lives free from commercial messages. Even public spaces, once shielded from private businesses, have become fair game for commerce, whether it is Detroit's Belle Isle turned over to Grand Prix auto racing or the huge corporate spectacles held in Central Park. New York City offered a poignant illustration of the new reach of the corporation into the public sphere when Mayor Rudolph Giuliani, a graduate of the Reagan administration, ordered

Central Park's Great Lawn closed to the public for two weeks in 1995 for the premiere of Disney's *Pocahontas* movie. Jimmy Breslin, the acerbic columnist who had witnessed every outrage the city had to offer in his five decades as a reporter, wrote in *Newsday* that few compared to this corporate usurpation of the public's space. "In all the history of Central Park," Breslin said, "the place never has been closed for two weeks for anybody. In all the history of Central Park, tickets never have been required for anybody to get in. Through Streisand and Shakespeare plays, through concerts and religious revivals, there has been no such thing, not even the first thought, requiring a ticket to use the sweeping lawn."

CHAPTER 8

The Spoils of Revolution

In late 1989, a widening scandal in the U.S. Department of Housing and Urban Development brought congressional investigators to the sleepy hamlet of Upper Deerfield, New Jersey. Their mission was to get a firsthand look at an apartment complex that had been refurbished with the help of $73 million from HUD's Moderate Rehabilitation Program, established in 1978 to encourage private developers to upgrade subsidized apartment units for the poor. This was no trivial sum of money. The Reagan administration having ended all new construction of public housing, mod rehab units—as they became known—were the only means of adding to the nation's federally subsidized housing stock, and even the funds for that work were in short supply. At the time in 1987 when mod rehab funds were approved for the 326-unit Seabrook Apartments, no other New Jersey project had been given such money for the previous three years. In competition with the vast slums of Newark, Jersey City, Paterson, and other large cities, Upper Deerfield, home to seven thousand people in rural Cumberland County, was chosen as the place that needed HUD most.

What the investigators found confirmed their worst suspicions: rows of drab cinderblock barracks standing like Stonehenge in the middle of the town's cornfields. The only entrance to the complex was an unlit and unpaved road that led to a weed-choked campus without curbing, sidewalks, or parking. The tenants, who paid up to $700 a month in rent, had to supply their own refrigerators. One woman who could not afford one was feeding her children entirely on canned goods. A supposed restoration of the roofing had consisted of tacking new shingles on top of old, in some cases on top of six previous layers. In places, the weight of the multiple layers of shingles was too much for the cheap gypsum board underneath, and there had been a ceiling collapse in one apartment.

Local officials, who had been kept in the dark about the project until it was too late to stop it, were aghast that precious federal money had been wasted on Seabrook. The complex had been constructed by the federal government in 1944 as temporary barracks for workers at Seabrook Farms, a food processor considered essential to the war effort. It was shoddy housing that was supposed to have a life of only ten years. "I think it's a horrible waste of taxpayers' money," Upper Deerfield mayor Bruce Peterson said in testimony before the Employment and Housing Subcommittee of the Committee on Government Operations. "The people in our area are outraged [that] this kind of money is being wasted on this project. . . . I think we would have preferred to see the majority of the units torn down, they were in such terrible shape."

But the townsfolk's confusion was not shared by the subcommittee's investigators, who by this time knew full well how such a boondoggle had occurred. A one-third share of CFM Development Corporation, the company that had purchased and joined in "restoring" Seabrook Apartments, was owned by Paul Manafort, a well-connected GOP consultant in Washington who had been a key fund-raiser in Ronald Reagan's 1980 campaign. Manafort's consulting firm, Black, Manafort, Stone & Kelly, had secured a federal commitment to the project in a single brief meeting with Deborah Gore Dean, another politically connected Republican who was executive assistant to HUD secretary Samuel Pierce. Laurance Gay, the Manafort subordinate who had met with Dean, would later recall that he told her nothing of the project, perhaps not even the name of the apartment complex, but the funding was nonetheless assured.

From there on, pilfering tens of millions of dollars from a program designed to help the poor was no great trick. All that was necessary was to continue working within a system of graft and cronyism that had been created by officials at the highest levels of the administration and sanctioned by Ronald Reagan himself. On November 18, 1986, four days after Gay's meeting with Dean, another Black, Manafort employee, Greg Stevens, who happened to be the former chief of staff to New Jersey Governor Thomas Kean, called New Jersey's Public Housing Authority to grease the skids for the project. Under the law, New Jersey had to formally submit an application for the project so local HUD officials could review its merits. The availability of HUD funding would also have to be publicly advertised so other developers could submit competing proposals.

But these requirements were hardly impediments. To keep officials in HUD's Newark office from raising any red flags, Stevens instructed New Jersey housing officials to bypass the usual protocol and apply to the New York City office, whose regional administrator, Joseph Monticciolo, had been installed by the White House as a favor to Republican senator Alfonse D'Amato. Monticciolo, D'Amato's chief Long Island fund-raiser in the 1980 Senate campaign, would see to it the funding was streamlined. On May 18, 1987, the New Jersey Public Housing Authority also complied with the requirement that the project be publicly advertised. The legal notice went into the *Millville Daily,* circulation seven thousand, and stated that "all projects must contain at least one hundred units and must be located in the city of Seabrook." Even if any other developers happened to be flipping through the *Millville Daily,* they would have found it hard to meet the requirements, since there is no city named Seabrook in the state of New Jersey.

The deal went swimmingly for Manafort. He not only received his share of the $31.2 million in rent subsidies that were to be paid to the developer over fifteen years, but Black, Manafort also picked up $326,000 in fees for intervening with Dean. When it came time for his testimony before the subcommittee, Manafort saw nothing wrong with the deal. "The technical term for what we do . . . is lobbying," he told the panel. "For purposes of today, I will admit in a narrow sense some might term it influence peddling."

It took Ronald Reagan only a few short years to reverse decades of efforts by reformers to bring honesty and accountability to the federal government. The 1980s HUD scandal, involving monstrous boondoggles like Seabrook across the country and ultimately costing the taxpayers an estimated $2 billion, was only the grossest example of the influence peddling and cronyism that infected the Reagan administration at almost every level. The right-wing ideologues and former corporate executives who larded the top layers of government in the Reagan years made a mockery of his promises to reduce government waste while preserving programs for the "truly needy." They were not wired to think in terms of democracy and the common well-being of Americans. Like their patron, they worshipped at the altar of self-interest. They had grown used to rationalizing their greed as the sacred ground of free-market economics. In their view, men like themselves had built this country with their relentless acquisitiveness, and they saw no reason to change their ways once they were appointed to public office. They would simply use government as an extension of their business interests.

Their mind-numbing disregard for the people of this country is well documented, although it seems to have disappeared from the public discourse, and it is inexplicably never mentioned as part of Reagan's legacy. The subcommittee investigating HUD's operations found "widespread abuses, influence peddling, blatant favoritism, monumental waste and gross mismanagement," as it noted in its final report. The moderate rehabilitation program,

> which was intended to benefit the poor, became a cash cow which was milked by former HUD officials and the politically well-connected. Projects pushed and lubricated by politically well-connected consultants and a cadre of ex-HUD officials received the lion's share of these increasingly scarce and valuable mod rehab funds. . . . It is the height of hypocrisy that individuals who, while in government, were ideo-

logically opposed to and beat up on federal housing programs benefited financially from the moderate rehabilitation program, and when called before the subcommittee became born-again advocates for low-income housing and sang the praises of the program.

The same verbiage could have been applied to any number of other agencies within the Reagan administration. By the end of Reagan's two terms, 138 members of his administration had been convicted, indicted, or investigated for criminal activity, a record of graft that far surpassed even the Nixon, Harding, and Grant administrations, Reagan's closest competitors in the sweepstakes for the most corrupt presidency. Federal banking regulators turned their heads as unscrupulous investors raided and bankrupted the savings-and-loan industry, costing the taxpayers $150 billion in a federal bailout. The Defense Department allowed contractors to overcharge the government tens of millions of dollars in military procurement deals, giving us the infamous $600 toilet seats and $400 hammers. Officials in the Environmental Protection Agency shielded politically connected firms from the enforcement of hazardous waste rules and then tried to keep the evidence from congressional investigators. National Security Council aides made secret arms sales to Iran, used the proceeds to fund the Nicaraguan Contras in defiance of Congress, and then lied about it, making a sham of the constitutional separation of powers. The list goes on and on, and does not even count people who enriched themselves in private industry by using their government connections after they left office.

President Carter had sought to restore faith in government in the post-Watergate era with the Ethics in Government Act of 1978, which established conflict-of-interest guidelines and a system of financial disclosure for federal appointees. Reagan approached the question of ethics as if it did not exist. He was silent on the issue in his campaign, said little on the subject as president, and left the discussion out of his memoirs. Ed Meese, who as presidential counselor and attorney general was so fond of lambasting the avarice and criminality of the poor, took a far more lax view of legal probity when it came to the conduct of administration officials. Meese himself narrowly—and some would say unfairly—escaped indictment in the Wedtech scandal, in which he helped the notorious Bronx defense contractor obtain a $32-million Army contract while his close friend, E. Robert Wallach, was a paid consultant for the company. How attentive was Reagan to Meese's transgressions? When William Weld, a Justice Department official who would later be governor of Massachusetts, met with Reagan in his second term to announce his resignation and explain why Meese should be indicted, the president dozed off during their conversation.

Meese was hardly alone among Reagan officials in condemning the moral transgressions of others while racking up his own record of graft. Former interior secretary James Watt's disdain for government was legendary. He once warned Americans to resist being "lured by the crumbs of subsidies, entitlements and giveaways." But upon leaving office, or rather being forced out, Watt went to work helping clients lap up those very crumbs. Joseph Strauss, who created a consulting firm, Phoenix Associates, a week after resigning from a high-ranking HUD position in 1983, admitted that he had hired Watt as a lobbyist despite the latter's utter lack of experience in housing issues. "I make no bones . . . about the fact that the reason that James Watt was hired . . . was not because of his housing knowledge or his technical knowledge or his legal skills, which may in fact have been there," he told the investigating subcommittee. "The reason was because of his access and influence." One of Watt's clients, Landex Corporation, had trouble securing mod rehab funds for a low-income project in Essex, Maryland, even though state officials had determined that it met all the proper criteria and had lobbied HUD unsuccessfully to fund the project for two years. But then Watt became involved and the funding suddenly materialized, to the tune of $28 million. By his own testimony, Watt earned his half of a $300,000 consulting fee paid to Phoenix Associates by meeting with Pierce for twenty minutes and following up with a half dozen calls to other HUD officials. He claimed in his testimony before the subcommittee that during their meeting he had obtained no commitment from Pierce to fund the project. But after the money was approved, he sent a letter to the secretary that read, "Thanks, you are a man of your word."

Behind the scandals that enveloped the federal government in the 1980s was a new breed of public servant that Reagan ushered into public life, one whose interests lay in serving not the public but the coterie of Republican contributors and wealthy businessmen who really mattered to the Reagan Revolution. The Employment and Housing Subcommittee report on HUD abuses found that "people appointed to positions of responsibility and power at HUD during Secretary Pierce's tenure were inexperienced, didn't believe in the programs they were administering, and cared little about meeting the nation's housing needs. HUD was used as a dumping ground for political castoffs."

None of those castoffs was more cynical, or more portentous of the new era taking shape in Washington, than Deborah Gore Dean, the young woman who became Pierce's chief aide and was to play the dominant role in the HUD scandal. Only twenty-nine years old when she was named Pierce's executive assistant in 1984, Dean had no experience in housing issues and no apparent interest in the subject. She had meandered her way through Georgetown University, taking eight years to earn her degree and finishing 507th in a class of 509. Along the way she had shown no curiosity about the problems of the poor or urban development. She was briefly in the drama club and took a tour of Ireland but mostly spent her time in Georgetown taverns and swank Washington restaurants. One hint of her lack of devotion to public affairs was that she did not register to vote until she was twenty-seven years old.

Dean was descended from an old southern family on her mother's side, which Dean claimed had been active in politics since arriving in this country in colonial days. Her maternal grandfather, H. Grady Gore, hailed from Tennessee and made a fortune on Washington-area real estate. Dean is a second cousin of Al Gore and a distant cousin of the writer Gore Vidal. But her wing of the family was decidedly more conservative. Her aunt, Louise Gore, was a onetime state senator and Republican powerbroker in Maryland. Her father, who died in a plane crash when Dean was three years old, had at various times been a Nazi war crimes prosecutor, chairman of the Atomic Energy Commission, and an executive for General Dynamics. One of her most important family connections in adulthood was the man she called her stepfather, former attorney general and Watergate conspirator John Mitchell, who began living with her widowed mother after leaving prison.

Dean had grown up in luxury. Among the properties still owned by her mother's family was the Fairfax Hotel on Washington's Embassy Row, the Jockey Club, an expensive restaurant near DuPont Circle, and the Guards, a Georgetown bar. In childhood she divided her time between the family's quarters in the Fairfax Hotel and Marwood, a thirty-three-room mansion set on two hundred acres overlooking the Potomac River in suburban Maryland, where she attended high school at the Holton Arms School for girls in Bethesda. An attractive blond with a forceful personality, a sense of entitlement, and the right social connections, Dean had little trouble gaining a toehold in the corridors of power in Washington. She had spent most of her twenties on the edges of high society, working as a hostess in her family's restaurants and at one point operating a society magazine. But then she focused on the real centers of power in Washington. She volunteered for the Reagan-Bush campaign in 1980 and accepted a job in John Mitchell's consulting firm, Global Research International. In 1981, Mitchell found her a job in Reagan's Energy Department. She moved to HUD a year later, hired by Lance Wilson, the man she would replace in 1984 as Pierce's executive assistant.

Created as part of Lyndon Johnson's Great Society in 1965, HUD even by its very existence was ideologically offensive to the conservative movement that Reagan rode into the White House, and no major agency was treated with more neglect during his eight years in office. Samuel Pierce had an esteemed career behind him. He was a graduate of Cornell Law School and a former federal prosecutor who in 1961 became a partner in Battle, Fowler, Stokes & Kheel, the first African American to hold such a position in a major New York law firm. That same year, he appeared before the U.S. Supreme Court to argue for the Reverend Martin Luther King Jr. and the *New York Times* in the landmark libel case *Times v. Sullivan*. A longtime Republican, Pierce had been brought to the attention of the White House by Reagan's friend and adviser Alfred Bloomingdale, who was impressed by legal work Pierce had done for one of his companies, Diners Club.

But the HUD position was something that held little interest for Pierce, especially in an administration that had so little regard for its mission. Administration officials all but admitted that he was a token minority member in a cabinet dominated by white males, and he was given little respect. Pierce was dutiful in carrying out the White House's plan for HUD's decimation. The agency's budget was slashed by 57 percent in Reagan's eight years in office, from $33.4 billion in 1981 to $14.2 billion in 1987. The number of employees plummeted from 16,323 in 1981 to a low of about 11,470 in 1986. Pierce got little thanks for this dirty work. He was denied the right to name his own deputies and forced to allow the upper ranks of the agency to become a dumping ground for political hacks. He occasionally fought losing battles over the appointments, but he largely took his marching orders from the White House and quickly became disenchanted with the job. Although he was the only member of Reagan's cabinet to stay through both terms, he was largely content to delegate the operations of the department to others while he traveled the country giving speeches or sat in his office watching soap operas.

Pierce's tenure was one of humiliation for career HUD employees. In early 1981, he assembled a group of them in a cherrywood conference room on the ninth floor of the agency's headquarters and introduced them to a room full of political appointees, most of them young, inexperienced, and ultimately contemptuous of HUD's mission. The old-timers took to calling them the Brat Pack. "This is the board of directors," Pierce told the agency's veterans. "We make all the policy decisions. You are to carry those orders out. And not ask questions."

The leader of the Brat Pack was Deborah Gore Dean. Pierce gave the twenty-something socialite the power to run roughshod over the agency's civil service personnel. He gave her an autopen, a device that would stamp his signature on documents, and turned her loose to make key decisions within the agency. "It's common knowledge on the Hill, if you wanted to get something done in the Secretary's office you talked to Deborah Dean," Democratic congressman Bruce Morrison of Connecticut said of that period. It remains a mystery how many of the abuses at HUD over the next three years were Dean's own doing and how many she carried out at Pierce's direction. It is also unknown whether Pierce abdicated so many of his decision-making powers to a young neophyte only after being forced to do so by White House officials. What is abundantly clear, however, is that Dean became the conduit for a parade of well-connected Republicans who wanted to pick at the bones of HUD's shriveling budget.

Every few months, Dean would summon employees from the mod rehab division to her ninth-floor office and sit down at a table with a clipboard listing the projects she wanted funded. As she read out the names, the employees would pore through their black binders to see whether the states that were hosting the projects had even submitted applications for funding. In many cases they had not, so HUD employees had to contact those communities and tell them to submit applications. It was a mere formality. As was the case with Seabrook, the fix was already in.

The most savvy developers quickly realized how important it was to "make the Dean's list," and that hiring a political consultant with ties to the Reagan administration, preferably a former HUD official, was the best way to make that happen. Dean even admitted as much to the *Wall Street Journal,* telling a reporter that mod rehab "was set up and designed to be a political program. . . . I would have to say that we ran it in a political manner."

One project that made the Dean's list was a 151-unit senior citizens' project in North Carolina known as the Durham Hosiery Mill. HUD staff had repeatedly turned down the project for funding because it was forty feet from an active railroad freight line and sat on a hazardous-waste site that would require expensive remediation. Stored inside the old mill were more than a hundred fifty-gallon drums of sulfuric acid, cyanide, and other toxins.

But things changed when the developer, John Allen, president of Boston-based Myerson/Allen and Company, followed the suggestion of North Carolina state Senator Harold Brubaker and hired Lou Kitchin, an Atlanta political consultant who had been the southern political director of Reagan's 1980 campaign. Assistant HUD Secretary Maurice Barksdale had rejected funding for the project three times, and his successor, Shirley Wiseman, had stood by the decision when she took over the job in 1985. But after Kitchin was hired, Dean met with Allen three times. After the last meeting, she told him to put in an application for funding. Dean called Wiseman and told her that Pierce was behind the project. But Wiseman still refused to free the funding, prompting a call from Pierce himself. As Wiseman later described the conversation, "I said I can't fund it, Mr. Secretary, and he said, 'I want the project funded,' . . . and I said, well, I am sorry, I can't fund it, but I will send it upstairs to you, and that was the end of the conversation."

Wiseman left the department a short time later. Dean gave her successor, Janet Hale, funding documents for the project on her first day in office and told her to sign them. The project was not only given $11.3 million in mod rehab money, a $2.3 million Urban Development Action Grant, and $3 million in tax credits; the developer was also given a series of waivers because the plans violated so many longstanding HUD requirements. One waiver allowed the developer to charge rent 132 percent above ordinary levels. When subcommittee members asked Hale later if any HUD officials besides Dean and Pierce thought the project should have been funded, she answered, "To my knowledge, there was no one else in support of the project within the building."

Another project that Dean streamlined benefited Fred Bush, who was chief of staff for Vice President George Bush in 1982 and 1983. Bush & Company had applied for a technical assistance grant of $267,933 so it could conduct planning studies for the city of San Juan, Puerto Rico. Like so many other HUD grants in the Reagan era, the proposal was driven by the developer rather than the community that was supposedly in need and would have to file the actual application for funding. HUD career staff had rejected the Bush & Company proposal six times. But DuBois Gilliam, a former HUD deputy assistant secretary who testified before the investigating subcommittee under a grant of immunity, said Dean intervened and told him to fund the program. He said he was glad to do so since Fred Bush was a friend of the administration: "What I looked at more or less was that Fred was a Republican, I was a Republican, he had been active in Republican campaigns, he had worked in the vice president's office, and so I was trying to help him for political reasons."

In yet another case, Gilliam testified, Vice President Bush's staff contacted Dean to ask that she ensure that Hector Barretto, a developer who was a longtime Bush supporter, would be given a technical assistance grant of $500,000 for a Kansas City project. "I received a call from Deborah Dean," Gilliam said. "Deborah Dean said he had been over visiting with the Vice President and she indicated that she had received a call from the Vice President's staff asking about the grant and indicating their desire to try to help to get this project funded." Gilliam said he had later met with Barretto and told him that the project did not qualify for a grant, and Barretto said he would take the matter back to the vice president. The grant was approved.

Dean was notoriously cocky and abrasive toward her underlings, the career HUD employees who were actually committed to the idea of housing the poor. She was known to banish employees to unpleasant jobs if they fell out of favor, once moving the furniture out of an official's office while he was away. "She liked power," Pierce himself told a reporter in 1989. "She liked the idea that, 'I can call the shots, I can get this for you if I want, I can stomp on you, I can kill you'—that's the kind of thing she liked." More than a few longtime HUD officials chafed at being forced to take orders from Dean, especially when those orders were to circumvent the agency's policies to benefit a favored developer. "I very strongly objected to being handed a scrap of paper and told to do something," said Thomas Demery, a former HUD official. "It was totally improper. I objected to that. I was the guy with the responsibility for it, but I didn't have the authority—she did."

But Dean knew how to turn on the charm for the officials who could make a difference in her career. On succeeding Lance Wilson as Pierce's executive assistant, she held a twenty-five-dollar-a-plate farewell party for him at the Four Seasons Hotel in Georgetown. Thanks to her habit of saving copies of her personal correspondence with administration officials, all of which was made available to congressional investigators, we have a revealing record of this obsequiousness. Typical of such correspondence was a letter she wrote to Patrick Buchanan on his resignation as White House director of communications in 1987. "Your contribution to this administration," she wrote, "will long be remembered not only for the superb manner in which you conveyed its philosophy, but as an achievement which will be emulated by others sharing the same concerns and commitment."

Dean was equally effusive in her praise of Donald Devine when he announced in 1985 that he would not seek another term as director of the Office of Personnel Management. "O.P.M.," she said, "has never had more outstanding direction than during the past four years." Less than two weeks later, she was saying almost the same thing to Devine's successor, Constance Horner: "I know that you'll be the best and brightest ever to serve as director of O.P.M."

At one point in 1986, Lee Atwater, who had been deputy director of the 1984 Reagan-Bush campaign, asked Dean to find a spot for Carter Bell, a young woman who had volunteered in the campaign. Dean dashed off a letter to one of Pierce's special assistants: "Carter Bell might call. She needs a 90-day consulting appointment at around $20,000. It's O.K." Bell got the job at exactly that salary. In a letter she sent off to the White House that same year, Dean put in a plug for another job candidate, writing, "She has a lot of political support—the real good kind!"

This young, inexperienced woman was given enormous influence over a sprawling agency that spends tens of billions of dollars a year in eighty field offices, and yet she had trouble managing her own affairs. Her personal finances were in such disarray that she could not qualify for credit and had to get her Diners Club card through HUD. Although the card was supposed to be limited to HUD business, she used it for personal expenses, such as making a purchase at Bloomingdale's and paying the tabs at bars. No one, it seems, bothered to school the young official on the ethical responsibilities that come with public office. In the summer of 1984, she made arrangements to share a beach house in Rehoboth Beach, Delaware, with Joseph Strauss, the former Pierce assistant who by that time had founded the Phoenix Associates consulting firm and was doing business with HUD. She also accepted a steady stream of gifts from business executives: flowers, plants, fruit, chocolates, and even a teddy bear. "Thank you very much for the splendid lunch today," she said in a note to George Ramonas of the lobbying firm Cassidy & Associates. "And then to return to the office to still another surprise—the Godiva chocolates! A woman could get spoiled by all of this, you know."

The operation of HUD in those years was one long pageant of disgrace. Among those making the most money pilfering from the agency were people who had been political appointees at HUD during Reagan's first term and left to become developers or consultants. Some of them were in the building so often that coworkers thought they still worked there. An internal HUD audit found that Lance Wilson, the man who hired Dean, was a partner in six mod rehab projects after leaving the agency, some obtained with Dean's help. Joseph Strauss was only twenty-four and had no housing experience when he used a connection he made in the 1980 campaign to get a job at HUD. He then formed a consulting business in 1983 and helped clients obtain funding for thirteen mod rehab projects, earning fees of $1.3 million.

While these young people were burnishing their résumés and cashing in on their connections, unscrupulous business executives took full advantage of an agency in disarray. The sale of foreclosed HUD properties was so poorly monitored that closing agents were able to steal millions simply by not turning over the proceeds of the home sales, a scam that cost the taxpayers more than $50 million. One agent, Marilyn Harrell of Prince Georges County, Maryland, was nicknamed "Robin HUD" because she diverted part of the $5.6 million she pocketed to charities.

HUD was a branch of government that Reagan and his aides would just as soon have seen disappear. But they could not get away with closing down such a large federal agency, so they did the next best thing: by allowing it to be plundered and neglected to such an unconscionable degree, they ensured it would have no effectiveness and lose its already anemic constituency. "It was a pathetic operation," one of Pierce's aides told the *Washington Post* in 1989. "It was a pathetic operation in that it was a government operation that was being run by a bunch of silly, young kids at public expense."

HUD may have been the center of the most outrageous of the domestic scandals that emanated from the Reagan administration, but it was hardly an isolated example. The ethos that Reagan transported to Washington, the contempt for government and exaltation of self-interest, meant that such self-serving behavior on the part of his appointees was inevitable. Three years into Reagan's presidency, more than two dozen senior EPA officials had been removed from office or resigned under pressure, most because of their ties with business interests they had shielded from environmental enforcement.

Like Pierce, Anne Gorsuch Burford, Reagan's first EPA administrator, was denied the right to name her own appointees so White House officials could install their political cronies. For the key position of assistant administrator of solid waste and emergency response, the division in charge of cleaning up the nation's hazardous waste, Ed Meese arranged for the appointment of Rita Lavelle, a public relations executive with Cordova Chemical, the subsidiary of a California company, Aerojet General, which had a long record of environmental violations. Lavelle came into office still dedicated to the job of handling public relations for polluters. Among the top goals for her office that she clumsily put down on paper were efforts to "provide credible proof that industries operating today are not dangerous to the public health" and "change perception (local and national) of Love Canal from dangerous to benign." Her knowledge of environmental issues was so negligible that Gary Dietrich, the highest-ranking civil servant in her division, described accompanying her in testimony before Congress as "the most embarrassing thing I ever had to do in the federal government." She was eventually convicted of perjury for lying to Congress about hazardous-waste cleanups and served three months in prison. Anne Burford, her boss, was cited for contempt of Congress for refusing to turn over internal documents related to the Superfund program, established to clean up the nation's worst hazardous waste sites.

In August 1984, the House Energy and Commerce Oversight Committee found that in the first three years of the Reagan administration, "top-level officials of the Environmental Protection Agency violated their public trust by disregarding the public health and the environment, manipulating the Superfund program for political purposes, engaging in unethical conduct, and participating in other abuses."

A similar atmosphere pervaded Defense Department procurement, which produced yet another scandal of momentous proportions, one that also seems to have been forgotten by the growing legions of Reagan worshippers. The public may have been briefly outraged at learning that the Pentagon was paying $600 for toilets seats and $400 for hammers, but that was just the tip of the iceberg. By the beginning of Reagan's second term, there were 132 separate investigations of alleged wrongdoing on the part of defense contractors. Not long after he had launched his trillion-dollar defense buildup, Reagan was warned by a blue-ribbon commission that collusion between defense contractors and procurement officials inside the government was generating an environment rife with kickbacks, overcharges in labor and other costs, false claims, and other abuses.

But the administration failed to heed the warnings, leaving the door open for a scandal aptly described by the journalist Haynes Johnson: "All the elements at work during the Reagan years combined to create an inevitable result in the Pentagon procurement case. It had money, politics, power, ambition, profits. It had consultants and contractors working hand in hand with procurement officers inside. It had power concentrated in a few hands. . . . It had the revolving door out of control as today's procurement officers of the government became tomorrow's weapons contract consultants."

In short, it bore the indelible stamp of Reaganism—the movement that decried government waste while allowing dishonest public officials and their corporate allies to squander billions of dollars of the public's money.

CHAPTER 9

The Great Enabler

Where was the president of the United States while his minions were busy setting records for corruption?

The character of Ronald Reagan and the ethics of his administration are usually treated as discrete phenomena, as if they bore no relation to one another. His administration may have been the most scandal-ridden ever, his policies may have offended Judeo-Christian values by blatantly favoring the rich over the poor, his aides may have lied to Congress, circumvented the Constitution, and regularly uttered phrases brimming with bigotry and contempt for democracy. And yet Reagan continued to be regarded by a large portion of the public as a man of pristine values. As *Nation* magazine columnist Eric Alterman once wrote, something inexplicable had caused America to "avert its eyes from the heart of darkness that beat beneath Ronald Reagan's congenial smile."

When it comes to Reagan's moral leadership, his apologists want to have it both ways. They have pointed to the recent release of his diaries and the handwritten notes of his prepresidential radio addresses as evidence that he was well versed in the government's affairs and in command of his presidency. The diaries do in fact reflect a steady day-to-day involvement in White House decision making, if not a nuanced understanding of the issues. And yet Reagan's propagandists want to absolve him of any responsibility for the ethical scandals of his administration on the grounds that he was not aware of the mischief being perpetrated in his cabinet or even within his own White House. They are apparently unbothered that this canard is thoroughly belied by the public record. The diaries and other strands of evidence show that Reagan, in some cases, was well aware of unethical practices within his administration and, in other cases, engaged in stupendous acts of self-deception to keep himself from knowing.

The HUD scandal is a perfect example. One of the most unconscionable acts of the Reagan administration in the whole affair was its decision virtually to cede control of the agency's New York regional office to Al D'Amato, one of the most unctuous and ethically challenged members of the Senate. The character of D'Amato is perhaps best exemplified by telephone calls he admitted making in 1984 and 1985 to then–U.S. Attorney Rudolph Giuliani to seek leniency for mobsters facing federal prosecution. Giuliani has confirmed that in the 1984 call D'Amato asked him to support shaving two years off the sentence of Mario Gigante, a reputed mob loan shark and brother of Genovese crime family boss Vincent Gigante. Giuliani said D'Amato called him again in early 1985 to urge that he drop a murder charge against Paul Castellano, boss of the Gambino family. Giuliani said he ignored both requests and told D'Amato that "it would be better for him and better for the office if he didn't talk to me about these things."

D'Amato was exactly the wrong man for Reagan to give power over HUD, since he had been misusing federal housing funds for years before he was even elected to the U.S. Senate. In the 1970s, while a town supervisor in Hempstead, New York, the future senator used HUD money to engineer what became known locally as the Black Removal Program in his hometown village of Island Park. According to an investigative biography of D'Amato by Leonard Lurie, he accomplished this by seeing to it that the village condemned and demolished—with federal money—any property where blacks lived, on the grounds that it was substandard housing. "Al D'Amato was the sole architect and implementer of the Black Removal Program in Island Park," said Jim Nagourney, who was the city manager of neighboring Long Beach, where the relocated black families tended to move. ". . . Every opportunity they had, they ripped down buildings in Island Park where blacks were living and built parking lots—God knows for what. They never had enough businesses for parking lots. There must have been ten parking spaces for every resident in Island Park."

The misuse of HUD money hardly stopped there. D'Amato secured federal money to build housing on some of those parking lots, with the construction contracts and many of the apartments themselves given to friends and contributors. Martin Bernstein, a D'Amato contributor and campaign aide, was awarded the contract to build and operate a senior citizens' complex. D'Amato made his friend and neighbor, Geraldine McGann, head of the Island Park Housing Authority, and she doled out HUD-subsidized apartments to D'Amato's political supporters and their relatives. The same fate awaited forty-four single-family homes that HUD funded for Island Park in 1980. Among the first applicants for these homes were two children of D'Amato's sister. William Sniffin, who was then married to D'Amato's cousin, Francine Ciccimarro, told the FBI that his wife called D'Amato about one of the homes. Putting down the receiver, she turned to her husband and said, "We got it." Squired by a village employee to choose a site a few days later, Sniffin and his wife selected a parking lot that was once the site of a boardinghouse with black tenants. A 1984 HUD audit found that most of the forty-four homes went to people because of their "relationships with village officials," and no blacks were among the group.

D'Amato's manipulation of HUD funds was known to the agency's employees and members of Congress. But when the Reagan administration came into office and sought to curry favor with influential Republicans by giving them power to recommend appointments, they turned over HUD's regional office to the newly elected senator from New York, Al D'Amato. HUD secretary Samuel Pierce turned the other way as the post of regional administrator went to D'Amato fund-raiser Joseph Monticciolo, who was so beholden to the senator that he installed a special button on his phone that would route his calls directly into D'Amato's Washington office. Monticciolo hired Geraldine McGann as his special assistant.

In the early 1990s, accusations that D'Amato interfered with HUD contracts during Monticciolo's tenure were under investigation by the Justice Department. One HUD audit of the New York regional office found that between 1986 and 1988, nearly two-thirds of the contracts to build senior citizen complexes had gone to developers that included a D'Amato contributor. The federal investigation never led to D'Amato's indictment, but details of the probe made their way to the press. One of the revelations was that a fund-raiser for former New York mayor David Dinkins told federal investigators that Monticciolo had told him D'Amato coached him to lie to the grand jury looking into the HUD contracting.

By the end of Reagan's second term in office, D'Amato's unseemly influence over HUD was well known to the White House. The scandal over HUD contracts was already beginning to take shape. The 1984 HUD audit of the Island Park homes had been quashed and never released to Congress or the public, but it was no secret within HUD. And yet, when it came time to name Monticciolo's successor in 1988, the Reagan White House again deferred to D'Amato and appointed Geraldine McGann. According to the report of the subcommittee investigating HUD abuses, even Silent Sam Pierce, normally willing to acquiesce to the administration's patronage requests, resisted the McGann appointment on the grounds that she was not qualified:

> Pierce explained to subcommittee staff that he eventually discussed it with Howard Baker, who was then White House chief of staff. Baker told Pierce that Senator D'Amato was pushing extremely hard for McGann, that the president needed D'Amato's support, that Pierce could take it to the president if he liked but the president would tell him the same thing. . . . Pierce stated that some time later when he was talking to the president about another matter, the president thanked him for appointing McGann regional administrator.

Reagan's own comments about the episode in his diaries are revealing. They confirm that he was well aware of the political nature of the appointment but either was clueless about what was happening inside

HUD or, more likely, willing to tell himself that McGann was suited for the job. "We have a problem concerning Sam Pierce & an appointment in New York re his dept.," Reagan wrote in a diary entry on March 9, 1988. "Our senators have mobilized in support of one candidate & Sam has a different choice. I have no choice but to give in to the senators. Both candidates are top rate."

The president also could not have been in the dark about another unethical manipulation of HUD funding since it took place right under his nose. The same Durham Hosiery Mill project for which Lou Kitchin had obtained funding in 1985 had been approved for a grant three years earlier but, according to a HUD memorandum, was "bumped due to higher priorities." When the subcommittee that investigated HUD questioned developer John Allen, he said he was told the money had been transferred to New Jersey to help Congresswoman Millicent Fenwick in her campaign for the Senate. How this came about was further explained in a memorandum that HUD secretary Samuel Piece received from a member of his staff on September 17, 1982. It stated that the staff member had got an urgent call from the White House telling him that Reagan was en route to New Jersey for a campaign event with Fenwick and wanted to announce that the congresswoman had obtained Section 8 funding for a 125-unit senior citizen housing project in Ewing Township. So much for North Carolina.

A September 18, 1982, article in the *Trenton Times* revealed that Reagan announced the funding with a flourish, surprising even the developer, who had no idea the project had been approved.

"In spite of all our cutting back," Reagan said, "the Department of Housing and Urban Development has agreed to supply public funds for 125 units of elderly housing at Park Place in Ewing, New Jersey." Then he turned to toward Fenwick and added with a smile, "If you don't elect her as senator, we'll take it away."

The procession of former Reagan aides who have written books on their years in the White House have for obvious reasons steered away from the question of ethics. It receives little mention in two books by former Reagan speech writer Peggy Noonan (one of them unctuously titled *When Character Was King*). Books by Peter King, Dinesh D'Souza, Larry Speakes, Michael Deaver, Donald Regan, and David Stockman are likewise silent on the issue. Reagan did not raise the issue in his memoirs, and Ed Meese, mute even on the ethical scandals that drove him from office, nonetheless had the audacity, in his memoir, to complain about the onerous background checks required for presidential appointees.

The closest any of these aides come to parsing the question of ethics is in their recollections of Reagan's personal character. This is a little odd, since there is not a lot to work with there. Measured in loyalty to people and communities, in how much he was willing to open himself to others and occasionally put their interests ahead of his own, Reagan never scored very high. When he wanted John Sears to run his 1980 primary campaign, he was willing to accede to Sears's suggestion that he jettison all of his most loyal California aides: Lyn Nofziger, Martin Anderson, and even Michael Deaver, the subordinate who had been closest to both him and Nancy throughout his public life. Only a strong stand by Ed Meese brought about Sears's downfall and allowed Reagan's longtime loyalists back into the fold.

As a father, husband, friend, or neighbor, Ronald Reagan had few personality traits that stood out in a moral sense. His former aides, trying to sell books and burnish the image of their movement's standard-bearer, were left to cite the most trivial matters as evidence of his character. Noonan titled her second book *When Character Was King* but strangely offered few examples of that character. She gave examples of his ever-present sense of humor, like the time aides had to burn the negatives when someone took a picture of Reagan in a clown hat at a cabinet meeting. Martin Anderson noted that Reagan rarely praised his employees for doing a good job, but he pointed out that their gratitude to *him* for being such a great leader was such that it didn't matter. Meese remembered him and Nancy supporting him after his son was killed in a car accident, as if any boss who had worked closely with a subordinate for more than two decades would not have done the same.

All these reminiscences really establish is that Ronald Reagan could be pleasant company, which is rather beside the point in measuring his moral value as a leader. A Mafia boss can be a loyal husband and loving father who never goes back on his word. Those admirable personal traits hardly mitigate the fact that his lifework is fundamentally evil. Conversely, John Kennedy's morals may have been deeply flawed. He was willing to lie to his wife and exploit women in the most abject manner imaginable, and yet he funded programs for the poor, promoted civil rights, supported the arts, faced down dangerously hawkish elements in the military, and inspired the country toward greater achievements in science and education. Despite the defects in his personal character, he set an example of public virtue.

The difference between private rectitude and public virtue is neatly summed up in a strange episode that took place early in Reagan's first term. On March 16, 1981, Dan Sullivan, the drama critic of the *Los Angeles Times,* walked into his newspaper's office just after lunchtime and was greeted by news that the White House had called for him and would be calling back later that day. As puzzled as he was, Sullivan thought he had a pretty good idea of what the call was about. He had penned a column a few days earlier that sharply criticized the Reagan administration's proposed cuts in federal arts funding. He assumed a White House aide was calling to challenge the accuracy of the article or put forth some kind of rationale for the cuts.

But something far more unusual was about to take place. When the call came later that day, a White House operator asked him to please hold for the president. "Then Ronald Reagan came on the phone," Sullivan said. "Right away it felt like someone I knew. This was a voice I had been hearing my entire adult life." Reagan did not seem to be aware of Sullivan's article on the arts funding. Instead, he was calling about the critic's review of a play called *Turn to the Right,* which was being performed in a Los Angeles theater. It happened to star Buddy Ebsen, an old pal of Reagan's from his Hollywood days.

Ebsen, best known for his role as Jed Clampett in the 1960s sitcom *The Beverly Hillbillies,* was a longtime Hollywood fixture who had once been part of a clique of right-wing actors that also included

Ronald and Nancy Reagan. Ebsen by this point was pretty much a has-been, a seventy-two-year-old man trying to milk his aw-shucks persona for a few more years. His eight-year stint in the police drama *Barnaby Jones* had ended the previous year. A *Beverly Hillbillies* movie, scheduled for release that year, was hardly new ground for him. He was counting on *Turn to the Right* to be a meaningful production to round out his career. However, as Sullivan would later find out, with the play tanking at the box office Ebsen had put in a call to the First Lady asking if she could help. Hence the president's intervention.

As Sullivan remembered the conversation, Reagan came off as genuine and gracious on the phone but took little time to get around to the purpose of the call. He thanked Sullivan for the review of *Turn to the Right* and said the president would consider it a favor if he gave the play more exposure. "I just wonder," Reagan said, "if there isn't some way you could let people know that I sure hope it's still playing next time I get home so I can see it."

Sullivan admits to having been a little starstruck when he first got on the phone with the president of the United States. But when Reagan delivered his pitch for Ebsen, and Sullivan suddenly realized the reason for the call, he became indignant, having just researched the shrinkage the administration was planning for the National Endowment for the Arts. "I'm ashamed of you," he told the president. "Here you go around cutting the arts programs and now you go around plugging a show." Reagan responded that he was sorry he felt that way, and the two then had what Sullivan described as a "nice dialogue" about funding for the arts.

The Ebsen affair is an instructive little parable, one that serves as a useful starting point for understanding the contempt for ethics and democracy that was the hallmark of the Reagan presidency. Reagan apologists might point to the Sullivan phone call as evidence of the president's personal character—his willingness to help an old friend salvage his career. But the episode has greater meaning in a public sense. Reagan was not only abusing the powers of the presidency in a most trivial way but was also suborning unethical behavior on the part of Dan Sullivan. He was asking an esteemed critic to promote a mediocre piece of theater because the lead actor happened to be a friend of someone powerful. The winners would be two men, Reagan and Ebsen, but the losers would be hundreds of thousands of *Los Angeles Times* readers who depended on Sullivan for honest reviews.

And that goes to the heart of how Ronald Reagan changed national politics and the society at large. By the personal example that he and his aides set for the nation, by the very words that he repeated throughout his first campaign—"Are *you* better off than you were four years ago?"—he exhorted Americans to think of themselves, not their country. He also transmitted that ethos to the people who made up the Washington establishment: the elected officials, bureaucrats, lobbyists, and reporters. And ultimately the ethos bled into society at large. It is no accident that what is known as the Decade of Greed coincided with the Reagan presidency.

The Reagan administration hardly invented influence peddling and other mechanisms for giving the rich their way in Washington. All the things that have shaken the public faith in government in recent years—the Reagan scandals, the unseemly workings of people like Jack Abramoff and Tom DeLay, the cozy relationship between the George W. Bush administration and unsavory companies like Enron and Halliburton—are hardly without precedent in the annals of American politics. What is new is that the rules of the game established by Ronald Reagan mean this graft can be carried out in plain sight, regarded as business as usual in Washington and eliciting little protest from an increasingly cynical public. In scandals that roiled Washington in the years before Reagan, the culprits became pariahs and were rarely seen again in public life. Senator Joseph McCarthy was censured by the Senate in 1954 and quickly disappeared from public view, ostracized by his fellow senators and condemned to deliver his speeches to near-empty chambers. He drank himself to death within three years. Most of the Watergate figures faded into obscurity after being driven from Washington, or started new careers well away from the public arena. Not so with the disgraced Reaganites. John Poindexter, who was indicted in the Iran-Contra scandal but had his conviction overturned on appeal, ended up serving under George W.

Bush. Another Iran-Contra figure, Oliver North, became a fixture on the lecture circuit and a radio talk-show host. Paul Manafort, the admitted influence peddler who played a large role in the HUD scandal, ended up running Bob Dole's 1996 presidential campaign and was the chief organizer of that year's Republican convention in San Diego, where he boasted how successfully he had manipulated the media. He later was treated by the national media as a political sage, making regular appearances on political talk shows.

This disdain for ethics is a huge part of Reagan's legacy. This is the class of people he put at the forefront of our society. The scandals of his administration were almost entirely ignored in the reminiscences of his presidency that appeared after his death. The question all the commentators should have been asking was quite simple: Could Reagan really have been a good man, deserving of the reverence he has been given by so many Americans, if his administration was steeped in such a miasma of corruption?

But outright corruption does not begin to tell the story of how Reagan changed the moral framework of Washington. Surveying the similarities between the 1920s and the 1980s, Arthur Schlesinger Jr. once referred to the "vulgarization which has been the almost invariable consequence of business supremacy." Nothing could better sum up the Reagan era, which injected a coarseness and incivility into our political culture that forever changed the way business is conducted in our nation's capital. Vulgarities and inanities flowed out of the mouths of Reagan administration officials on a regular basis: "We have every kind of mixture you can have. I have a black, I have a woman, two Jews and a cripple" (James Watt); "The poor homosexuals. They have declared war on nature and now nature is exacting an awful retribution" (Patrick Buchanan); "Trees cause more pollution than automobiles do" (Ronald Reagan). Reagan called the corrupt and butcherous Nicaraguan Contras "the moral equivalent of the Founding Fathers" and once opined that the apartheid regime in South Africa had "eliminated the segregation that we once had in our own country."

The Reagan years brought us the "steak and jail" luncheon hosted by Paula Hawkins, the right-wing senator from Florida. As the *New York Times* described it, Hawkins invited reporters, lobbyists, and others to a private Senate dining room of "mahogany and marble and crystal chandeliers" for a feast of New York sirloin, asparagus, strawberries and apple pie; then she put down her linen napkin and "announced her plan to send food stamp chiselers to jail unless they made restitution."

Washington was once a cordial place where politicians from rival parties respected each other's views and socialized at the end of the workday. But the Reaganites brought a new breed into the capital, whose credo was to mock the enemy and win at all costs. Reagan's staff recruited dozens of members from the College Republicans and the Young Americans for Freedom, two sophomoric groups that made a mockery of government service as a sacred vocation. The Young Americans convention in August 1981 at the Park Plaza Hotel in Boston should have sent a chilling message about the caliber of people who were taking over America's leadership. After watching speeches by Lyn Nofziger and other Reagan administration officials, and hearing a taped message from their most famous advisory board member, Ronald Reagan himself, the members began singing "Deck the halls with Commie corpses . . . 'Tis the time to be remorseless . . . Wield we now our sharp stiletti . . . Carve the pinks into confetti." Or how about "God Bless free enterprise, / System divine. / Stand beside her, don't deride her, / Just so long as the profits are mine."

The election of Ronald Reagan opened an era of mediocrity in the Congress. Dozens of candidates whom all of Washington recognized as unfit for the job were elected as senators and representatives on Reagan's coattails. And a handful of incumbents well known for their political extremism or slippery ethics, like Tom DeLay, Newt Gingrich, and Jesse Helms, suddenly had enormous influence, key committee chairmanships, or both. The new crop of lawmakers were so slavish in their devotion to Reagan's policies that they were dubbed the "Reagan Robots." Their political coarseness and win-at-all-costs mentality would produce ugly scenes in Washington over the next two decades: Newt Gingrich's unseemly crusade against House Speaker Jim Wright, who was forced to resign over an ethics lapse far less serious than those later committed by Gingrich; the stalking and ultimate impeachment of Bill Clinton; and the tawdry fund-raising scandals and outright bribery of lawmakers on both sides of the aisle by corporate interests.

Even John Sears, Reagan's campaign manager during the primaries in 1980, lamented the quality of some senators who were swept into office by the Reagan Revolution. "In the wee small hours of election night," he said in 1985, "we thought, 'Had all of us known the Republicans were going to do so well, we would have run some different guys'" The stately oration of the Senate chamber devolved into the triviality of political hacks, like Senator Alfonse D'Amato, part of the class of 1980, bringing a stuffed pig onto the Senate floor and singing "Old McDonald Had a Farm."

In the House, the Reagan Robots were led by the likes of Representative Duncan Hunter of San Diego. Hunter admits to riding Reagan's coattails to a Republican House seat in 1980. One of the centerpieces of his campaign was a photograph of him with the presidential candidate, arranged by his politically connected father. And Hunter's subsequent career no doubt made Reagan proud. By the 1990s, Hunter was a member of the Armed Services Committee and one of the most successful fund-raisers in the House, his campaign chests flush with cash from the defense industry. As a result, he was a friend to every weapons program that came his way. After the Abu Ghraib scandal, Hunter was one of a handful of influential congressmen who lobbied President George W. Bush to forgo an investigation of the prisoner abuse. In his media statements on the issue, Hunter never mentioned that among those alleged to be complicit in the abuse were employees of Titan Corporation, a San Diego–based company supplying translators to the U.S. military in Iraq. (A federal judge later dismissed the lawsuit that victims of the abuse had filed against Titan.) According to the Center for Responsive Politics, Titan's political action committee was the top contributor to Hunter's campaigns in 2002 and 2004.

Another California congressman with a debt to Reagan is Dana Rohrabacher, who served in the Reagan White House before being elected in 1988. "Reagan influenced a whole generation of people here," Rohrabacher told the *Los Angeles Times* after Reagan's death. "I'm 56, and my whole life has been influenced by the man." He certainly influenced Rohrabacher's lackadaisical attitude toward ethics. It was revealed in April 2005 that Rohrabacher paid his wife, Rhonda, a yearly salary of $40,000 to run his campaign. Over a four-year period, she earned $114,894. "I need a campaign manager I can trust," he told a reporter when confronted about the expenditure. The one thing that can be said in Rohrabacher's defense is that he was not as greedy as Tom DeLay, another Reagan Robot. DeLay used campaign funds to pay his wife and daughter $473,801 over two election cycles.

In the mid-1990s, Rohrabacher was fond of attacking the belief that global warming was man-made, even though scientists then were already in virtual agreement on the dangers of greenhouse gases. He assured a reporter that the 104th Congress, with Newt Gingrich as Speaker, was a "new gang in town" and would not be taken in. "Our FY-96 budget does not operate on the assumption that global warming is a proven phenomenon," he said. "In fact, it is assumed at best to be unproven and at worst to be liberal claptrap, trendy, but soon to go out of style in our Newt Congress." Could his position have had something to do with the money from energy and transportation companies that made up at least 10 percent of his $180,000 in campaign receipts in 1994?

There can be no doubt that the quality of elected officials plummeted in the post-Reagan era and that the president's loose ethics and disdain for government, ringing like a clarion call across cities and towns, statehouses and city halls, were the prime agents of change. It is palpable in the very halls of the Capitol, a place where politicians of the two parties used to socialize at the end of the day but now engage in bitter personal attacks, where no one gathers anymore to hear what was once spellbinding oration on the Senate floor. "There are almost no great debates in the Senate anymore," Elizabeth Drew wrote in 1999. "When Hubert Humphrey and Everett McKinley Dirksen debated, people came to listen. There's virtually no one who people come to the Senate chamber to listen to when word spreads that a certain senator is about to speak. There are no oratorical descendants of Daniel Webster."

The game in Washington became slitting the other guy's throat and winning at all costs. It began with the 1980 campaign. Reagan's invention of soft-money fund-raising to subvert the post-Watergate reforms made a huge difference in his victory over Jimmy Carter. By election day, $15 million in unregulated contributions had been poured into Reagan's coffers. It was not a huge sum by today's standards, but it helps to remember that FEC rules at the time limited the Reagan and Carter campaigns to $29.4 million apiece for the general election, so $15 million mattered. Soft money, with all the abuses it promised for the future, had been introduced into American politics.

Reagan's supporters added an additional $12 million to his campaign by finding another loophole in federal election law: its failure to regulate fund-raising and expenditures by independent committees. As long as such committees were not working directly with the candidate's campaign, they could spend as much as they wanted on advertising and other efforts to promote their candidate. Carter, who made little use of the soft-money loophole, also got little help from independent political action committees, a grand total of $50,000. But millions of dollars were poured into the Reagan effort by a series of independent groups, including the National Conservative Political Action Committee, Americans for Change, and the Fund for a Conservative Majority. In some regions, like Harris County, Texas, the PACs outspent Reagan's campaign.

Gerald Rafshoon, Carter's advertising adviser, said the independent committees had severely damaged Carter in southern states and far eclipsed any help the incumbent received from organized labor. Reagan used unregulated money to nearly double the $29.4 million he was legally authorized to spend on his campaign, while soft money and independent committees added less than $2 million to Carter's effort. The lesson for political candidates after 1980 was clear—to be competitive, they would have to load up on soft money and independent expenditures. Federal election law would become a joke.

More than in any recent administration, politics came before merit in the appointment of federal officials. Cabinet-level officials routinely sent the Republican National Committee names of prospective appointees to departmental boards and commissions as part of a computerized patronage system designed to purge Democrats from the government. Interior Secretary James Watt gave the RNC fourteen names for a board overseeing offshore drilling. Only four were found to be acceptable, and only they were reappointed. James Baker, the White House chief of staff, even went so far as to announce publicly that the administration was going to pay more attention to politics in hiring. "We insist, of course, that people are qualified," he said. "We're not compromising on that. But we were getting criticized by political people, many of them strong conservatives, and justifiably, for not taking politics into consideration on appointments. We felt we had to make sure we didn't forget the people who got us where we are."

Anyone looking for the antecedents of the Red State–Blue State divide in America need look only to the style of governance Reagan introduced in his first term. To convince rural and blue-collar whites to support his elitist agenda, Reagan relied on a politics of paranoia and distraction, establishing what would become known as *wedge issues* as a cornerstone of conservative rule. In his stump speeches Reagan never mentioned his real plans for the country: the selling of national parks, tax cuts skewed toward the rich, the deregulation of the financial industry, the gutting of environmental enforcement, or the promotion of mergers between companies. Instead, he spoke broadly of attacking big government and, more than any president before him, distracted attention from his real agenda by focusing on controversial issues that his handlers knew would drive a wedge between traditional Democratic constituencies.

For Reagan, race was the biggest wedge issue of all. He made his appeals to bigotry with coded phrases like "welfare queen," "state's rights," and "affirmative action," but there was never any doubt that this was a deliberate strategy. Reagan's first speech after the 1980 Republican convention was an address on state's rights in Philadelphia,

Mississippi, a city known nationally for only one reason: the 1964 murders of civil rights workers James Chaney, Andrew Goodman, and Michael Schwerner. There was some precedent for this approach in Richard Nixon's "southern strategy," but Reagan was more audacious in its use, making wedge issues an enduring GOP tactic. Their use would become notorious in the 1988 presidential campaign, when Lee Atwater, the first President Bush's campaign manager and a graduate of the Reagan administration, used the Willie Horton ad to frighten whites into voting against Michael Dukakis. The younger Bush continued Reagan's legacy, using terrorism, abortion, and the canard of "family values" to distract southerners and other Red State Americans from his elitist agenda.

Progressive commentators have often marveled at how gullible Americans are in not seeing through this blatant manipulation of their prejudices. But they underestimate the power of the propaganda that the Reagan administration unleashed on the country. The first plank of this strategy was an effort to sharply curtail the people's right to know. The Reagan administration moved on a wide number of fronts to reduce the amount of information that the public receives from the federal government. The administration tried to justify the greater secrecy by saying it lowered the cost of government and improved national security. But it amounted to a cynical disregard of the public's need to be informed about the workings of its own government. Indeed, Reagan, in an interview early in his first term, called Washington "one giant ear" and said his greatest frustration as president was that the press was finding out too much about the workings of the White House.

The moves to curtail the flow of public information included Attorney General William French's instruction to federal agencies to offer firm resistance to any Freedom of Information Act requests, along with a new requirement that even *former* employees of federal agencies that handled classified material submit any of their books, magazine articles, and speeches for government review. Reagan also set a new precedent in American history by banning the press from coverage of the invasion of Grenada.

Other moves promoted secrecy with less fanfare, like the canceling of dozens of programs for gathering statistics and the permanent elimination of hundreds of government publications. Officials said the publications had been canceled to save on the costs of printing. The truth was that many of them were eliminated due to corporate pressure. Assistant Labor Secretary Thorne Auchter announced that a series of publications that "no longer represent agency policy" were being scrapped, such as "Cotton Dust: Worker Health Alert" and a poster entitled "Cotton Dust Can Destroy Your Lungs." It was not that cotton dust had suddenly disappeared as a grave health problem. The cotton industry just had more clout in Washington. Dr. Jean Mayer, president of Tufts University and former chairman of the White House Conference on Food, Nutrition and Health, complained that dietary publications popular among schools and other institutions had been killed because "the producers of eggs, milk and meat were dissatisfied with the guidelines that advised less consumption of these foods because of their cholesterol content."

While reducing the level of information available to the public, the administration went further than any previous administration in its efforts to deceive and manipulate the press. The wiretapping of reporters by the Kennedy and Nixon administrations posed a grave danger to freedom of the press, but these programs were conducted in secret and, in the case of Nixon, were the stuff of scandal when they were revealed. Reagan's loathsome treatment of the press, his blatant scripting of events, his endless falsehoods, and his constant distortion of reality were out in the open and forever changed the way press relations would be handled in the capital.

Reagan's presidency was the first to fully adopt the corporate model of public relations in its communications with the public. Some elements of showmanship and deception—the guiding principles of modern public relations and advertising—have been present in virtually every presidential election. Dwight Eisenhower kept an advertising firm on retainer in his first term, and Richard Nixon's use of television advertising techniques in his 1968 campaign was famously chronicled in Joe McGinniss's *The Selling of the President.* But no administration before Reagan's extended these techniques beyond the campaign and into the realm of governance, packaging its message and selling its programs in precisely the same fashion that a corporation might push cars or toasters. His was the first administration that had public opinion polls taken thrice weekly, the president's image the subject of a meeting every morning. "The whole thing was PR," said Leslie Janka, a deputy White House press secretary under Reagan. "This was a PR outfit that became president and took over the country. And to the degree that the Constitution forced them to do things like make a budget, run foreign policy and all that, they sort of did it. But their first, last and overarching activity was public relations."

Reagan was the perfect vehicle for such a strategy. His years with General Electric had been spent projecting a broad and simplistic message to his white middle-class audience: that unfettered free enterprise was the greatest good for America. It was in that era that advertisers and public relations specialists had begun to grasp how effectively mass media could be used to shape the public's consciousness. Edward Bernays, a blood nephew of Sigmund Freud who is often referred to as the father of public relations, wrote an influential 1946 essay, "The Engineering of Consent," that portrayed the public as little more than a bovine herd in need of shepherding by the elite: "If we understand the mechanism and motives of the group mind, is it not possible to control and regiment the masses according to our will without their knowing about it?"

Among Bernays's clients was General Electric, a company famous for its wholesome image and its ability to create a longing in the American household for its products. And Ronald Reagan, the public face of that giant corporation throughout the 1950s, the personification of its effort to engineer consent, was at the center of this revolution in public relations. When a group of Southern California businessmen pushed Ronald Reagan into politics in the 1960s, they were recognizing the obvious. Just as the nation's business elite could indoctrinate the masses to sell hair cream and electric can openers, they could use the same methods to sell a political candidate—one who would look after their interests.

In the Reagan White House, the engineering of consent was accomplished in part by manipulation of the press. Michael Deaver, David Gergen, and other media strategists made it their goal every morning to control that day's story. They would develop a "line of the day" and push it at the press corps, usually scheduling a highly visual event that would please the television networks. The effort was extremely successful in setting the agenda for the media, which spent little time analyzing the implications of Reagan's sweeping transformation of federal policies. "Ronald Reagan enjoyed the most generous treatment by the press of any president in the postwar era," Deaver wrote in his memoirs. "He knew it, and liked the distinction."

But denying the press information was also part of the strategy. The Reagan administration placed unprecedented controls on the the flow of information from the federal government and sharply limited Reagan's unscripted appearances before the media. News conferences were a rarity, and Reagan's aides sometimes went to absurd lengths, like pulling the plugs on television lights or stepping in front of reporters, to prevent Reagan from being exposed to questions. Elizabeth Drew, the *New Yorker*'s longtime Washington correspondent, wrote after covering the 1980 campaign that she had never before seen a candidate who was forbidden to talk to the press. "This is an eerie campaign," Drew wrote. "It's not just that Reagan is cordoned off and protected from the press; it's a question of why his aides feel he must be protected from the normal give-and-take of political life—of what it is they are afraid will be revealed."

The answer, of course, is that the last thing they wanted the public to find out was that Reagan, by the time he was elected president, could articulate few political ideas beyond his disdain for communism, taxes, and big government. But it was the very simplicity of those beliefs that made him the perfect pitchman. Thus we have Ronald Reagan in his speeches speaking in simple platitudes that often cloaked the real intentions of the administration, intentions that he never completely understood. He would not tell the American people that his administration planned to gut environmental protections or drastically reduce business taxes or set off a rash of corporate mergers. In fact, he rarely mentioned corporations at all. He would just tell his audience things that anyone would want to hear. "All across the land," he said in a typical moment of his 1980 campaign, "I've found a longing among our people for hope, a longing for a belief in ourselves and the vision that gave birth to this nation. For the values of family, work, neighborhood, peace, and freedom. Jimmy Carter would have us believe that dream is over . . . or at least in need of some drastic change." It was the type of bromide sure to bring a warm glow to anyone who heard it, but it was essentially meaningless.

And so the pattern was set: Every president who followed Reagan would be squired by image consultants and pollsters; the Washington press corps would not be informed of the government's real activities but distracted and manipulated; speeches would be filled with meaningless drivel; and the public would come to regard politicians as no more worthy of trust than used-car salesmen.

CHAPTER 10

"The Man with the Badge"

On a spring morning in 2002, elementary school students in the tiny South Dakota town of Wagner, population sixteen hundred, were getting out their pens and paper for the day's instruction when they were suddenly given a lesson on the U.S. Constitution that they would not find in their history books.

The voice of their principal, Neil Goter, a stout, ruddy-cheeked man known as a stern disciplinarian, came over an intercom and warned that their school was on "lockdown." What the term *lockdown* meant most students had no idea, particularly the kindergartners and first-graders. All they knew was that they were confined to their desks, not even allowed to go to the bathroom. But the penal imagery turned out to be well suited to what came next.

Within moments of the principal's edict, Wagner police officers swept into the school with a German shepherd and began a painstaking search of every classroom, from kindergarten through twelfth grade. As officers spent hours leading the dog up and down the aisles between desks, they warned the pupils to keep their hands at their sides and not make any sudden moves, lest the animals attack. Some students reported the dog was growling as it stopped by their desks. In one kindergarten class, the dog broke free from its handler, jumped up on desks, and chased terrified students into a corner, causing some of them to burst out crying. One child wet his pants he was so scared.

After the parents of seventeen students, mostly Native Americans from a nearby reservation, persuaded the American Civil Liberties Union to file suit against the district, school officials justified the canine sweep by saying they had received a report of drugs in the school. But no drugs or other contraband was found. The same dog again sniffed through the school's lockers and classrooms a few days later and still never picked up the scent of anything more dangerous than sweaty gym socks.

Kindergartners rousted in their classrooms by police dogs may seem an abomination, but it is part and parcel of Ronald Reagan's vision for America. The ACLU's only hope of prevailing in its lawsuit was to prove that the dogs had searched the students without any reasonable suspicion, for the U.S. Supreme Court, siding with arguments put forth by Reagan's solicitor general, had ruled in 1985 that it is perfectly legal for police and school authorities to rummage though students' personal effects. It is also perfectly legal—and done all the time around the country—to search schools with dogs. No real probable cause is needed, just a vague belief on the part of school authorities that drugs, weapons, or other illegal items might be on the premises.

Solicitor General Rex. E. Lee intervened in the 1985 case, *New Jersey v. T.L.O.,* as part of an effort by administration officials to chip away at a raft of liberal precedents that had emanated from the Court in the previous three decades, especially those involving abortion, affirmative action, and the rights of criminal defendants. Ideologues like Ed Meese and William Bradford Reynolds, assistant attorney general for civil rights, were disdainful of the court's tradition, under a doctrine known as *stare decisis,* of steering away from issues that had been settled in previous decisions. For them, the ideal solicitor general was one who would crusade for the reversal of any precedent the Reaganites might not like, while lecturing the Court on its past liberalism.

Rex Lee was notably uncomfortable with this approach. A Mormon who was the dean of the Brigham Young University law school in Utah, he had been chosen for his post on the basis of his conservative legal writings. He had no quarrel with the administration's embrace of "judicial restraint," the idea that the Supreme Court should create no rights that the founders had not expressly intended as they drafted the Constitution. But he was loath to press the court to break from its tradition of stare decisis. He understood the perils of attempting to rewrite the law of the land every time there was a shift in the political winds. And he felt that haranguing justices about previous rulings would only diminish the credibility of his office and work to the detriment of the administration in the long run. By the time he resigned in June 1985, Lee had had enough. "There has been this notion that my job is to press the Administration's policies at every turn and announce true conservative principles through the pages of my briefs," he told an interviewer. "It is not. I am the Solicitor General, not the Pamphleteer General."

But Lee could not help but be influenced by constant pressure from right-wingers in the Justice Department, whom he accommodated by filing friend-of-the-court briefs in a larger number of cases than had his predecessors in the Carter, Nixon, and Johnson administrations. One of those cases was *New Jersey v. T.L.O.* The underlying criminal case originated when a high school principal in Piscataway, New Jersey, searched the purse of a teenage girl suspected of smoking in the bathroom. After discovering a pack of Marlboros in the purse, he dug deeper and found marijuana, a pipe, a wad of bills, and a list of students she had been selling joints for a dollar apiece. Her arrest on juvenile delinquency charges ended up before the Supreme Court, an important test case on the Fourth Amendment rights of students.

Lee's brief argued that students have no such rights, that teachers and school administrators are free to act in loco parentis, in the place of parents. The brief also placed the issue in the context of national concerns about school safety, arguing—not a little hysterically—that "disorder and crime in the schools have reached epidemic proportions." The solicitor general is no ordinary litigant before the Supreme Court. His influence is so well accepted that he is sometimes called the "tenth justice." And Lee had been more successful than most of his predecessors in convincing the Court to back the government's position.

In this case, by a vote of six to three, the Court rejected Lee's argument that students are not protected by the Fourth Amendment on school grounds. But Justice Lewis Powell wrote for the majority that school officials, even though they are government agents, are not bound by the same restrictions as law enforcement personnel. They may search students without a warrant or even probable cause as long as their intrusiveness is based on reasonable suspicion. The implications of the decision were profound. A citizen, albeit one under eighteen, could be charged with a crime and even sent to jail on the basis of evidence whose seizure in any other context would be deemed an affront to the Constitution. The decision was too much for Justice William Brennan, whose dissent called it an "unclear, unprecedented, and unnecessary departure from generally applicable Fourth Amendment standards." He said the "Rorschach-like balancing test" that Powell laid down for weighing privacy interests against those of school security "portends a dangerous weakening of the purpose of the Fourth Amendment to protect the privacy and security of our citizens."

Brennan could not have called it better. While the case did not address broad and random searches of school hallways and lockers, focusing mainly on the actions of school officials rather than police, *New Jersey v. T.L.O.* helped pave the way for a widespread police assault on the nation's schoolchildren. The Wagner schools were hardly alone in treating their pupils like inmates in a penal institution. By the end of the 1980s, Gestapo-like tactics geared to finding drugs and weapons in schools were being used all over the country. One Michigan school district strip-searched every member of a gym class when money was found to be missing from a locker room. Outside Kansas City, Missouri, teachers were accused of strip-searching two dozen third-graders in 2002 in a quest for missing lunch money.

In the fall of 2000, students in Clearwater, Florida, returned to school after summer break and found their high school's central campus enclosed with thick metal fencing and locking gates, with forty-eight surveillance cameras keeping watch over their movements. Clearwater is part of the Pinellas County school district, which at the time had a twenty-member campus police department with five dogs that would make random sweeps of every school in the district. In one of the district's schools, parents hatched a plan to sell candy bars and wash cars to raise enough money to have their own drug-sniffing dog work full time. "It is not an Orwellian leap," observed Diane Steinle, an editorial writer for the *St. Petersburg Times,* "to imagine schools of the future as places where students will be subjected to strip searches, forced interrogations, mandatory drug tests—perhaps even cavity searches. . . . But is this really what we want—schools that look like correctional institutions and kids who feel like criminals?"

Whether or not this is what we want, this is our country in the post-Reagan era, and the victims are not just schoolchildren. The last two decades have seen a rollback of civil liberties and a dramatic empowerment of police in the name of fighting criminal threats that seem to shift with every political season. Reagan pledged to take government off the backs of the people, but for many Americans, that government is more intrusive than ever. Its emissaries are searching our children at school, stopping and questioning us at roadway checkpoints, rummaging through our bank accounts, gathering profiles of us in cyberspace, collecting samples of our urine, spying on us with cameras mounted in public places, and putting record numbers of us behind bars.

Some Americans are privileged enough not to notice these harshest aspects of the new law-and-order regime. Dogs tend to search schools in poor and working-class school districts while the children of the affluent go unmolested. Cameras don't watch over the public in affluent Ridgewood, New Jersey; they hang on telephone poles in working-class Harrison. But the gradual disregard of our freedoms eventually ends up affecting us all. In middle-class Glen Rock, New Jersey, where the author lives, teachers search student bags before school trips and watch over schoolchildren with video monitors in the hallway, the latter made possible by a $200,000 homeland security grant. The lone parent who complained about the bag searches at an assembly was heckled and shouted down by the crowd.

And that is precisely the tragedy of Reagan's America. It's not just the changes that Reaganism brought to the law, but the public's blithe acceptance of the new restrictions on its freedom. A recent survey by *Family Circle* magazine found that 76 percent of the respondents favored random drug testing in schools and 94 percent supported the placing of metal detectors in the hallways. With right-wing politicians and their media allies regularly stoking the public's paranoia over drugs or carjacking or kidnapped children or abusive day-care centers or terrorism—the menace shifts with the political winds—citizens are frightened into giving up liberties jealously guarded by previous generations of Americans. Does anyone really believe that the terrorist threat to Glen Rock justifies putting schoolchildren under surveillance? Is the chance that one or two students will be caught trying to sneak liquor on a school trip worth subjecting two hundred well-behaved children to a warrantless search? We treat the Constitution as a sacred text in the classroom and then, through these pointless exercises, teach the students that in real life it is meaningless.

It is hardly as if these measures were absolutely necessary to battle a crime problem spiraling out of control. Crime was falling at the time Ronald Reagan took office. As will be shown below, except for a six-year period, 1985 to 1991, it has done nothing but fall in the past two and half decades. While the reasons for the particularly dramatic reduction in the 1990s have been widely debated, most serious scholars attribute the decline to demographic and socioeconomic factors like the aging of the population, the waning of the crack epidemic, and low unemployment rates in the 1990s. In New York City, where the number of murders dropped from 2,245 in 1990 to 572 in 2004, innovative policing deserves a share of the credit. Former New York City police commissioner William Bratton pioneered the computerized mapping of crime trends, known as CompStat, and an emphasis on the prosecution of quality-of-life crimes to reduce general lawlessness. But none of this is consistent with the Reagan agenda of locking up multitudes of young men and exposing the poor to increased surveillance.

The entire landscape of criminal justice in America was shaped by Ronald Reagan. The prison-building boom, the exponential increase in the number of Americans behind bars, the billions poured down the drain in the so-called war on drugs, the racial-profiling scandal on the nation's highways, the attacks on habeas corpus and the exclusionary rule, the exaggerated hero worship of the police officer—all of these can be laid at Reagan's doorstep. The law-and-order debate in America has always been a spawning ground for demagoguery, but the forces of reason and dispassion had the upper hand for much of the middle decades of the last century. Reagan helped make sure that criminal justice questions would close out the century steeped in hysteria. Since he established crime as a potent wedge issue, politicians across the country have been falling over one another to press for tougher criminal statutes, whether they make sense or not. It is no coincidence that the elder George Bush made the war on drugs the centerpiece of his presidency at the very time when other wedge issues were suddenly unavailable. The widening budget deficit meant he could not cut taxes. His pledge to be "kinder and gentler" than his predecessor took the welfare queen out of his arsenal. And the fall of the Soviet Union deprived him of the communist menace as a bludgeon to use against Democrats. So he escalated Reagan's war on drugs, hiring thousands of new federal agents and, for the first time, creating a federal death penalty for crimes having nothing to do with national security. Bill Clinton also recognized a political winner when he saw it and adopted the Reagan-Bush approach as his own. He created fifty new federal offenses eligible for the death penalty, restricted the use of habeas corpus, promoted boot camps for federal offenders, and earmarked money for cities to hire a hundred thousand new police officers.

Politicians at the state level have been just as retrograde. When a new law makes a media splash in one state, elected officials across the country jump on the bandwagon. So-called three-strikes laws, which mandate life in prison for conviction of a third violent crime, were adopted in twenty-six states after such a statute first appeared in California. Megan's laws, named for a seven-year-old New Jersey girl raped and murdered by a neighbor in 1994, are now on the books in every state. And no issue has been a bigger source of shameless politicking than the death penalty, at least until DNA technology began to show just how often it has been applied to wrongly convicted defendants. When William Weld, a former official in Reagan's Justice Department, ran against John Kerry for Massachusetts governor in 1996, one of his chief campaign issues was the restoration of the death penalty. Since Kerry opposed the death penalty, he had to prove to voters that on the issue of crime he could foam at the mouth just as rabidly as his opponent. After Weld brought up the mother of a murdered police officer during a debate and challenged Kerry to "tell her why the life of the man who murdered her son is worth more than the life of a police officer," his adversary was ready for him. "It's not worth more. It's not worth anything. It's scum that ought to be thrown into jail for the rest of its life," Kerry responded.

Who was this "scum" that Kerry referred to as an "it" rather than a person? Johnny Ortiz was a twenty-three-year-old with a clean record who made the mistake of trying to restrain his teenaged brother, Eduardo "Crazy Eddie" Ortiz, when the younger man picked up a gun and left their home in a rage. The youths' father told Johnny to go after Eddie and calm him down. So Johnny was in the car when Eddie was pulled over and ended up shooting and killing two Springfield police officers.

Eddie Ortiz shot himself to death the next day, leaving his brother to absorb the public's outrage over the police shootings. A prosecutor used a novel argument to charge Johnny Ortiz with second-degree murder, claiming he was in joint possession of the gun, even though there was no evidence that he ever touched it. The jury bought the argument, and Ortiz went off to prison. This "scum" who became the poster boy for death penalty advocates in Massachusetts would never even have been eligible for death under any state's laws. But in the world of politicized law and order that Reagan bequeathed to us, such subtleties hardly matter.

All the vote-getting strategies of tough-on-crime politicians have little to do with getting tough on crime. It has been established by endless studies that the death penalty is not a deterrent. A 1996 study of three-strikes laws by the Campaign for Effective Crime Policy, a private Washington research group, found that they were rarely used in most of the twenty-two states that have adopted them. The reason, said Charles Dickey, a University of Wisconsin law professor who coauthored the study, was that most people who committed two violent felonies tended to be old men by the time they got out of prison. "My bottom line on three-strikes laws is that they are much ado about nothing," Dickey said. "There is not a lot of substance behind them since there is already authority to put people away for a long time."

No serious criminologist believes Megan's laws protect children. If a sex offender is going to strike again, the fact that his neighbors know who he is does not stop him from going to another neighborhood. What Megan's laws—and the related trend toward indefinite civil commitment of sex offenders after they have completed their prison terms—have accomplished is a dangerous precedent in American jurisprudence. Certain criminal defendants are being designated as permanent undesirables, subject to punishment and public scorn even after they have paid their debt to society. In her dissent from a Supreme Court ruling that upheld Megan's laws, Justice Ruth Bader Ginsburg said that "however plain it may be that a former sex offender currently poses no threat of recidivism, he will remain subject to long-term monitoring and inescapable humiliation." There are now countless recorded instances of released sex offenders' being exposed to vandalism and even physical attack after their addresses have become public.

Reagan did not have to personally draw up an elaborate blueprint for a martial regime that would slowly eat away at the constitutional rights of Americans. For that he had more devious intellects at work, like that of Edwin Meese III, the banal, self-effacing but fiercely ideological man who had been eager to carry forth his vision for nearly two decades. Meese was famously a law-and-order zealot and doctrinaire conservative who closely identified with right-wing groups like the John Birch Society and the Heritage Foundation. Even Nancy Reagan, in her memoirs, dismissed him as "a jump-off-the-cliff-with-the-flag-flying conservative." He was an unabashed ideologue who would walk around the West Wing with a bust of Adam

Smith embroidered on his tie. With his round middle and plump red cheeks, Meese had the looks of an Irish cop and the political sensibilities of a Rotarian, convinced that America had been run down by hippies, blacks, gays, feminists, and welfare cheats. But he had a serviceable intellect and an ardor for his conservative beliefs that would wear down his bureaucratic opponents. Many years earlier, when Meese was chief of staff to then-governor Reagan in California, the state's Assembly Speaker, Robert Moretti, described him as having "a stick-to-itiveness that can sometimes drive you up a wall." In the White House, he applied this diligence to his role as ideological gatekeeper, the man whom orthodox conservatives depended on to guard against the dreaded pragmatism of James Baker and Michael Deaver, the other two members of the "troika" running the administration. Meese was the most in tune with Reagan politically, and he used that symbiosis to nudge the president to the right on many issues. Baker and Deaver were interested in promoting Reagan, Meese in promoting Reagan's revolution.

Meese was an unlikely architect of that revolution. Demure in his manners and amiable to everyone, even those he secretly loathed, he had none of the guile and charisma that usually prevail in bureaucratic infighting. He was the consummate team player, always willing to "roundtable" important questions with other Reagan aides. He had few of the qualities that normally propel a man to the top of a highly competitive organization. He was notoriously disorganized—prone to taking on too many tasks at once and not delegating enough his to aides. A long-running joke in the White House was that documents would never again see the light of day after being popped in Meese's briefcase, which political operative John Sears called the "black hole of Calcutta." Even in their days together in Sacramento, Governor Reagan would crack jokes about Meese's clutter. "Now, Ed, don't lose this one on your desk," he would say after assigning him a task. Meese's tendency to get lost in a miasma of details probably accounts for the arrest warrant the Los Angeles Police Department issued for him in 1985. One of the most powerful men in Washington had forgotten to pay a jaywalking ticket.

Meese socialized little with his colleagues and, like the president himself, was something of a loner. He did not lunch with congressmen or banter with reporters in the manner of Deaver and Baker. He viewed the press corps and much of the Washington establishment with suspicion, convinced they were thick with liberals out to get the new president. He infuriated Baker and Deaver by being ideologically rigid and tone-deaf to the reaction of the press and the public to many of Reagan's policies. They felt he would urge the president into extreme positions on meaningless issues that would unnecessarily stir up damaging controversy. It was Meese who ignited a political firestorm in January 1982 by convincing Reagan to support tax exemptions for private schools, like Bob Jones University in South Carolina, that discriminated against blacks. He set off another round of controversy when he told reporters that the administration "had considerable information that people go to soup kitchens because the food is free and that's easier than paying for it." Baker and Deaver were cordial to Meese to his face but made him the butt of jokes behind his back, in a not-so-subtle effort to undermine his influence. Baker, in off-the-record chats with reporters, called him "Poppin' Fresh, the doughboy."

But Meese was able to exert an enormous influence over policy in those first few months in the White House because of his unique relationship with the president. No one was more simpatico with Reagan's views nor more loyal to his revolution. Reagan knew that Meese was his ideological soul mate and would be the last man to turn on him to advance his own agenda. While many of Reagan's former aides took potshots at the president after they left the White House, making light of his befuddlement and gullibility, Meese continued in his banal defense of everything Reagan ever said or did, right down to insisting that his old boss was correct when he said trees cause pollution. In his 1992 memoirs (which somehow managed to avoid any mention of the ethical conflicts that eventually forced his resignation as attorney general), Meese accused liberals of "a blatant attempt to distort the impact of Ronald Reagan's leadership during this period and to derogate or deny his accomplishments."

Meese had been with Reagan through all of the controversies of the California years. He was the loyal chief of staff in Sacramento, standing in the wings in press conferences, quietly mouthing the words Reagan needed to finish his sentences. He had been by his side through two presidential campaigns and had been the key player in the White House transition in 1981. More than any other aide, he knew how Reagan's mind worked. He knew how to present issues to him lyrically, conveying ideas with anecdote and parable instead of facts and figures. And he knew how to translate Reagan's own lyricism into concrete programs. Meese was able to win Reagan over in policy debates, to the frustration of Baker and Deaver, by uttering the words that could have just as easily come out of Reagan's mouth. "When someone talks to Ed," his wife, Ursula, once said, "they have a pretty good idea of what Ronald Reagan would be saying. So often it is one and the same. . . . Almost ninety-five percent of the time, in fact, they could speak for one another."

Nowhere was Meese's influence applied more diligently than in the realm of criminal justice. He had his hand in all manner of domestic affairs, but cops and robbers were his greatest passion. He had been a police buff from the time of his boyhood in Oakland, California, the former prosecutor who preferred riding in squad cars to arguing law in the courtroom. He loved showing visitors to his White House office his collection of toy police cars and porcelain pigs, his little joke at the expense of political protesters he was so fond of locking up in his days in California. Meese's views on law and order were startlingly reactionary even by the standards that Richard Nixon had set for Republicans a few years earlier. He had contempt for habeas corpus, the exclusionary rule, the *Miranda* rule, and any other constitutional right that could inconvenience the police. He believed that power to decide the fate of criminal defendants should be shifted from judges to prosecutors. "We must increase the power of the prosecutors," he once stated baldly. In a speech before the California Peace Officers Association in 1981, he called the American Civil Liberties Union a "criminals' lobby." In another interview he let it be known that Supreme Court decisions were not the "supreme law of the land," and he once told

U.S. News and World Report that the *Miranda* rule should be done away with because most suspects are guilty. "The thing is," he said, "you don't have many suspects who are innocent of a crime. That's contradictory. If a person is innocent of a crime, then he is not a suspect." He later called his comments a "bad choice of words," but his actions while in office left little doubt that they perfectly summed up his attitude toward the rights of criminal defendants.

And his attitude was perfectly in synch with that of his boss. From his days as California governor through his campaign for the presidency in 1980, Reagan's views on crime and punishment remained consistent. Like Meese, his answer to crime in California in the 1960s, or across the United States in the 1980s, was the crack of the policeman's baton, the slamming of the cell door, and the hum of the electric chair. "Let us have an end to the idea that society is responsible for each and every wrongdoer," Reagan said in a speech to the National Sheriff's Association in 1967. "We must return to a belief in every individual being responsible for his conduct and his misdeeds with punishment immediate and certain. With all our science and sophistication, our culture and our pride in intellectual accomplishment, the jungle still is waiting to take over. The man with the badge holds it back."

Meese had every reason to believe that he would be named chief of staff in the Reagan White House. He had been the loyal lieutenant, always by Reagan's side during the campaign and never far out of touch in his years out of office. If neither man's personality allowed them to become close friends, they were nonetheless joined at the hip ideologically. Meese had emerged from the campaign as Reagan's most powerful aide, in no small part because of a coup he had helped engineer at a crucial moment in the campaign: the firing of Reagan's campaign manager, John Sears, on the day the candidate finished first in the New Hampshire primary, and his replacement by William Casey, who would become CIA director.

Meese entered the transition as the power broker. The chief-of-staff position seemed to be his for the taking. Indeed, it was the newly elected president's plan to give him the post. But Michael Deaver, Nancy Reagan, and Stuart Spencer, who had been giving political advice to Reagan since his first gubernatorial campaign, were determined that Meese not get the job. To their credit, they recognized that his lack of organizational skills, his ideological rigidity, and his tin ear for politics made him unsuited for such a sensitive position. So they came up with the idea of the troika and sold it to the president-elect. James Baker, who had managed Vice President George Bush's 1980 campaign, would be chief of staff, the man who would make the wheels turn in the White House. Deaver, as deputy chief of staff, would handle the stagecraft. Meese would be the counselor to the president, sharing the stewardship of the White House with Baker under a written power-sharing agreement.

The arrangement bitterly disappointed Meese and meant his relationship with Deaver and Baker would never be anything but one of mistrust. But it also left him with enormous power to place his ideological stamp on the nation's affairs. Neither Baker nor Deaver was fiercely driven by ideology, and their concerns about policy details were outweighed by their desire to help Reagan succeed politically. To them, a half victory was always better than standing firm on principle and losing a legislative battle. Their agnosticism in many of the key policy debates left the field wide open to Meese. He injected himself into the full range of decision making in the Reagan White House, using his close access to the president to ensure that his views would be at the forefront of domestic policy discussions. When a cabinet official received marching orders from the White House, the directives tended not to come from the president or the chief of staff, but from Meese or a member of his staff. Meese also used his longtime relationship with Pendelton James, the White House personnel chief, to place his ideological surrogates in key administration positions. Most of the attention in Reagan's first term may have been paid to David Stockman's budget cuts, Alexander Haig's strong-arm policies as secretary of state, or Jeanne Kirkpatrick's ideological crusade at the United Nations, but it was Meese's policy positions that would arguably have a greater impact on the country.

This was especially true in matters of criminal justice. Reagan's attorney general, William French Smith, was a smooth, immaculately tailored man who cut an elegant figure in the briefing room. He served in his position with more aplomb than had most of his predecessors. He decorated his office with paintings borrowed from the Smithsonian, including a California landscape that he lovingly placed on the wall behind his desk. Smith was no shrinking violet in issues that mattered to him. He could summon more than a little pluck in fighting for his department's budget. But he was no hands-on attorney general. He was better known in Washington for his social calendar than for his dynamism as a policy man. The key initiatives came from Meese and his aides in the White House and were carried out by Lowell Jensen, Meese's old buddy from Alameda County, who was strategically placed as head of the Justice Department's criminal division.

And those initiatives were sweeping. Most important among them, because it was the foundation of so many of the others, was the huge financial boondoggle, enemy of constitutional freedoms, and instigator of racial injustice known as the war on drugs. Confronting the sale of illegal drugs was a natural for the Reaganites. Nothing was a greater symbol of what they viewed as the new immorality of America. Drugs were the nectar of the counterculture, the ghetto, and the gay salon, the bastions of licentiousness that Meese and Reagan believed were shredding the nation's moral fiber. Their crusade to stamp out drug use would lay the ground for the law-and-order society that they had been fighting for since the 1960s. Their ideas on criminal justice had not mellowed since the California days. Reagan was still harping on the idea that one's position on the socioeconomic ladder had no bearing on criminal behavior. He said in a 1982 speech that he rejected "utopian presumptions about human nature that see man as primarily a creature of his material environment. By changing this environment through expensive social programs, this philosophy holds that government can permanently change man and usher in an era of prosperity and virtue. . . . This philosophy suggests in short that there is crime or wrongdoing, and that society, not the individual, is to blame." No longer would this permissive philosophy hold sway in America. Banished would be the do-gooder sociologist, driven into seclusion in the academy, and the man with the badge would finally take his rightful place at the pinnacle of society.

But there was another, more important reason for declaring war on drugs: it was smart politics. It was the ultimate wedge issue, the perfect vehicle for instilling fear in the populace and distracting attention from the administration's procorporate agenda. As *Harper's* editor Lewis Lapham once wrote, "The war against drugs provides them with something to say that offends nobody, requires them to do nothing difficult, and allows them to postpone, perhaps indefinitely, the more urgent and specific questions about the nation's schools, housing, employment opportunities for young black men—i.e., the condition to which drug addiction speaks as a tragic symptom, not a cause. They remain safe in the knowledge that they might as well be denouncing Satan or the rain."

Portraying the poor as criminals would also help win support for curtailing social welfare programs, one reason Reagan made spending on law enforcement one of two areas of government—the other being national defense—that would be exempt from budget cuts. David Stockman learned how serious Reagan was in this commitment when he suggested during one of the first cabinet meetings that the Justice Department's staff of fifty-four thousand be cut by two thousand. William French Smith responded angrily—with a slap of his palm on the oak cabinet table—that the Justice Department was not a domestic agency but an important component of the national defense. Besides, Smith said, "Restoring a strong federal law enforcement capability is going to be highly popular with the American people." Reagan, sitting at the head or the table, ended the debate in Smith's favor. "Bill is right," he told Stockman, "Law enforcement is something we have always believed was a legitimate function of government."

So began the war on drugs. In 1982, Reagan designated Vice President Bush to head up the South Florida Task Force, designed to coordinate the local and federal assault on Latin American drug traffickers in the Sunshine State. But that was just the beginning. The war would continue to escalate, as would the rhetoric used to support it. "It's high time that we make our cities safe again," Reagan said in his 1983 State of the Union address. "This administration hereby declares an all-out war on big-time organized crime and the drug racketeers who are poisoning our young people." The martial imagery was no accident. Rather than fund programs for drug treatment, child care, job training, education, and housing, which might actually have made a difference in drug-abuse patterns, Reagan chose to militarize the cities. By 1984, thirteen regional task forces modeled on the South Florida effort were up and running, and inner-city neighborhoods were turned into armed encampments. Raiding parties made up of state and local police and federal agents were sweeping young black and Hispanic men off the street corners, kicking down doors, and making mass arrests. Reagan also for the first time authorized the use of the military in domestic law enforcement, amending the Posse Comitatus Act so the Navy and Coast Guard could assist in stopping suspect vessels in U.S. waters. The military's expenditures on prosecuting the drug war grew from $4.9 million in 1982 to more than $1 billion eight years later.

The public was whipped up into a fury against the poor. Young drug dealers—people with few skills to compete in the knowledge-based economy, who chose to make hundreds of dollars a week on street corners instead of $175 at Burger King—were suddenly as vile as rapists and child molesters. As the years went on, the true believers would come to consider no punishment too extreme for these young people of color. William Bennett, who was the first person to fill the drug czar post created by the elder George Bush, said on a radio show that he had no moral objection to the beheading of drug dealers. The Delaware legislature seriously considered a bill that would allow them to be publicly flogged. Darryl Gates, Los Angeles police chief, recommended they be shot.

Among the casualties in the war on drugs were the civil liberties of Americans, especially those of the poor. One of the first criminal justice initiatives to come out of the White House, the Criminal Justice

Reform Act of 1982, was a deeply controversial bill that would have sharply limited habeas corpus—the legal doctrine that allows inmates to have their imprisonment reviewed by the courts—and weakened the exclusionary rule, which bars convictions based on evidence seized without a warrant or probable cause. Both of these core American principles, essential elements of the Constitution and our sense of what it means to live in a free and open society, had long been on Meese's hit list. He promoted a "good-faith exception" to the exclusionary rule. A police search may have lacked probable cause or a search warrant may have targeted the wrong apartment, but as long as the officers *believed* they were acting lawfully, why should a simple mistake allow a criminal to go free? Civil libertarians pointed out that a minuscule fraction of criminal convictions were overturned because of honest police mistakes in applying search warrants or probable cause. The bill, they said, was a political charade that would undermine an important Fourth Amendment protection—diminishing it in the eyes of law enforcement and the public—while having virtually no impact on crime.

With the Democrats in control of the House, the bill never made it out of Congress. But as with so much of his agenda, Reagan and his faithful kept up the fight, and their views ultimately prevailed. In 1996, President Clinton, who put the finishing touches on so much of Reagan's agenda, signed legislation limiting habeas corpus appeals. The exclusionary rule would be dealt with more quickly. On July 5, 1984, the Supreme Court, by a vote of six to three, established a good-faith exception to the exclusionary rule, siding with arguments put forth by Reagan's solicitor general, Rex Lee. Once again, it was up to Justice Brennan to lament the further erosion of the U.S. Constitution. In his dissent, which was joined by Justice Thurgood Marshall, Brennan said he had long been dismayed by the court's gradual "strangulation" of the exclusionary rule. "It now appears that the Court's victory over the Fourth Amendment is complete," he wrote. "That today's decisions represent the piece de resistance of the Court's past efforts cannot be doubted, for today the Court sanctions the use . . . of illegally obtained evidence against the individual whose rights have been violated—a result that had previously been thought to be foreclosed."

Undeterred by the defeat of the 1982 crime bill, Reagan pushed successfully for an even broader package of crime legislation, with strong support from both the Democrats and the Republicans in Congress. The Comprehensive Crime Contract Act of 1985 was the most sweeping overhaul of the nation's criminal laws ever adopted by Congress. Within the bill's 635 pages and ninety separate provisions were measures that would affect the justice system for years to come. It would make it much tougher for criminal defendants to mount an insanity defense, abolish parole in federal sentencing, toughen sanctions for dealing drugs outside a school, and make it easier for prosecutors to achieve the civil forfeiture of property. In short order, the public would be treated to the spectacle of federal authorities seizing cars, houses, and bank accounts of people caught with even small amounts of drugs. One Kentucky man who grew a small amount of marijuana to treat his glaucoma received only a year in jail after his arrest in 1987—but U.S. District Judge Ronald Meredith seized the ninety-acre farm he had owned for eighteen years and gave his family ten days to clear off the property.

But the most significant element of the bill was the establishment of guidelines that judges were required to follow in sentencing defendants, including the creation of mandatory minimum penalties for a host of drug crimes. The new measures removed the discretion of judges in sentencing and put the power in the hands of prosecutors, just as Ed Meese had always wanted. If there were extenuating circumstances that drove a defendant to commit a drug crime, if he had become a drug mule to pay for a cancer operation for his wife and did not even know the amount of heroin he was carrying through an airport, only a prosecutor could offer him leniency, as part of the plea-bargaining process. The judge would become an automaton, with little room to depart from the sentence dictated in the guidelines. Most prosecutors, of course, see a longer sentence as a greater victory and a means of moving up the career ladder. Leniency would not be applied for reasons of compassion or fair play, but only as a means of ensuring a guilty plea or winning cooperation against more significant offenders. The result was more federal offenders in prison for longer periods of time. The administration moved ahead with this legislation despite ample warnings that it could have an adverse outcome. In 1983, Reagan's own Justice Department issued a report questioning whether the push for "collective incapacitation"—that is, uniformity in federal sentencing—would reduce crime. The lead author reported that the "most striking finding is that incapacitation does not appear to achieve large reductions in crime," but that its use could "cause enormous increases in prison populations." When these guidelines were copied by state legislators across the country—with mandatory minimums applied across a wide array of state crimes—it set up the framework for the imprisonment of multitudes of young minorities, often for nonviolent drug offenses. The number of people in state and federal prison increased from about 600,000 in 1980 to 2.2 million at the end of 2002. Beginning in 1985, federal and state correctional authorities spent the next ten years opening a new prison every week. Even as crime across the country plummeted, beginning in the early 1990s, the number of people being put behind bars has continued to escalate. For people of color, Reagan created an American gulag.

At a time when the scourge of crack cocaine had begun to take hold of the nation's inner cities, such measures seemed to make sense to the federal lawmakers of both parties who supported the bill. Democrats had lined up in support of the 1985 crime package, partly because it provided for the establishment of sentencing guidelines as a way to bring uniformity to the punishment of federal criminals, a goal long supported by Edward Kennedy, Joseph Biden, and other Democratic senators. The senators wanted to see underprivileged defendants get the same outcome in court as well-heeled criminals convicted of the same offenses. But any benefits the poor derived from the guidelines were far outweighed by the devastating effects the bill had on inner-city communities.

The idea that the public was clamoring for a federal war on drugs is simply a fiction. The Reagan and first Bush administrations—with help from the sensational media—deliberately drummed up national hysteria to justify a harsher approach. *Time* and *Newsweek* each featured cocaine on their covers five times in 1986, *Time* in one article calling the drug war "urgent and necessary," even while noting that cocaine use had peaked and that consumption of all drugs together was declining. And yet the public was slow to realize the extent of this "menace." In July 1989, a *New York Times/CBS* poll found that only 20 percent of the respondents considered drugs a pressing issue. But then the first President Bush delivered a speech two months later in which he called drugs "the gravest domestic threat facing our nation today" and pledged to "enlarge our criminal justice system across the board." In advance of and shortly after the president's address, which was devoted solely to the topic of drugs, the major television networks ran an average of three to four stories a night on the issue. Shortly after the address, 64 percent of people polled now believed drugs to be our biggest problem. This was not a response to a real crisis. It was a triumph of scare politics, designed to make drugs a potent political issue.

The spread of the gulag to the states could not have been accomplished without the likes of Frank Graves, one of countless state legislators across the country who quickly latched onto Reagan's criminal justice model as a sure vote getter. Graves, who served simultaneously as a state senator and the mayor of Paterson, New Jersey, a crumbling old mill town nestled within a sharp curve of the Passaic River, was a pit bull of a politician whose exploits were legendary. The son of a police reporter for the Paterson *News,* he was a Runyonesque character who loved the rough-and-tumble of being mayor of a hard-luck city. He would cruise the streets in an unmarked police car with a gun on his side and a readiness to bring the law, Frank Graves's law, to anyone threatening order in his city. A copy boy for the Paterson *News* found this out late one night in 1984 when his girlfriend jumped out of his car in a huff in the city's downtown. Refusing to let her walk home through tough neighborhoods, the copy boy lifted her up by the waist, planning to put her back in the car. Suddenly that familiar black detective's car screeched up to the scene, and out bounded the mayor with a black pistol in his hand. "Hold it right there, buster," the mayor shouted, his gun pointed at the shocked young man.

Graves was a master at manipulating the press. When one of Paterson's tenements caught fire, the mayor would be helping carry the victim on a stretcher when the news cameras arrived. If a child was reported missing, Graves would be at the command post and was not shy about pointing it out to local reporters. "Remember," he would say, jabbing his finger at a reporter's notebook, "Mayor Frank Graves is leading the search for the missing girl." One of his favorite tricks was to call the Paterson *News* city room on a Sunday night and report his latest legislative achievement in Trenton, the state capital. He knew that a reporter could not check the accuracy of his claims on a Sunday night and would put whatever he said in the next day's paper. Invariably, his legislative victory was less dramatic than he had reported, if it existed at all.

By the mid-1980s, few issues were more prominent in New Jersey than crime. The national media's attention on crack cocaine as a potent new source of violence and pathology in the inner cities had hit home with the state politicians. No one seemed to be concerned that crack cocaine had not produced a spurt of violent crime in the Garden State. The number of murders in the state averaged 399 between 1985 and 1990, the prime years of the crack epidemic, compared with 445 in the period from 1975 to 1980. The number of murders in Paterson, the heart of Graves's legislative district, had been falling even more precipitously. But Graves and other lawmakers, like their counterparts around the country, were not about to miss out on the political gravy train created by Ronald Reagan and Ed Meese. The New Jersey legislature approved a crime package incorporating many of the same elements as Reagan's crime bill. It even had a similar name, the Comprehensive Drug Reform Act of 1987. The most important of the bill's provisions was the creation of a mandatory three-year prison sentence for selling drugs within a thousand feet of a school. "I personally believe that anyone selling drugs to school-aged children should be buried alive or hung by the neck in front of city hall," Graves said at one legislative hearing. As on the federal level, the tough talk was politically popular, and subsequent bills added similar thousand-foot zones around public housing complexes and public buildings.

The effect on the prison population was immediate. What neither Graves nor anyone else took into account when considering the school zone law was that virtually every square inch of crowded New Jersey cities like Newark, Jersey City, and Paterson were within a thousand feet of a school. The law essentially created a mandatory prison sentence for drug dealing in an inner city, while setting no such penalty for suburban dealers. What followed was a dramatic increase in the number of young men going to prison for nonviolent crimes. New Jersey's prison population, about 6,000 in 1977, grew to more than 27,000 by 2004, with most of the increase due to incarceration for drug crimes. A recent study by the Urban Institute, a Washington-based research group, found that the number of imprisonments per 100,000 residents of New Jersey was 331 in 2002, compared with 76 in 1980. The cost of this new penal state was staggering. The state built four new prisons between 1981 and 1997, and the cost of corrections, parole, and juvenile justice reached $1.2 billion by 2004, compared to $92.3 million in 1980.

Whatever else the taxpayers may have gotten from that boom in prison construction, they did not get lower crime rates. In fact, the opposite occurred. Crimes of violence had been falling in New Jersey throughout the first half of the 1980s. The number of violent crimes per 100,000 residents dropped from 604 in 1980 to 572 in 1986, with the absolute number of murders declining from 504 to 399. Between 1987 and 1992, the five years following the passage of New Jersey's comprehensive drug bill, those numbers went in the opposite direction. The number of violent crimes per 100,000 people climbed from 541 to 625, and murders went from 351 to 397. Whatever was driving an increase in violent crime across the country produced the same effect in New Jersey, even with the harsh new sentencing laws. Reagan's idea of criminal justice did not work for New Jersey any more than it worked for the rest of the country.

Reagan's war on drugs spread its tentacles across society in a multitude of ways. In 1984, the U.S. Drug Enforcement Administration launched Operation Pipeline, a national effort to use state highway patrol officers to interdict drug couriers on the country's freeways. The theory behind the program was that couriers for the Colombian and Mexican drug cartels, as the DEA put it, often "shared many characteristics, tendencies, and methods" that a trained police officer could spot during a vehicle stop. Those characteristics, according to the DEA's literature, included the use of rented cars, a look of fatigue from driving long distances, and food wrappers littering the floor. What was not spelled out in the literature, but became the standard operating procedure of highway officers around the country, was the emphasis on pulling over lone drivers of Hispanic and African descent.

More than twenty-seven thousand state highway patrol officers across the country were trained under Operation Pipeline. Turning highway officers into shock troops for the war on drugs was ill advised from the start. While the DEA boasts to this day of the amounts of drugs seized under the program—thirty-five thousand seizures between 1986 and 1998—any first-year criminology student should know that picking off a few couriers would put hardly a dent in the flow of drugs into this country. No drug user in this nation ever went a day without a fix because of Operation Pipeline. It was like so many other elements of the war on drugs: politically attractive but of no real efficacy in reducing drug traffic or violent crime.

But the program had a big impact on countless Americans of color. As racial-profiling scandals broke into public view in the late 1990s on either coast, states released figures showing that minorities were pulled over in higher proportions than whites but showed no greater likelihood to have drugs or other contraband in their vehicles. Statistics released by the Maryland State Police as the result of a lawsuit showed that blacks made up 73 percent of the motorists stopped by troopers between January 1995 and September 1996, even though blacks were responsible for only 17.5 percent of traffic violations. The searches turned up contraband in 28.4 percent of the vehicles of blacks, compared with 28.8 percent of cars driven by whites. In New Jersey, where the racial-profiling scandal toppled the New Jersey State

Police superintendent and led to sweeping changes in policies on motor vehicle stops, a report by the state's attorney general in 1999 found that nearly eight of every ten people searched after a vehicle stop were minorities. One black state police sergeant complained to his superiors that he had been pulled over by fellow troopers forty times. Statistics from two state police barracks on the New Jersey Turnpike showed that between 1994 and 1999, 77.2 percent of the drivers who had their cars searched were black or Hispanic. Only 19.2 percent resulted in arrests. In other words, more than four out of five minorities searched in that five-year period were innocent victims of Reagan's extension of his drug war onto the nation's highways, collateral damage in a battle that was all about right-wing politics and not in the least about curbing the availability of illegal drugs in America.

All of us were asked to sacrifice some of our liberties to control drugs. By the end of the 1980s, Americans were putting up with roadway stop checks, searches of their automobiles, and as was noted above, the warrantless searches of their children in the schools. In 1986, Reagan signed an executive order, titled Drug Free Workplace, that ordered federal agencies to test the urine of all employees whose jobs involved "a high degree of trust and confidence." The measure helped spur the spread of drug testing across the private sector. As the journalist Dan Baum put it, "The contents of one's bladder would now be the boss's business." In many major cities, police took to rounding up every young man on a street corner when drugs were found on only one, or even nearby on the ground. Under civil forfeiture laws, the suspects' money and other property could be seized at the whim of the police, often not to be returned even if they were acquitted. Laws sprung up that made loitering in a known drug zone a crime, even by those who lived in the neighborhood. Police began "reverse stings," going undercover to offer drugs to people and then arresting them if they accepted. Cities took to demolishing homes used as crack dens. None of this, of course, was focused on drug dealers in the suburbs, only the inner-city poor.

No sensible person would ever argue that authorities should not target murderous drug gangs for prosecution. But those have been precisely the expensive and time-consuming investigations that have often been neglected in favor of the low-level sweeps of drug dealers. The people arrested are quickly replaced by other small-fry, but the police officials and politicians get their press conference, which is the whole point.

Billions upon billions have been spent on the drug war since Reagan launched the South Florida Task Force, hundreds of thousands of young black and Hispanic men have been put in prison for nonviolent crimes, and Americans have given up an untold number of constitutional freedoms. And to what end? The supply of drugs was never interrupted. Drugs like cocaine and heroin were cheaper and more plentiful by the late 1990s than they were at the start of the Reagan years. Nor have surveys shown a sustained reduction in drug use patterns among children and adults. The drug war was at best a tragic mistake and at worst a cynical use of fear mongering to help the Reagan Revolution achieve its larger political goals.

The proposition that putting vast numbers of Americans behind bars is the answer to our crime problems has simply not stood the test of time. The best evidence that supporters of a harsher law-enforcement climate point to as a vindication of the Reagan program is the dramatic reduction in national crime rates that began in 1992. This reduction, they say, could not have occurred had not the United States incarcerated a higher number of citizens than any other country in the Western world. But the reality is far more complex, and not easily reduced to the simplistic slogans of right-wing demagogues.

Decades of research have established conclusively that fluctuations in crime are usually driven by a labyrinth of factors that even the best criminological minds despair of ever fully comprehending. The best they can hope for is to identify and hopefully reshuffle a few pieces of the puzzle. Law enforcement strategies are clearly one of those pieces. And there is no doubt that broad economic conditions also play a role, with crime levels sometimes corresponding with an increase in unemployment. But any responsible criminologist knows that a search for the real antecedents of rising crime must plumb deeper. The most dramatic increases in crime in America occurred between

1960 and 1974, a period that for the most part was marked by economic prosperity, a decline in poverty levels, and greater efforts by the federal government to care for its neediest citizens.

It was that period of escalating crime in the 1960s that shaped the views of Ronald Reagan and Ed Meese, and it was no mirage. The United States had 9,110 murders in 1960, compared to 23,040 two decades later. Serious crimes per 100,000 people also more than doubled, going from 1,187 to 5,950. Up through the early 1950s, it was safe to walk the streets at night even in the toughest big-city neighborhoods. Two decades later, only the foolhardy or the very menacing would tarry after hours on the streets of the South Bronx or Chicago's South Side. Aggressive action to combat such deterioration in the quality of life in our cities was obviously needed, and it is not hard to see why Democrats and Republicans were ready to blame the criminal justice system for coddling criminals.

But serious research has ferreted out a more nuanced explanation for rising crime in this period. The Harvard criminologist William Julius Wilson wrote an influential book toward the end of the Reagan era that collated the best research on the causes of the social pathology afflicting African American communities. Wilson concluded that the problems of big-city ghettoes were rooted in a massive social upheaval occasioned by the migration of rural southern blacks to big cities in the preceding six decades. Such a vast dislocation of people to crowded inner-city neighborhoods had always produced social pathology in the past, beginning with the gangs of hooligans that terrorized Irish American ghettoes in the middle of the nineteenth century.

The black migration had unique characteristics. The racism that oppressed and isolated black migrants—even more than their white counterparts—is obvious and does not need to be explored here. But racism was hardly the only hurdle facing black migrants. A disproportionate number of people forced from the fields of Dixie by the mechanization of agriculture were young people, whose domination of black neighborhoods in Detroit, Chicago, New York, and other cities created its own dynamic. The number of inner-city blacks between the ages of fourteen and twenty-four increased by 78 percent between

1960 and 1970, while the number of urban whites in that age range increased by only 23 percent. "In short, much of what has gone awry in the inner city is due in part to the sheer increase in the number of young people, especially young minorities," Wilson concluded.

He based his conclusion in part on the 1970s research of another Harvard criminologist, James Q. Wilson, who found that such a concentration of young people has "an exponential effect" on crime and other social problems that can bring about effects in even greater proportion than their numbers. "In other words," William Julius Wilson wrote, "there may be a 'critical mass' of young persons in a given community such that when the mass is reached or is increased suddenly and substantially, 'a self-sustaining chain reaction is set off that creates an explosive increase in the amount of crime, addiction, and welfare dependency.'"

On top of this age dynamic lay another factor that continues to bedevil minority communities to this day. Blacks had accumulated in northern cities in the 1960s at the very time that manufacturing jobs, which had long sustained migrant and immigrant populations, had begun to disappear. The nation was embarking on its path to a service-oriented economy that offered far fewer jobs to people without skills or education, and what jobs were available increasingly existed in suburban areas not easily accessible to the inner-city poor.

One of the most intriguing of Wilson's propositions is that since the substantial migration of blacks to inner cities had largely come to an end by 1970, the pathologies occasioned by the transience and youthfulness of the population should have begun to disappear. There is some evidence that this is exactly what occurred, as is shown in Tables 2 and 3. Table 2 shows that rates of overall crime and violent crime climbed steadily for the two decades after 1960. But by the time Ronald Reagan was elected in 1980—before he had a chance to enact his criminal justice agenda in the middle of the decade—crime had begun to decline in the United States. The dropping levels of crime—including violent crime—continued even through the deep recession of 1981–1982. This bears repeating: *Crime was falling at the very time Reagan and Meese were hatching their plan to curtail the rights*

TABLE 2 United States Crime per 100,000 Inhabitants, 1960–2000

Year	*Overall Crime*	*Violent Crime*
1960	1,887.2	160.9
1965	2,449.0	200.2
1970	3,984.5	363.5
1975	5,298.5	487.8
1980	5,950.0	596.6
1985	5,207.1	556.6
1990	5,820.3	731.8
1995	5,274.9	684.5
2000	4,124.8	506.5

Source: U.S. Department of Justice, *Crime in the United States, 1960–2000,* FBI Uniform Crime Report.

of Americans in the name of fighting crime. After 1985, with Reagan's policies clearly in place on the federal level, and replicated on the state level, with the new police state in full flower, crime began a period of increase that would last for the next six years. Then, in the decade after 1990, crime went into a period of decline.

Table 3 shows the percentage of the black male population between the crime-prone ages of age of fifteen and nineteen in five selected cities. (The author used that age group because census data in 1960 and 1970 were not broken down for ages twenty to twenty-four, another crime-prone cohort.) In each of the five cities, the percentage of black males between ages fifteen and nineteen roughly doubled between 1960 and 1980. The percentage then began to decline after 1980, which could help explain the reduction in crime in the first few years of the 1980s. Why crime spiked in the second half of the 1980s while the percentage of young black people continued to decline is explained by the crack epidemic, with its accompanying violence. Once the use of crack waned, crime continued the downward pattern that it had begun in 1980, commensurate with the lower percentage of young people in the black male population. A Justice Department study found that crack use went into decline in New York City beginning in 1990, at almost the same time that crime began to fall.

TABLE 3 Percentage of Black Male Population, Ages 15 to 19, Selected Cities, 1960–2000

City	*1960**	*1970*	*1980*	*1990*	*2000*
New York	6.0	9.6	11.3	8.7	8.6
Los Angeles	5.7	9.0	10.4	7.4	7.3
Chicago	5.8	9.9	11.6	9.6	9.3
Philadelphia	6.6	9.8	11.3	8.1	8.3
Detroit	6.1	10.2	10.1	10.0	8.0

* Census data for 1960 combined blacks, Asians, and other racial groups into the category "nonwhite."

Source: U.S. Census Bureau, Decennial Census, 1960–2000, General Population Characteristics.

And the study's authors also found that the drug began disappearing because its ill effects made it fall out of favor with young people, not because incarceration was a deterrent.

Other factors may also have contributed to the reduction in crime in the 1990s. It was a decade marked by an overall improvement in the social and economic well-being of black Americans. The usual benchmarks of ghetto pathology—poverty, infant mortality, out-of-wedlock births, high school dropout rates, median income, and scores on standardized tests in schools—all showed statistical improvement for black people by the mid-1990s. Whether because of the strong economy, the gains of the civil rights movement finally coming to fruition, or some other dynamic, the socioeconomic status of blacks was rising, and it is not surprising that crime within their communities saw a corresponding decline.

To debunk Reagan's belief that out-of-control crime was due to an overly permissive criminal justice system does not suggest that police strategies don't matter. New York City has achieved its historic reductions in crime at least in part because of two innovations in policing. In 1994, former New York police commissioner William Bratton introduced Gotham to the "broken-windows" theory of policing, which held that crime was bred in an atmosphere of overall disorder in a community and that paying attention to small things like public drinking, noise complaints, and fare beating in subways would help lower the rates of more serious crime. Bratton's second innovation was CompStat, which combined computerized tracking of criminal trends with weekly meetings in which precinct commanders were held accountable for crime spikes in their districts. The program has been replicated in big cities across the country. Neither strategy requires the use of mandatory minimum penalties, the mass incarceration of young black men, or the denial of defendants' rights, although all these also occurred in New York City. Rutgers University professor George Kelling, cooriginator of the "broken-windows" theory and a longtime Bratton adviser, made it clear to the author that he felt no allegiance to the proponents of mass incarceration. In fact, Kelling said he was in favor of having the police tolerate low-key, nonviolent drug sales and instead focus their efforts on drug dealers who engage in violence or otherwise disrupt their communities. "Drugs are part of our culture," said Kelling. "They are going to be available, and they are going to be sold. You have to find ways to manage drug dealing so it doesn't lead to violence and doesn't intimidate neighborhood life."

Reagan's answer to crime in America was to place a huge percentage of one racial minority behind bars. The Sentencing Project, a Washington research group, found in a 1995 study that one in three black males between ages twenty and twenty-nine was either in prison, on probation, or on parole. There can be no doubt that putting such unprecedented numbers of young people behind bars had some impact on crime, even violent crime. Some of the people incarcerated for selling crack on street corners would no doubt have committed violent crimes if they had been on the street.

But what has been the cost of achieving this partial and ephemeral victory over crime? Most of the people locked away for drug crimes eventually return to the community. Indeed, the number of people being released from incarceration—the flip side of the prison-building boom—has been at record highs in recent years. And the people returning to the streets are not prepared for life on the outside. In the post-Reagan era, correctional authorities largely did away with any programs designed to prepare offenders for a law-abiding life after prison. No longer can most inmates take college courses in prison or learn a trade. Incredibly shortsighted politicians dispensed with the entire concept of rehabilitation, seeing it as coddling criminals.

The prison experience has also become far harsher than it was before 1981. Authorities have greatly expanded the use of so-called control units, where inmates suspected of being security threats or being punished for an infraction are locked in solitary confinement for up to twenty-three hours a day and allowed no contact with another human being. Some prisons, such as the notorious Pelican Bay in California, keep every inmate in that status. Since many of the people who end up in these control units already have severe emotional disorders or outright mental illness, the damage to their psyches from such isolation can be extreme, which is why some international human rights groups have deemed the practice a form of torture. And prison authorities are taking away exercise equipment and cutting back on phone calls and family visitation even for those in the general prison population.

So the record numbers of inmates returning to society are doing so without any education, counseling, or job training, many of them deeply angry and psychologically wounded by their experience in prison. Because new public databases make their criminal records available to potential employers, most have difficulty finding work. Federal laws now deny them welfare, public housing, and student loans if they have drug convictions. Most states have recognized prisoner reentry as a major issue facing the nation's big cities. There has been much recent talk of the need for job training, drug treatment, and education programs to help ease them back into society. Should it not be obvious that a little job training, drug treatment, and education on the front end might have obviated the need for incarceration in the first place, at a much lower cost to society?

And then the final irony. The reentry of these angry and ill-equipped young men into society appears to be driving a resurgence in violent crime. City after city has reported an increase in murder rates in recent years, with police blaming a dramatic influx of ex-convicts, many of whom became affiliated with gangs in prison. The city of Newark, where the author spent years as a daily newspaper reporter, provides a vivid example. Newark traditionally was a city without a discernible gang problem. It had violent drug organizations, but no turf gangs like the Bloods and Crips of Los Angeles or the Folk and People of Chicago. But the prison gulag changed all of that. The Bloods gang gained a toehold in the New Jersey prison system in the mid-1990s, having spread from New York's prisons, and by the latter part of the decade had been transported to the streets by released inmates. Newark and other New Jersey cities are now awash in Bloods gangs, and murder rates were steadily climbing in the first few years of the millennium.

Gangs, of course, are just a symptom. The real cause of increasing crime across the country is the failure of Lockdown America. Reagan's answer to dealing with a surplus population of young black men without skills to compete in the global economy was not to train and educate them but to lock them away. But they couldn't be locked away forever. They are returning to the streets as angry and frustrated criminals—in many cases far more dangerous than when they went to prison. Their anger should be our own. Their victimization is potentially our victimization. When the state greatly expands its power to persecute the poor and fills up prisons at a time when crime is falling, and when this happens in America, which Reagan once called "the last, best hope of man on earth," human freedom everywhere is at stake.

CHAPTER 11

The Second-Rate Society

Commerce, luxury, and avarice destroyed every republican government.

—JOHN ADAMS

We are in the midst of a crass and vulgar epoch, proof of the axiom that corruption and decay await all great civilizations. If it is true that republics live or die by their virtue, ours may soon be on life support. The predictions of political commentators that the Age of Reagan has run its course—that a new American Enlightenment is beckoning—is wishful thinking that underestimates the changes his presidency brought to the country. Few portents of such a renewal emerged from the two presidential nominating conventions in the summer of 2008, with their smarmy stagecraft and vague promises of incremental change.

And it is here that we find the most destructive element of the Reagan legacy: America's utter loss of national purpose. National purpose cannot exist when the anarchy of laissez-faire has created a war of all against all. By discrediting government as a legitimate and meaningful presence in the lives of Americans, Reagan repudiated the very concept of national leadership. By exhorting Americans to place self-interest above all, he undermined the spirit of sacrifice and the possibility of a common effort to solve our most pressing national problems.

No great civilization has ever arisen or persevered without forceful national leadership. It was true in the Rome of Caesar Augustus, who boasted on his deathbed, "I found Rome of clay; I leave it to you of marble." It was true of Great Britain, whose national government shepherded the rise of industrial capitalism. And it was undeniably true of the United States of America, whose federal government played a strong role in important phases of the nation's growth—in the laying of the transcontinental railroads, the development of the computer, the fostering of the aviation industry, the launching of the New Deal, and the spearheading of the Marshall Plan. A probusiness Republican like Herbert Hoover not only established the Reconstruction Finance Corporation but sought to rationalize American industry through large trade associations. One of the most luminous of our Founding Fathers, Alexander Hamilton, envisioned the government directing wealth toward its most productive uses. He regarded the idea of a self-regulating economy as a "wild speculative paradox." The list goes on and on. The ending of slavery and the civil rights struggle began as grassroots movements but achieved real success only when the government was compelled to make those struggles its own.

The postwar leaders of the United States—that generation of "tax and spenders" so often derided by the Reaganites—were unafraid to use the resources of the federal government to fulfill the nation's potential. Within months of the Soviet Union's launch of *Sputnik* in 1957, the government poured enormous sums of money into the funding of scientific research, establishing the National Aeronautics and Space Administration in 1959 and landing a man on the moon a decade later. In the same era, the Eisenhower administration began work on the interstate highway system, the largest public works project in the history of the world, eventually encompassing more than forty-six thousand miles of highway.

The Johnson administration took up an even more audacious challenge: the elimination of poverty in the world's wealthiest nation and the founding of a "Great Society" dedicated to social welfare, the arts, the sciences, and the vast expansion of secondary and higher education. The Reaganites mock the campaign against poverty as a failure, as a vindication of the view that government has little ability to make a difference in the lives of the poor. But as Johnson aide Joseph Califano wrote a few years ago, "If there is a prize for the political scam of the 20th century, it should go to the conservatives for propagating as conventional wisdom that the Great Society programs of the 1960s were a misguided and failed social experiment that wasted taxpayers' money."

In fact, the proportion of American families living in poverty in the United States dropped from 17.9 percent in 1963 to 10.9 percent in 1970, the period encompassed by Johnson's Great Society programs. In the early 1960s, few among the poor and elderly had health insurance, but Medicaid and Medicare have brought medical care to hundreds of millions of Americans. Johnson steered federal aid to local school districts for the first time and made higher education possible for millions of poor and working-class students with the help of federal grants and loans. Public broadcasting, funding for the arts, environmental enforcement, Head Start and child nutrition programs, millions of acres of national parks, and the National Institutes of Health are all part of the Great Society legacy.

It is true that Johnson failed to eradicate the ghettos or integrate the black urban poor into mainstream society. The War on Poverty was aborted by America's deepening involvement in Vietnam and negative publicity generated by poorly executed programs like those of the Office of Economic Opportunity. Although many valuable programs remain in place to this day, the aggressive effort by the federal government to combat poverty lasted only a half decade. That is a paltry amount of time to erase the legacy of more than two centuries of racism, to uplift a people that Tocqueville described as "condemned by law and opinion to a hereditary state of degradation and wretchedness." Conservatives make a mockery of an effort that never had time to flower. If some Great Society programs misfired, new strategies should have been developed in their place. "It is common sense to take a method and try it," said Franklin Roosevelt. "If it fails, admit it frankly and try another. But above all, try something."

Reagan's answer was to try nothing. American leaders no longer reach for the moon, set aside parkland, nurture manufacturing, or harness ingenuity and resources to the task of eradicating poverty or rebuilding the cities. We are told, most recently by John McCain, that the federal government must stand aside and let big business shape the nation's destiny. The market will educate the children, the market will care for the poor, and the market will protect the environment. Reagan was unsuccessful in gutting all of the New Deal and Great Society programs—he criticized almost every one of them at one time or another in his career—but he ensured the failure of any proposals in Washington over the next two and a half decades to improve the lives of the poor. He brought down the curtain on the Great Society.

That curtain came down in the first few months of Reagan's presidency, the seminal period in America's decline. His animus toward the public sector was funneled through David Stockman and his little black notebooks. Stockman convinced Congress to accept a reduction of $35 billion in the budget for 1982, including the paring of millions of recipients from the food stamp rolls, a $1-billion cut in Medicaid, the elimination of 107,000 subsidized housing units, and the removal of 400,000 families from welfare rolls and a reduction in benefits for 258,000 others. Opponents of the budget cuts pointed out that the majority of the recipients of the main welfare program, Aid to Families with Dependent Children, were in fact children—as if this would somehow prick the nation's conscience. But children were among the biggest losers in the Reagan budget cuts. The Women, Infants, and Children Program, one of the most effective of the nation's food programs, was cut by nearly a third. Notoriously, the administration obtained cuts in the school lunch program, in part by suggesting that ketchup be classified as a vegetable. Overall, child nutrition programs were cut by 42 percent in Reagan's first budget. The new president quietly pulled the plug on the White House Conference on Children and Youth, a national gathering that had been held in Washington once a decade since 1909. Among other programs that took severe hits in the Reagan budget were funding for the arts and humanities, public broadcasting, and health care, including an end to the federal operation of eight public health service hospitals.

Stockman also sought, and a compliant Congress accepted, reductions in mass-transit funding and development funds for urban and rural areas. Funding for legal services for the poor was eliminated entirely. Unemployment insurance was cut from thirty-nine to twenty-six weeks at a time when unemployment was rising, and the administration slashed funding for college student loans, which Stockman called "middle-class welfare." "Why should some steelworker pay taxes to help his plant manager send his kid to a private school out of state?" he said. Even as it laid the groundwork for the flight of U.S. industry abroad, the administration also ended trade adjustment assistance for workers displaced by foreign competition. Overall, public funding for job training in the United States was halved in the 1980s, going from $13.2 billion to $5.6 billion.

One of the budget cuts that most offended advocates for the poor was the complete elimination of an employment program created under the Comprehensive Employment and Training Act of 1973. CETA had brought seventeen public works programs under one umbrella so state and local governments could use the funds for their most pressing training and employment problems. The program, originally aimed at providing training to the hard-core unemployed, was expanded in 1974 and again in 1977 to include temporary employment of skilled workers who had been laid off from manufacturing jobs. By 1978, CETA was funding 750,000 jobs across the country. But it was also a favorite whipping boy of Ronald Reagan, one he had been flogging before he entered the White House. In a 1978 interview with *U.S. News and World Report,* he made it a prime example of bloated government: "Then you come down to waste: Comprehensive Employment and Training Act funds, for instance. Do we really need—in Eugene, Oregon—a 31-foot cement monolith for rock and mountain climbers to practice on? That is funded with CETA money, which is supposed to be used for training people for future employment."

More responsible critics had indeed faulted the program for drifting from its original intent to train the hardcore unemployed. State and local governments had begun using CETA funds to pay skilled workers that they would have hired anyway. In response to this criticism, the Carter administration tightened eligibility requirements, and by 1980 a larger percentage of recipients were young minorities with little in the way of skills or education. "By and large, the amendments have been quite successful in improving the program," William Mirengoff, who studied the program for the National Academy of Sciences, told the *National Journal.* "The major goal of serving the most needy appears to have been accomplished."

But when more skilled workers were removed from the program, the jobs that were funded were also less useful to communities and had fewer friends in Washington outside the Congressional Black Caucus. "There's just no constituency for the program on Capitol Hill any more," a former congressional aide told the *National Journal.* "Members of Congress get none of the credit for financing the jobs dished out by state and local governments and catch all the blame when abuses are uncovered in the program." In the harsh climate Ronald Reagan brought to Washington, giving jobs to young minorities was not enough. CETA never had a chance and disappeared from the budget by the end of 1981, costing three hundred thousand people their jobs.

Reagan's assault on discretionary spending was not as dramatic as Stockman and other zealots had hoped, nor as some of their opponents claimed. In the first place, only a limited portion of the federal budget was eligible for reduction. Of the $700-billion federal budget in 1982, 48 percent was earmarked for Social Security, pensions, reimbursements to medical providers for the poor, and other entitlements that were immune from reductions. Another 25 percent went to defense spending, which Reagan planned to increase, and 10 percent went to interest on the national debt. That left only 17 percent of the budget for Stockman's axe, and even some of those areas were off-limits because of Reagan's political commitments. Some of the program reductions were restored in later budgets or picked up by state governments, lessening some of the pain for the poor.

But Reagan's broad swipes at the federal budget created a momentum that would last long after he left office. He virtually took Washington out of the business of promoting the welfare of its citizens. No subsequent administration has proposed any serious programs to rebuild the cities, house and educate the poor, or shore up the nation's infrastructure, let alone adopt an industrial policy.

In July 1981, just as Reagan was in the process of decimating CETA and other job-training programs, *Time* magazine published a major article on the shortage of skilled labor that threatened the nation's economic well being. "At a time when one in 13 U.S. workers is unemployed, jobs by the hundreds of thousands in many of the economy's most vital sectors are going begging for the lack of trained people," the article said. A machinist union president feared that the United States was "in danger of becoming a nation of industrial illiterates who do not know how to a stop a running toilet, replace a burned-out fuse or identify anything on a car more complicated than the gas-tank cap." A federal program to train workers to manufacture machine tools or service aircraft engines would not seem beyond the capability of a government that put a man on the moon, but no one in Washington was in the mood for such a program. Said Dan Quayle, then chairman of the Senate Subcommittee on Employment and Productivity, "The more that government gets involved in training, the worse the problem gets."

And what happens when the government doesn't get involved? The answer to that question can be found in places like Newark, New Jersey. Newark has long been in decline, beginning with the disappearance of its heavy industry, the white flight of the 1950s, the riots of the 1960s, and the state takeover of its schools in the 1990s. But one trend stands out above all: Newark's young people are dying at an alarming rate.

The gang warfare that has consumed Newark in recent years has confounded local criminologists. For much of the last decade, the city saw a steady decline in burglaries, robberies, larcenies, auto thefts, and even nonfatal shootings. And yet homicide continued to rise. It is a baffling phenomenon: murder as a discrete social malady, disembodied from every other criminal trend. Law enforcement experts seek to explain this anomaly, which has also occurred in other cities, by pointing to gangs, the easy availability of handguns, and the incitements of gangster rap. Each may have its place in the equation, but the real impetus for murder in Newark is hopelessness.

Young people kill each other in Newark because they simply have no expectation of a future. They have grown up in families shattered by generations of joblessness, their fathers absent and their mothers defeated. Too many have suffered physical and emotional abuse, undetected or poorly addressed by an overburdened child welfare system. Newark's children are isolated from mainstream society by what Jonathan Kozol has called the "restoration of apartheid schooling in America." Their peers on the street become their substitute families and violence their rituals. They fly the colors of the Bloods and Crips and don't fear the consequences of murder because they expect to follow their street-corner idols into a prison cell.

Nothing about Newark is unique; the same lessons that arise so brutally from its streets can also be found in Detroit, Baltimore, New Orleans, Gary, Flint, East St. Louis, and scores of other communities forgotten by our national leaders. But in Newark the lessons are especially poignant in that they fester literally within sight of the towers of Wall Street. While hundreds of billions of dollars have been amassed in the great financial houses in the past two decades, and hundreds of billions more have disappeared in market meltdowns; while the federal government has spent billions subsidizing and bailing out the kingpins of finance; while bought-and-paid-for legislators have labored into the night to do the bidding of the rich, the vast majority of America's cities—once the lifeblood of the nation—have been allowed to degenerate into maelstroms of despair.

From their birth in the Neolithic world, through their flowering in Athens and Rome, to the emergence of the great metropolises of London, Paris, Berlin, New York, cities have been the progenitors of all that is grand and sublime in our world, great throbbing centers of life that—as Lewis Mumford once wrote—"convert power into form, energy into culture, dead matter into the living symbols of art, biological reproduction into social creativity." What will history say of Reaganism, the political movement that rid public policy of all efforts to preserve these centers of culture and consigned so many of their citizens to the bleakest of human environments? What kind of future can we expect from a nation where millions of residents live in communities devoid of sound education or meaningful economic activity, known to the rest of the citizens only as crime stories on the evening news?

It is easy to misunderstand the crisis facing urban America if the world is viewed solely from the gentrified neighborhoods of Chicago, Philadelphia, Boston, San Francisco, Seattle, and other fashionable cities. The centers of those cities have become the playgrounds of the affluent, peopled with young professionals at home in art galleries and trendy bars and restaurants but without any social or cultural links to the poor and working-class neighborhoods that house the bulk of those cities' population. Far more typical of America's urban landscape are the battered old mill towns of the Northeast and Midwest, whose rooftops and faded skylines Americans see only from the interstates, tableaus of poverty, ignorance, and social isolation that make a mockery of our pretensions of prosperity. It is these communities that adherents of Reaganism suggest are better off left to their own devices, as if the ghettoes and gang warfare and abused children will not one day be viewed the way we now see slavery or child labor—as emblems of America's barbaric past.

The Age of Reagan will not be erased by empty promises of change followed by business as usual. It will have passed only when our leaders regain a sense of national purpose and contemplate real public investment in science, infrastructure, education, and job training—investment in the people of America. Human investment means not just education and health care but also increases in the minimum wage and government strategies to promote unionization in the service and manufacturing sectors.

It seems vaguely utopian to speak in such terms, but that only shows how far Reagan pushed the country to the right. Not long ago these were the enunciated policies of the federal government, fully accepted by *centrist* politicians, not just those on the left. Reagan's demagoguery was so skillful that these policies were virtually banished from public life.

Their exile was wholly unwarranted. Countless researchers, Robert Reich among them, have made sound arguments for public investment as a way to help the United States attract high-paying, white-collar jobs in the global economy, but less attention has been paid to the need for public employment of the unskilled and semiskilled. No one has to be a fan of welfare handouts to accept the wisdom that public works projects have a better chance of stimulating the economy and bringing relief to economically depressed areas than financial deregulation and tax cuts for the rich. The image of the layabout leaning on a shovel while taking home the taxpayers' money every week is galling to some, but is it really a greater evil than tax shelters for the earnings of hedge fund billionaires?

William Julius Wilson has amassed evidence that chronic unemployment, not welfare, is the principal force behind the disintegration of ghetto families—the joblessness stemming from the disappearance of manufacturing. Paying people high wages in public works projects would not only stimulate the economy, and heal families by boosting the self-esteem of inner-city parents, but also help rebuild America's neglected infrastructure.

In 2008 testimony before a House subcommittee studying economic inequality, Jared Bernstein, a senior economist at the pro-labor Economic Policy Institute, noted that his researchers had identified a backlog of thousands of infrastructure projects that could quickly be implemented upon passage of an economic stimulus package. The researchers identified three thousand state highway projects, totaling $18 billion, ready to lift off within thirty days of being funded, and 772 communities in thirty-three states with a total of 9,471 combined-sewer overflow problems that were spewing an estimated 850 billion gallons of sewage into waterways every year. Also on the list were six thousand structurally deficient bridges and the deferred maintenance of 76 percent of the nation's school buildings.

America's restoration, including a reversal of widening income disparity, may still be within our powers, if we accept—as a first step—

that something went horribly wrong on election day in 1980, the day our country was turned over to mean-spirited religious zealots, thinly veiled racists, law-and-order extremists, warmongers, and a class of people shamefully willing to act as handmaidens of the wealthy at the expense of the ordinary citizen. The loudmouths in this brigade, the conservative talk-show hosts and Fox News commentators, ridicule "experts" and "professors" and the "scientific elite," as if they want to tear down all the pillars of our once-great civilization.

They were all there at the 2008 Republican National Convention, at their ignorant and mean-spirited best, mocking Barack Obama for being a "community organizer" and offering nothing in the way of policy prescriptions except repeated cries for offshore oil drilling and victory in Iraq. They couldn't talk about education because John McCain's plan was to allocate no new money for schools. They couldn't talk about rebuilding infrastructure because they had no such intention. No vision. No sense of national purpose. They are content with what the world saw in our response to Hurricane Katrina, in our subprime mortgage scandal, in our continuing blindness and bungling in the war in Iraq and the war on terror—an increasingly second-rate society.

They pretended to be running against the party in power, but it was their own party, which McCain had the temerity to call "the party of Lincoln, Roosevelt, and Reagan." By his side was the most cynical and irresponsible choice for vice president in the history of the republic, the ethically challenged Christian ideologue who introduced herself to the nation by arrogantly mocking the press for daring to examine her past. As she did so, the crowd roared and the celebrity-loving press anointed her a star. But with the historic victory of President Barack Obama, the star has fallen and the smirk has been wiped off her face. At long last, we may dare to hope that the retrograde politics of John McCain, Sarah Palin, and their legions of followers in the cultural backwaters of America—the pandering and the shallowness and the contempt for progress that oozed forth from the convention stage—was the last hoarse utterance of Reaganism.

ACKNOWLEDGMENTS

This book could not have been written without the excellent reporting by hundreds of my colleagues in newspapers, wire services, and magazines who chronicled Ronald Reagan's years in the White House. At a time when aggressive reporting on public affairs is threatened by the decline of the American newspaper, I can only hope that such a resource will be available to authors in the future. I also wish to extend my gratitude to a number of people who gave their support to this project. Howard Zinn, my former professor at Boston University and an inspiration to progressives around the world, and the late New Jersey congressman Peter Rodino, who both agreed to read and comment on early drafts of this manuscript even though I was a complete stranger to them. Leo Diehl, the former chief of staff to House Speaker Tip O'Neill, and the Speaker's son, Thomas P. O'Neill III, were extremely helpful in their recollections of the Reagan years.

Several of my colleagues at the Newark *Star-Ledger*, Steve Chambers, John Hassell, Tom Moran, Guy Sterling, and Russell Ben-Ali, read portions of the manuscript and gave me valuable advice, and Christine Baird, the editor of news research at the paper, helped me more than she probably realizes. Invaluable support, and research assistance, came from Michael Dunn and Charles Granoff, friends and comrades for thirty years, and my fellow journalist Padraic Cassidy has been e-mailing me minutiae about Reagan's legacy for more years than I can remember.

I would like to thank Carl Bromley, the editorial director of Nation Books; John Sherer, the publisher of Basic Books; and my agent, Gail Ross, for recognizing the importance of this book and shepherding it into print. There are not enough people like them in the publishing industry. My thanks also go to Margaret Ritchie for excellent copy editing.

Finally, I would like to express my gratitude to my wife, Margarita, our son, Christopher, and our daughter, Danica, for all their love, support, and *patience* in the years I was engrossed in the writing of this book.

NOTES

INTRODUCTION

ix **"The cataclysm has happened":** D. H. Lawrence, *Lady Chatterley's Lover* (New York: Penguin Classics, 1994), 5.

x **"I am a conservative Republican":** John McCain, *Meet the Press,* NBC, November 12, 2006.

x **"I took the exact same path":** Lou Cannon and Carl M. Cannon, *Reagan's Disciple: George W. Bush's Troubled Quest for a Presidential Legacy* (New York: PublicAffairs, 2008), 322–323.

x **"embodied the idea that":** Karen Tumulty, "How the Right Went Wrong," *Time,* March 26, 2007, 26.

x **"the greatest living American":** Joshua Green, "Reagan's Liberal Legacy: What the New Literature on the Gipper Won't Tell You," *Washington Monthly,* January 1, 2003.

x **most popular former president:** "Poll Names America's Best Presidents," *Associated Press Online,* February 19, 2001, http://w3.nexis.com/new/results/docview/docview.do?docLinkInd=true&risb=21_T4765983105&format=GNBFI&sort=BOOLEAN&startDocNo=1&resultsUrlKey=29_T4765983108&cisb=22_T4765983107&treeMax=true&treeWidth=0&csi=147876&docNo=3. Reagan usually finishes near the top in the annual Gallup polls. In 2008, he was a close second to John F. Kennedy.

xiii **"Ronald Reagan rode in":** John Hockenberry, *Dateline NBC,* June 5, 2004, http://w3.nexis.com/new/results/docview/docview.do?docLinkInd=true&risb=21_T4781454988&format=GNBFI&sort=BOOLEAN&startDocNo=1&resultsUrlKey=29_T4781454991&cisb=22_T4781454990&treeMax=true&treeWidth=0&csi=157446&docNo=1.

xiv **"Reagan was Illinois come to California":** Lou Cannon, *President Reagan: The Role of a Lifetime* (New York: PublicAffairs, 2000), 23.

xiv **An exhaustive survey of wealth:** Lawrence Mishel, Jared Bernstein, and John Schmitt, *The State of Working America, 2000–2001,* biannual report of the Economic Policy Institute (Ithaca, N.Y.: Cornell University Press, 2001), 257–261.

xv **new census figures in May 2002:** U.S. Census Bureau, *Profile of Selected Economic Characteristics: 2000* (Washington, D.C.: U.S. Government Printing Office, 2002).

xv **Newspapers across the country:** Sue Kirchhoff and Bill Dedman, "90s Boom Bypassed Many Mass. Regions, Census Shows," *Boston Globe,* May 22, 2002; Paul Zielbauer, "In Much of Connecticut, Go-Go 90's Went Nowhere, Data Show," *New York Times,* May 22, 2002; Janny Scott, "Census Finds Rising Tide, and Many Who Missed Boat," *New York Times,* June 17, 2002.

xvi **While 52 percent of Americans:** Mishel, Bernstein, and Schmitt, *State of Working America,* 266–270.

xvii **And this is what they found:** Michael L. Dertouzos, Richard K. Lester, Robert M. Solow, and the MIT Commission on Industrial Productivity, *Made in America: Regaining the Productive Edge* (New York: HarperPerennial, paperback edition, 1990).

xviii **"Only an extraordinary optimist":** Ibid., 39.

xviii **the portion of national income invested:** Benjamin M. Friedman, *Day of Reckoning: The Consequences of American Economic Policy under Reagan and After* (New York: Random House, 1988), 28–29.

xix **"a people's capitalism":** Max Lerner, *America as a Civilization,* vol. 1 (New York: Simon & Schuster, 1963), 267.

xix **The historian Howard Zinn has noted:** E-mail to the author by Howard Zinn, December 5, 2004.

xx **"You want the ordinary man":** José Ortega y Gasset, *The Revolt of the Masses* (New York: W. W. Norton, 1932), 16–17.

xxi **"war of all against all":** Christopher Lasch, *The Culture of Narcissism: American Life in an Age of Diminishing Expectations* (New York: Warner Books, 1979).

xxii **"In a nation that was proud":** Jimmy Carter, Address to the Nation on Energy and National Goals ("The Malaise Speech"), *July 15, 1979, American Presidency Project,* http://www.presidency.ucsb.edu/ws/index.php?pid=32596&st=Address+to+the+Nation+on+Energy+and+National+Goals&st1=.

xxii **"Ask not what your country":** John F. Kennedy, Inaugural Address, January 20, 1961, American Presidency Project, http://www.presidency.ucsb.edu/ws/index.php?pid=8032&st=Ask+Not+What+Your+Country&st1=.

xxii **"Are you better off":** One such moment was in the presidential debate in Cleveland on October 28, 1980, American Presidency Project, http://www.presidency.ucsb.edu/ws/index.php?pid=29408&st=Are+you+better+off+than&st1=.

xxiii **"dependence effect":** John Kenneth Galbraith, *The Affluent Society*, 3rd ed. (Boston: Houghton Mifflin, 1976), 126.

xxv **"With individuals . . . natural strength":** Thomas Carlyle, *The Works of Thomas Carlyle* (London: Chapman & Hall, 1899), 61.

xxvi **"a great national illusion":** Robert L. Heilbroner, *An Inquiry into the Human Prospect* (New York: W. W. Norton, 1980), 7.

xxvi **"The true," wrote William James:** Alfonso Morales, *Renascent Pragmatism: Studies in Law and Social Science* (Hampshire, UK: Ashgate Publishing, 2003), xv.

xxvi **"To believe your own thought":** Ralph Waldo Emerson, *Essays* (Philadelphia: Henry Altemus, 1895), 43.

xvii **"gray spirit of compromise":** Cited in James T. Kloppenberg, *Uncertain Victory: Social Democracy and Progressivism in European and American Thought, 1870–1920* (New York: Oxford University Press, 1986), 413.

CHAPTER 1: FORGOTTEN ROOTS

1 **It was as if the entire city:** Descriptions of the election day celebrations come from the *Dixon Evening Telegraph*, November 4–10, 1980.

2 **The city's median family income:** Comparisons of median family income and percentages of college graduates in Dixon are from the U.S. Census, 1970 and 1980; U.S. Census Bureau, *1970 Census of Population* (Washington, D.C.: U.S. Government Printing Office, 1972).

3 **the real assets of farmers:** Susan DeMarco, "A Fresh Crop of Ideas: State Sows the Seeds of a New Agriculture," *The Progressive*, January 1989, 26–31.

3 **"quagmire of federal farm programs":** Ronald Reagan, Radio Address to the Nation on the Farm Industry, August 17, 1985, *American Presidency Project*, http://www.presidency.ucsb.edu/ws/index.php?pid=39004&st=&st1=.

4 **carried the aroma of opportunism:** Anne Edwards, *Early Reagan: The Rise to Power* (New York: William Morrow, 1987), 1–13, 410–411; Edwards describes the motivations behind both the 1941 and the 1950 visits.

5 **the Dukes were not invited:** "Dixon HS Band Excluded from Reagan's Inauguration," United Press International, December 13, 1980.

5 **"We're concentrating entirely on television":** Lynn Rosellini, "A Preview of the Reagan Inauguration," *New York Times*, December 10, 1980.

6 **forced the closing of the center:** Steve Huntley, "How Reagan Rates Now in His Hometown, *U.S. News and World Report*, September 20, 1982, 22; "Budget Cuts to Hit Reagan's Hometown Hard, Union Official Says," Associated Press, March 16, 1981.

6 **"I deeply regret the problems":** "Reagan's Hometown Voters Give Boost to School Athletics," Associated Press, February 27, 1985; Leon Daniel, "President Running Strong In Hometown," United Press International, November 4, 1984.

6 **financial struggle continues to this day:** Author interview with James Brown, Dixon school superintendent, March 22, 2006.

7 **"Every time I look":** Laurent Belsie, "Small US Steel Mills Show Glimmer of Vitality, but Import Threat Looms Large," *Christian Science Monitor*, June 26, 1984.

7 **running at 40 percent capacity:** Harry Anderson, "Getting Tough on Steel," *Newsweek*, November 1, 1982, 71.

8 **half the company's operations:** Robert B. Reich, *The Next American Frontier: A Provocative Program for Economic Renewal* (New York: Penguin Books, 1983), 183.

9 **$170-million government-guaranteed loan:** Gayle Worland, "Tumble of the Steel Industry," *Rockford (IL) Register Star*, January 7, 2002.

9 **"We are going to feel this":** Todd Welvaert, "Steel Mill's Closing Ripples through Area," *Dispatch-Argus* (Davenport, Iowa).

9 **The local carpenters' union reported in 1982:** Huntley, "How Reagan Rates."

9 **"Reagan's forgotten where he came from":** Daniel, "President Running Strong."

10 **"He's no buddy of mine":** John Dowling, "Hometown Folks Still Back Reagan—But with Reservations," Associated Press, January 19, 1983.

10 **"The answer to our farm problems":** Reagan, Radio Address to the Nation on the Farm Industry, August 17, 1985.

11 **benefit not of the small farmer:** Jay Walljasper, "Farmers and the Left: A Little Cell on the Prairie," *The Nation,* October 25, 1986, 402.

11 **Corn, which at that time cost:** Ibid.

11 **The farm bill failed miserably:** Randolph Nodland, "Farm Programs: A Back-to-the-Future Road to Reform," *Chicago Tribune,* July 9, 1990; Nancy Dunne, "U.S. Aims to Build on Success of Agricultural Policy," *Financial Times,* July 28, 1989; Don Kendall, "Spending on Corn Price Supports Adding Up," Associated Press, July 25, 1989.

11 **Food processing and wholesaling became:** Randolph Nodland, "Design Farm Bill to Aid Family Farms," *St. Louis Post-Dispatch*, July 13, 1990.

12 **increased its profits by 66 percent:** "Company Notes: Cargill Profits," *New York Times,* February 28, 1987.

13 **Rural development programs:** Dennis Roth, Anne B. W. Effland, and Douglas E. Bowers, *Federal Rural Development Policy in the Twentieth Century* (U.S. Department of Agriculture, Economic Research Service, 2002).

13 **"He agreed to accept the post":** "Reagan Hometown Offers Bounty to Lure Business," Associated Press, December 14, 1984.

14 **But none of that opulence:** Median family income figures are from the U.S. Census, 1980, 1990, and 2000; U.S. Census Bureau, *Decennial Census* (Washington, D.C.: U.S. Government Printing Office, 1982, 1992, 2002).

15 **One company that utilizes:** Judy Newman, "Tale of 2 Cities and 2 Factories," *Wisconsin State Journal,* June 22, 2003.

16 **"the hard pills to swallow":** Author interview with Jim Thompson, March 21, 2006.

16 **The portion of Dixon's adults:** U.S. Census Bureau, *Decennial Census.*

17 **state and federal aid to Dixon's schools:** Figures provided by Dixon school superintendent Robert Brown, March-April 2006.

17 **"We are in a world economy":** Author interview with Robert Brown, March 22, 2006.

18 **"Then you've got the haves":** Ibid.

19 **"We're talking about work":** Flynn McRoberts, "Reagan Home Is a Historic Site: Now Bill Comes Due," *Chicago Tribune,* February 7, 2002; Tim Ruzek, "Transfer of Reagan Home in Question: Foundation Unhappy with Interior's Offer," *Washington Post,* January 27, 2003.

CHAPTER 2: TWO VIEWS OF AMERICA

23 **"the ultimate presidential commodity":** Mark Hertsgaard, *On Bended Knee: The Press and the Reagan Presidency* (New York: Schocken Books, 1988), 6.

23 **Eisenhower kept an advertising firm:** Joe McGinniss, *The Selling of the President 1968* (New York: Trident Press, 1969), 27.

24 **"Politics boiled down to one thing":** Thomas P. O'Neill Jr., *Man of the House: The Life and Political Memoirs of Speaker Tip O'Neill* (New York: Random House, 1987), 11.

26 **"dismays the humble man":** Diane Ravitch, *The American Reader: Words That Moved a Nation* (New York: HarperCollins, 2000), 392.

26 **"not whether we add more":** Franklin D. Roosevelt, Second Inaugural Address, January 20, 1937, Avalon Project, Yale Law School, http://avalon.law.yale.edu/20th_century/froos2.asp.

26 **"One man in three":** Frederick Lewis Allen, *Since Yesterday: 1929–1939* (New York: Harper & Row, 1940), 128.

27 **"Without this sustained tradition":** Richard Hofstadter, *The Age of Reform: From Bryan to F.D.R.* (New York: Vintage Books, 1955), 18.

28 **"had considerable information that people":** Associated Press transcript of remarks, *New York Times,* December 15, 1983.

28 **"the welfare queen":** Lou Cannon, *President Reagan: The Role of a Lifetime* (New York: PublicAffairs, 2000), 457.

28 **"Substantial parts of it":** "Mr. Reagan's War on Poverty," *New York Times,* October 2, 1981.

29 **Reagan proposed a $7.2-billion:** *Annual Survey of Corporate Taxpayers and Corporate Freeloaders* (Washington, D.C.: Citizens for Tax Justice, October 1989).

29 **By 1983 the portion of federal tax receipts:** Kevin Phillips, *The Politics of Rich and Poor: Wealth and the American Electorate in the Reagan Aftermath* (New York: Random House, 1990), 78.

29 **"Voodoo economics, George":** O'Neill, *Man of the House,* 341.

30 **"Max said, 'Reagan's gonna be our next nominee'":** Author interview with Leo Diehl, former chief of staff to Tip O'Neill, July 6, 2000.

31 **so many negative letters:** Ibid.

31 **"Leave the president alone":** O'Neill, *Man of the House,* 351.

32 **"Tip is reeling":** Robert Ajemian, "Tip O'Neill on the Ropes: The Failed Strategy of an Out-of-Touch Leader," *Time,* May 18, 1981, 17.

32 **"too proud to quit":** Ibid.

32 **"He was very pointed":** Author interview with Thomas P. O'Neill III, July 7, 2000.

33 **"I can read Congresses":** Martin Tolchin, "It's Reagan's Strong Suit against the Odds," *New York Times,* May 3, 1981.

34 **"The Reagan Revolution is over":** Peter Osterlund, "Democrats Not Planning Senate Revolt, *Christian Science Monitor,* November 6, 1986.

35 **"Don't give me that crap":** O'Neill, *Man of the House,* 362.

36 **"tall and austere":** John A. Farrell, *Tip O'Neill and the Democratic Century* (Boston: Back Bay, 2002), 35.

36 **"Even Jimmy Carter got to know":** O'Neill III interview.

36 **"one of those rare Huck Finn–Tom Sawyer":** Ronald Reagan and Richard G. Hubler, *Where's the Rest of Me?* (New York: Duell, Sloan & Pearce, 1965), 13.

37 **"The New Deal bailed":** Garry Wills, *Reagan's America: Innocents at Home* (Garden City, N.Y.: Doubleday, 1987), 63.

37 **play alone with lead soldiers:** Cannon, *President Reagan,* 178.

37 **no lifelong friends:** Ibid., 141, 143.

37 **little access to Reagan:** Edmund Morris, *Dutch: A Memoir of Ronald Reagan* (New York: Random House, 1999), 638.

38 **"His charm was overwhelming":** Anne Edwards, *Early Reagan: The Rise to Power* (New York: William Morrow, 1987), 66.

38 **"He had an inability to distinguish":** Morris, *Dutch,* 121.

39 **"I discovered that night":** Reagan and Hubler, *Where's the Rest of Me?* 28.

40 **"always had the feeling that I was with him":** Haynes Johnson, *Sleepwalking through History: America in the Reagan Years* (New York: W. W. Norton, 2003), 42.

40 **"There were two things about Ronnie":** Edwards, *Early Reagan,* 398.

40 **joined HICCASP's board:** Wills, *Reagan's America,* 290–293.

41 **a clip from the *People's World:*** Ibid., 292–293.

41 **"near hopeless hemophiliac liberal":** Reagan and Hubler, *Where's the Rest of Me?* 139–141.

41 **"Well, sir, I found myself":** Ibid., 167.

42 **became an FBI informant:** Ibid., 170; Wills, *Reagan's America,* 293; Edwards, *Early Reagan,* 305.

43 **"he has been made a member":** Wills, *Reagan's America,* 301; Wills cites the Reagan FBI File, Office Memorandum of November 14, 1947, LA 100-138754-314.

43 **"I think of people now":** Ibid., 307.

44 **to buy Reagan's ranch:** "Film Company Paid the Candidate a Steep Price for Some Steep Land to Make Him a Millionaire," *Wall Street Journal,* August 1, 1980; Wills, *Reagan's America,* 320; Dan E. Moldea and Jeff Goldberg, "The Deal's the Thing," *Los Angeles Reader,* November 2, 1984.

46 **a major player in the Republican Party:** Edwards, *Early Reagan,* 488–489.

46 **"The night we first met":** James Barron, "Justin Dart, the Industrialist and Friend of Reagan, Dies," *New York Times,* January 27, 1984.

46 **Williams said Reagan acknowledged for the first time:** Edwards, *Early Reagan,* 197.

47 **Reagan found his finances suddenly precarious:** Cannon, *President Reagan,* 69.

47 **"So we all quit working":** David A. Stockman, *The Triumph of Politics: How the Reagan Revolution Failed* (New York: Harper & Row, 1986), 10.

48 **"the time we came up with":** Reagan and Hubler, *Where's the Rest of Me?* 256.

48 **"I was seeing how government":** Ronald Reagan, *Ronald Reagan: An American Life* (New York: Simon & Schuster, 1990), 128.

50 **"big-issues guy":** Edwards, *Early Reagan,* 488.

50 **"After the speech, we were swamped":** Lou Cannon, *Ronnie and Jesse: A Political Odyssey* (New York: Doubleday, 1969), 72.

51 **"They were rich, but":** Sidney Blumenthal, *The Rise of the Counter-Establishment: From Conservative Ideology to Political* Power (New York: Times Books, 1986), 62.

CHAPTER 3: THE INVASION

53 **The banner of free enterprise:** Descriptions are culled from the inaugural coverage of daily newspapers and newsweeklies, most notably the *New York Times* and the *Washington Post.*

55 **"A gala celebration":** Jerry Adler, "Hitting the Ground Dancing," *Newsweek,* February 2, 1981, 55.

55 **Nancy Reagan's inaugural wardrobe:** Nina Hyde, "Nancy Reagan's $25,000 Designer Wardrobe," *Washington Post,* January 19, 1981.

55 **"hotel coat racks like giant furry beasts":** Elisabeth Bumiller, "The Inaugural Weekend: The Furs! The Food! The Clout!" *Washington Post,* January 19, 1981.

55 **"Ostentatious," growled Barry Goldwater:** Mary Battiata, "The Republicans Hit the Receiving Line, Running," *Washington Post,* January 19, 1981.

56 **"as blatant a presidential conflict":** Robert Parry and Ann Blackman, "Private Donations May Cost Government More Than Federal Stipend," Associated Press, March 27, 1981.

56 **Regan attended twenty-eight social functions:** Lynn Rosellini, "Reagan Aides Show Capital Luxury Style," *New York Times,* April 16, 1981.

57 **"During the Depression":** Ibid.

57 **"torch had been passed to a new generation":** John F. Kennedy, Inaugural Address, January 20, 1961, American Presidency Project, http://www.presidency.ucsb.edu/ws/index.php?pid=8032&st=Ask+Not+What+Your+Country&st1=.

58 **"It's getting a little tiresome":** John Duka, "A New Opulence Triumphs in Capital," *New York Times,* January 22, 1981.

60 **a colossal fund-raising effort:** Thomas B. Edsall, "Reagan Campaign Gearing Up Its 'Soft Money' Machine for '84," *Washington Post,* November 27, 1983; Maxwell Glen, "Republicans and Democrats Battling to Raise Big Bucks for Voter Drives," *National Journal,* September 1, 1984, 1618.

61 **"Instead of playing golf":** Jason DeParle, "The First Primary," *New York Times Magazine,* April 16, 1995, 29.

62 **vast majority of Washington's regulatory agencies:** Ronald Brownstein and Nina Easton, *Reagan's Ruling Class: Portraits of the President's Top One Hundred Officials* (Washington, D.C.: Presidential Accountability Group, 1982).

63 **"Good faith bargaining simply means":** Ibid., 277.

63 **Auchter Company had had forty-eight safety violations:** Susanna McBee, "When Outsiders Take Over the Bureaucracy," *U.S. News and World Report,* July 13, 1981, 37.

63 **"Reagan didn't say many of the things":** Frank W. Slusser, "Stocks Plunge in Disappointment over Reagan's Inaugural Speech," United Press International, January 20, 1981.

66 **"aligning himself with Jerry Falwell":** David A. Stockman, *The Triumph of Politics: Why the Reagan Revolution Failed* (New York: Harper & Row, 1986), 49–50.

67 **"I was alarmed":** Jude Wanniski, "With Reagan in January 1980," *Polyconomics,* October 6, 1999, http://www.polyconomics.com/memos/mm-991006.htm.

67 **"an across the board reduction in tax rates":** Ronald Brownstein and Nina Easton, *Reagan's Ruling Class: Portraits of the President's Top One Hundred Officials* (Washington, D.C.: Presidential Accountability Group, 1982), 8.

68 **"based on a Carter debate staff":** Martin Schram, "Reagan Ex-Aide Names 2 Sources of Carter Memo," *Washington Post,* July 17, 1983.

69 **"Like the Confederacy":** Sidney Blumenthal, *The Rise of the Counter-Establishment: From Conservative Ideology to Political* Power (New York: Times Books, 1986), 85.

69 **"That was red meat":** Author interview with Wayne Valis, May 14, 2004.

69 **"would come at us like a battalion":** Stockman, *Triumph of Politics,* 248.

69 **"Jim Baker would call":** Valis interview.

70 **"I used to walk into the congressional offices":** Ibid.

CHAPTER 4: YEAR ZERO

74 **study by the Federal Trade Commission:** John Kenneth Galbraith, *American Capitalism: The Concept of Countervailing Power* (Boston: Houghton Mifflin, 1956), 38.

74 **"An economy where the typical industry":** Ibid., 36–37.

75 **"There was nothing natural":** Karl Polanyi, *The Great Transformation: The Political and Economic Origins of Our Time* (Boston: Beacon Press, 1944), 136–139.

76 **"Ames, you take hold of this":** Stephen E. Ambrose, *Nothing Like It in the World: The Men Who Built the Transcontinental Railroad, 1863–1869* (New York: Simon & Schuster, 2000), 132.

76 **An Interior Department auditor found:** Ibid., 377.

76 **The proposal would have gone nowhere:** Scott McCartney, *ENIAC: The Triumphs and Tragedies of the World's First Computer* (New York: Walker, 1999), 52–61.

78 **"New York apartment houses":** Samuel Eliot Morison, *The Oxford History of the American People* (New York: Oxford University Press, 1965), 944.

78 **"People will work harder":** Ibid., 945–946.

80 **"countervailing power has become":** Galbraith, *American Capitalism,* 136.

81 **"utterly destroyed by American indifference":** Brooks is quoted in Frederick Lewis Allen, *The Big Change: American Transforms Itself, 1900–1950* (New York: Harper & Brothers, 1952), 5.

82 **a time when Andrew Carnegie:** Ibid., 27.

82 **"The state," wrote Richard Hofstadter:** Richard Hofstadter, *The Age of Reform: From Bryan to F.D.R.* (New York: Vintage Books, 1955), 234.

82 **"the widest distribution of prosperity":** Allen, *Big Change,* 6.

83 **some two-thirds of the U.S. economy:** Robert Kuttner, *Everything for Sale: The Virtues and Limits of Markets* (Chicago: University of Chicago Press, 1996), 225.

83 **called for the outright abolishment:** Ibid., 232.

83 **"Every time an American dials":** Jack Newfield and Jeff Greenfield, *A Populist Manifesto: The Making of a New Majority* (New York: Warner Paperback Library, 1972), 75.

83 **the "vital center":** Arthur M. Schlesinger Jr., *The Vital Center: The Politics of Freedom* (Boulder, Colo.: Westview Press, 1982).

84 **"This is a moment for which":** Alex Brummer, "Six Men in Kuwait Detonated an Oil Price Explosion 25 Years Ago That Gave the World Monetarism and an Inflation Obsession," *The Guardian,* October 17, 1998.

85 **The first faint rumblings:** Allen J. Matusow, *The Unraveling of America: A History of Liberalism in the 1960s* (New York: Harper Torchbooks, 1984), 161.

85 **But on top of all this:** Ibid., 159–161.

85 **The annual spending on the Vietnam War:** Douglas Brinkley, "The Stain of Vietnam: Robert McNamara, Redemption Denied," *Foreign Affairs,* Summer 1993, 190.

86 **To make sure he would not:** Michael Harrington, *Decade of Decision: The Crisis of the American System* (New York: Simon & Schuster, 1980), 47–48.

86 **"The Watergate affair was shocking":** Ibid., 47.

88 **"Those of us who were":** Milton Friedman, *Capitalism and Freedom* (Chicago: University of Chicago Press, 2002), xi.

88 **Among the government programs:** Ibid., 35–36.

89 **"The fact is that the Great Depression":** Ibid., 38.

89 **The about-face embittered Friedman:** Sidney Blumenthal, *The Rise of the Counter-Establishment: From Conservative Ideology to Political* Power (New York: Times Books, 1986), 109–111.

90 **The Code of Federal Regulations doubled:** Lou Cannon, *President Reagan: The Role of a Lifetime* (New York: PublicAffairs, 2000), 820.

91 **"The danger had suddenly escalated":** Thomas Byrne Edsall, *The New Politics of Inequality* (New York: W. W. Norton, 1984), 113–114.

91 **By the 1970s, what had once been:** Blumenthal, *Rise of the Counter-Establishment,* 35–42.

92 **In the late 1970s, Dow Chemical Company assembled:** Susan J. Tolchin and Martin Tolchin, *Dismantling America: The Rush to Deregulate* (Boston: Houghton Mifflin, 1983), 6.

92 **blaming government regulation for curtailing:** Timothy B. Clark, "The Costs and Benefits of Regulation—Who Knows How Great They Really Are?" *National Journal,* December 1, 1979, 2023.

92 **Business groups seized on the estimate:** Ibid.

92 **"one of the most widely accepted estimates":** Mark Green, "The Trouble with Murray: Weidenbaum's Figures Are 'Largely Conjectural,'" *Washington Post,* January 21, 1979.

92 **The estimate was based on:** Clark, "Costs and Benefits," 2023.

93 **Weidenbaum's estimate of $666:** Green, "Trouble with Murray."

93 **A 1976 survey of automakers:** Ibid.

93 **hired the Arthur Andersen accounting firm:** Clark, "Costs and Benefits."

93 **assessment of Weidenbaum's study:** Green, "Trouble with Murray."

93 **the Congressional Research Service found:** Clark, "Costs and Benefits."

93 **"His emphasis on costs":** Green, "Trouble with Murray."

93 **A 1979 University of Wyoming study:** Clark, "Costs and Benefits."

94 **yielded $36 billion in benefits:** Ibid.

94 **When Anaconda Copper Company closed:** Tolchin and Tolchin, *Dismantling America,* 2.

94 **"By the late 1970s, complaints":** Ibid., 4.

95 **"Japanese steel firms spent twice":** Robert B. Reich, *The Next American Frontier: A Provocative Program for Economic Renewal* (New York: Penguin Books, 1983), 182.

95 **"Regulatory rollbacks will not restore":** Ibid., 181–182.

95 **"The commission's sectoral studies":** Michael L. Dertouzos, Richard K. Lester, Robert M. Solow, and the MIT Commission on Industrial Productivity, *Made in America: Regaining the Productive Edge* (New York: HarperPerennial, paperback edition, 1990), 110–111.

95 **"A somewhat larger number felt":** Ibid., 110–111.

96 **a Regulation Analysis Review Group:** Tolchin and Tolchin, *Dismantling America,* 48.

96 **"For 90 percent of the population":** Edsall, *New Politics of Inequality.*

97 **"progressive rate system that was":** *Ibid.,* 211.

97 **"coming through the windows":** Blumenthal, *Rise of the Counter-Establishment,* 267.

97 **Reagan uttered scores of inaccurate statements:** Mark Green and Gail MacColl, *Reagan's Reign of Error: The Instant Nostalgia Edition* (New York: Pantheon Books, 1987).

98 **He was quoted in the *Washington Star:*** Ibid., 80.

98 **"Well, it's a good story, though":** Ibid., 82–83.

98 **"Those who have for so long":** Remarks at a Fundraising Dinner Honoring Former Representative John M. Ashbrook in Ashland, Ohio, May 9, 1983, http://www.reagan.utexas.edu/archives/speeches/1983/50983b.htm.

CHAPTER 5: THE LOOTING OF AMERICA

105 **"The future of banking":** Chet Currier, "Reagan's Treasury Choice Heads Wall Street Giant," Associated Press, December 11, 1980.

105 **"I have some very strong personal convictions":** *Competition and Conditions in the Financial System,* hearings before the Committee on Banking, Housing, and Urban Affairs, U.S. Senate, Part 1, April 28, May 6–7, 1981. (Washington, D.C.: U.S. Government Printing Office, 1981), 31–35.

105 **"I think most of you know":** Ibid., 29.

106 **"Most small businesses in the towns":** Ibid., 30.

108 **"None of the lawyers I know":** Jeff Gerth, "Is Business Regulation Now in Friendly Hands," *New York Times,* March 30, 1981.

108 **"one of the most pernicious":** Penina Migdal Glazer, *The Whistleblowers: Exposing Corruption in Government and Industry* (New York: Basic Books, 1989), 14.

109 **OSHA's inspections of manufacturing concerns:** Frank Donner and James Ledbetter, "Deregulation by Sleaze: Ronald Reagan's Attempts to Dismantle Certain Government Agencies," *The Nation,* February 6, 1988, 163.

109 **"If you go to the agency":** Susan J. Tolchin and Martin Tolchin, *Dismantling America: The Rush to Deregulate* (Boston: Houghton Mifflin, 1983), 58–59.

110 **"like a list of the Fortune 500":** Ibid., 64.

110 **excerpt from the June 1981 testimony:** Ibid., 66.

111 **"We've lost direction":** Ward Sinclair, "Budget Cuts Hit Safety Enforcement like a Ton of Kentucky Coal: Coal Mining Deaths Are Rising," *Washington Post,* February 15, 1982.

111 **"favorite bad guy":** Chris Mooney, *The Republican War on Science* (New York: Basic Books, 2005), 102–105.

112 **"There's a nerd over at Army":** Dan Davidson, "Nixon's 'Nerd' Turns Regulations Watchdog," *Federal Times,* November 11, 2002, 22.

112 **"We would ask ourselves":** "Profile—OMB's Jim Joseph Tozzi," *Environmental Forum,* May 1982, 12, http://thecre.com/pdf/20060612_ELI_Environmental Forum.pdf.

112 **"I don't want to leave fingerprints":** Peter Behr, "If There Is a New Rule, Jim Tozzi Has Read It," *Washington Post,* July 10, 1981.

113 **"You have not made your case":** Larry Doyle, United Press International, "Aspirin-Reye's Chronology: Threat of Suits Delayed Warning Process," *Los Angeles Times,* May 31, 1987.

113 **after pressure from the Committee:** Appellate brief in *Public Citizen Health Research Group v. Commission, Food and Drug Administration and Aspirin Foundation of America,* United States Court of Appeals for the District of Columbia Circuit, 238 U.S. App. D.C. 271; 740 F.2d 21; 1984.

114 **"They wanted to make it very clear":** Pamela Warrick, "Health: If You Can't Read the English Label, How Will You Know of a Product's Dangers?" *Los Angeles Times,* May 25, 1993; Doyle, "Aspirin-Reye's Chronology."

114 **"Procedurally," he said:** Doyle, "Aspirin-Reye's Chronology."

114 **"We don't know the other side":** David Segal, "Lemon Laws; Idiotic Legislation," *Washington Monthly,* January 1, 1993, 25.

114 **he was in full denial:** Barbara Hinkson Craig, Ralph Nader, and Alan B. Morrison, *Courting Change: The Story of the Public Citizen Litigation Group* (Washington, D.C.: Public Citizen Press, 2004), 305, 309.

115 **"These 1,470 deaths":** Paul Raeburn, "Nearly 1,500 Children's Deaths Blamed on Government Inaction," Associated Press, October 23, 1992.

117 **"It took minutes":** Matthew Miller, "The 100 Grand Illusion: The Problem with the Banks and Thrifts That They Still Haven't Fixed," *Washington Monthly,* July 1, 1990, 22.

117 **pushed legislation and regulatory changes:** Lou Cannon, *President Reagan: The Role of a Lifetime* (New York: PublicAffairs, 2000), 742.

118 **"All in all, I think":** Joe Conason, "The Corporate Financiers Are Wrong," *Salon,* September 19, 2008, http://www.salon.com/opinion/conason/2008/09/19/market/.

118 **"This was a failure of government":** Cannon, *President Reagan,* 742.

118 **"patsy for the industry":** Ibid., 743.

119 **"one more roll of the dice":** Robert Kuttner, *Everything for Sale: The Virtues and Limits of Markets* (Chicago: University of Chicago Press, 1996), 174.

120 **mounted their own campaign against Glass-Steagall:** "The Long Demise of Glass-Steagall," *Frontline,* May 8, 2003, http://www.pbs.org/wgbh/pages/frontline/shows/wallstreet/weill/demise.html.

120 **"One of the more attractive features":** Alan Greenspan, address before a conference on bank structure and competition, Federal Reserve Bank of Chicago, May 12, 1988. http://fraser.stlouisfed.org/historicaldocs/ag88/download/27752/Greenspan_19880512.pdf.

121 **Greenspan continued the Fed's dismantling:** "Long Demise of Glass-Steagal."

121 **$300-million lobbying effort:** Stephen Labaton, "Congress Eases Bank Laws," *New York Times,* November 7, 1999.

121 **$70-billion stock swap:** Bill Atkinson, "Citicorp Plans Record Merger with Travelers," *Baltimore Sun,* April 7, 1998.

122 **Weill met with Greenspan before announcing:** Peter Pae, "Bank, Insurance Giants Set Merger: Citicorp, Travelers in $82 Billion Deal," *Washington Post,* April 7, 1998.

122 **"You're buying the government":** Carol J. Loomis and James Aley, "'One Helluva Candy Store,'" *Fortune,* May 11, 1998, 72.

122 **"When this potentially historic agreement":** Bill Clinton statement on modernization of financial laws, U.S. Newswire, October 22, 1999, http://w3.nexis.com/new/search/newssubmitForm.do.

122 **Gramm and two other UBS lobbyists:** Lisa Lerer, "McCain Guru Linked to Subprime Crisis," *Politico,* March 28, 2008, http://www.politico.com/news/stories/0308/9246.html.

123 **"Consider WorldCom's support":** Robert Sherrill, "Why the Bubble Popped," *The Nation,* April 15, 2004, 57.

124 **"Why We Had Glass-Steagall" was the headline:** Jeanne Cummings, John R. Emshwiller, Tom Hamburger, Scot J. Paltrow, Jathon Sapsford, Ellen E. Schultz, Randall Smith, and Rebecca Smith, "Why We Had Glass-Steagall," *Wall Street Journal,* January 15, 2002.

124 **"Might J. P. Morgan and Citi":** "Conflicts, Conflicts Everywhere," *The Economist,* January 26, 2002.

125 **"Innovation has brought about":** Remarks by Alan Greenspan on consumer finance at the Federal Reserve System's Fourth Annual Community Affairs Research Conference, Washington, D.C., April 8, 2005, http://www.federalreserve.gov/BoardDocs/speeches/2005/20050408/default.htm.

126 **"You know these practices":** *60 Minutes,* CBS News Transcripts, September 16, 2007.

126 **"He was opposed to it":** Greg Ip, "Did Greenspan Add to Subprime Woes," *Wall Street Journal,* June 9, 2007.

126 **"it was clearly a mistake":** Steven Mufson, "Greenspan Stands His Ground: Ex-Chairman Says Fed Policies Didn't Cause Current Woes," *Washington Post,* March 21, 2008.

127 **"People who had taken out loans":** Excerpts from an interview with former Federal Reserve chairman Alan Greenspan, *Washington Post,* March 21, 2008.

127 **"The Federal Reserve could have stopped":** Edmund L. Andrews, "Fed and Regulators Shrugged as the Subprime Crisis Spread," *New York Times,* December 18, 2007.

129 **"As California Starved for Energy":** Scott Thurm, Robert Gavin, and Mitchel Benson, "As California Starved for Energy, U.S. Businesses Had a Feast," *Wall Street Journal,* September 16, 2002.

129 **"We have had enough experience":** Robert J. Samuelson, "The Joy of Deregulation," *Newsweek*, February 3, 1997, 39.

130 **The two decades after deregulation:** Carole A. Shifrin, "Tough Policy Questions: A Deregulation Legacy," *Aviation Week and Space Technology,* November 9, 1998, 50.

131 **Clifford Winston of the Brookings Institution:** Steven A. Morrison and Clifford Winston, "The Remaining Role of Government Policy in the Deregulated Airline Industry," in Sam Peltzman and Clifford Winston, eds., *Deregulation of Network Industries: What's Next?* (Washington, D.C.: Brookings Institution, 2000), 1–40.

132 **"This is the continued working out":** Micheline Maynard, "Two Major Airlines Seen Near Filing for Bankruptcy," *New York Times,* September 14, 2005.

132 **"The problem with the previous system":** Panel Two of a hearing of the Senate Commerce, Science, and Transportation Committee, January 9, 2003, *Future of the Airline Industry* (Washington, D.C.: U.S. Government Printing Office, 2006).

132 **"It's time to move away":** Deborah Potter, "The Big Get Bigger," *American Journalism Review,* August-September 2003, 72.

133 **"not the captive of any industry":** Merrill Brown, "Fowler: FCC Is No Censor: Applied Reaganism at the FCC," *Washington Post,* June 27, 1981.

133 **reviewed or abolished 89 percent:** "1985: A Year like No Other for the Fifth Estate: Changes in the Broadcasting Industry," *Broadcasting,* December 30, 1985, 38.

134 **"I have never seen anything":** Roger McChesney, "The Political Economy of Radio," in Ron Sakolsky and Stephen Dunifer, eds., *Seizing the Airways: A Free Radio Handbook* (Oakland, Calif.: AK Press, 1998), 23.

134 **Instead, cable rates went up:** Common Cause Education Fund, *The Fallout from the Telecommunications Act of 1996: Unintended Consequences and Lessons Learned* (Washington, D.C.: Common Cause Education Fund, May 9, 2005).

CHAPTER 6: MERGER MANIA

136 **"Mr. Shad will rock no corporate boats":** "When Wall Street Talks, Shad Listens," *The Economist,* February 28, 1981, 80.

137 **"B.S.," he wrote in the margins:** Details of Shad's speech and the reaction it set off in the Reagan administration are from David A. Vise and Steve Coll, *Eagle on the Street: Based on the Pulitzer Prize–Winning Account of the SEC's Battle with Wall Street* (New York: Scribner's, 1991), 186.

137 **"In today's corporate world":** David A. Vise and Steve Coll, "After 8 Years, a Chance to Return to the Fray," *Washington Post,* February 8, 1989.

139 **"the movement towards totalitarianism":** Friedrich A. Hayek, *The Road to Serfdom* (New York: Routledge, 2001), 200.

140 **"a few hundred business suzerainties":** Cited in Jack Newfield and Jeff Greenfield, *A Populist Manifesto: The Making of a New Majority* (New York: Warner Paperback Library, 1972), 48.

140 **"Bigness doesn't necessarily":** Walter Adams and James W. Brock, *Dangerous Pursuits: Mergers and Acquisitions in the Age of Wall Street* (New York: Pantheon Books, 1989), xii.

140 **pledged to review twelve hundred:** Charles R. Babcock, "New Antitrust Policy: Bigness Isn't Badness: Baxter's Enforcers Seek 'More Bang for the Buck,'" *Washington Post,* February 7, 1982.

140 **"It was almost like he was":** Author interview with Albert Foer, October 19, 2000.

141 **Of the 10,723 mergers that came:** Adams and Brock, *Dangerous Pursuit,* 27–28.

141 **Americans' investment in productive capacity:** Benjamin M. Friedman, *Day of Reckoning: The Consequences of American Economic Policy under Reagan and After* (New York: Random House, 1988), 28–29.

142 **Reagan's alma mater:** Citizens for Tax Justice, *Annual Survey of Corporate Taxpayers and Corporate Freeloaders* (Washington, D.C.: Citizens for Tax Justice, October 1989); William Greider, *Who Will Tell the People: The Betrayal of American Democracy* (New York: Touchstone, 1992), 341–342.

142 **Citizens for Tax Justice, a liberal advocacy group:** Citizens for Tax Justice, *Annual Survey;* Greider, *Who Will Tell the People,* 341–342.

143 **"vigorous, nonpartisan independence":** Jeff Gerth, "SEC's Future Focus in Doubt," *New York Times,* January 29, 1981.

143 **It was on Sporkin's advice:** Ibid.

143 **clip Sporkin's wings:** Ibid.

143 **A three-hundred-page report:** Ibid.

144 **"It was improper":** David A. Vise and Steve Coll, "Remaking the Nation's Markets: In Six Years at S.E.C. Shad Spurred Radical Change," *Washington Post,* February 5, 1989.

144 **"the oddest thing I ever saw":** Ibid.

145 **"Every corporate boardroom":** Merrill Sheils, "The New Urge to Merge," *Newsweek,* July 27, 1981, 50.

146 **"Millions of ordinary Americans":** "Washington Dateline," Associated Press, October 2, 1982.

146 **More than ten thousand mergers:** Roy C. Smith, *The Money Wars: The Rise and Fall of the Great Buyout Boom of the 1980s* (New York: Dutton, 1990), 106.

146 **"in 1983, Esmark":** Adams and Brock, *Dangerous Pursuits,* 17.

148 **"It does not create new wealth":** Robert B. Reich, *The Next American Frontier: A Provocative Program for Economic Renewal* (New York: Penguin Books, 1983), 141.

148 **After DuPont paid $7.8 billion:** John Greenwald, "The Great Takeover Debate," *Time,* April 22, 1985, 44.

149 **"My experience," the takeover lawyer:** Leonard Silk, "The Peril behind the Takeover Boom," *New York Times,* December 29, 1985.

149 **"All this frenzy":** Ann Crittenden, "The Age of Me-First Management," *New York Times,* August 19, 1984.

149 **"In 1981, $30 billion to $38 billion":** Ronald Brownstein, "Merger Wars: Congress, SEC Take Aim at Hostile Corporate Takeover Moves," *National Journal,* July 23, 1983, 1538.

150 **"The whole idea of corporate accounting":** Clemens P. Work and Jack Seamonds, "What Are Mergers Doing to America?" *U.S. News and World Report,* July 22, 1985, 48.

150 **"It doesn't take a revolutionary":** Crittenden, "Age of Me-First Management."

150 **"The human toll was vast":** Work and Seamonds, "What Are Mergers?" 48.

151 **The Association of Outplacement Consulting Firms:** Ibid.

151 **"The undiluted pursuit of personal gain":** Crittenden, "Age of Me-First Management."

153 **A study commissioned by the *Wall Street Journal:*** Robert Frank and Robin Sidel, "Firms That Lived by the Deal in '90s Now Sink by the Dozens," *Wall Street Journal,* June 7, 2002.

153 **"Our goal is not to capture":** Amy Barrett and Peter Elstrom, "Making Worldcom Live Up to Its Name," *Business Week,* July 14, 1997, 64.

CHAPTER 7: THE EFFLUVIA OF COMMERCE

156 **"the organized creation of dissatisfaction":** Juliet Schor, *The Overworked American: The Unexpected Decline of Leisure* (New York: Basic Books, 1993), 120.

157 **"rising tide of mediocrity":** National Commission on Excellence in Education, *A Nation at Risk: The Imperative for Education Reform, A Report to the Nation and the Secretary of Education,* U.S. Department of Education, April 1983, http://www.ed.gov/pubs/NatAtRisk/index.html.

157 **a study by the National Association of Partners in Education:** Cited in Elinor Mills, "School Volunteers and Business Partnerships Flourishing," Associated Press, March 17, 1992.

157 **Center for the Analysis of Commercialism:** Mills, "School Volunteers"; Alex Molnar and Jennifer Morales, "The Third Annual Report on Trends in Schoolhouse Commercialism," Center for the Analysis of Commercialism in Education, September 2000, http://epsl.asu.edu/ceru/Annual%20reports/cace-00-02-exec-summary.pdf.

158 **"public skepticism toward business":** Thomas Ferguson and Joel Rogers, "The Myth of America's Turn to the Right," *Atlantic Monthly,* May 1986, 43–53.

158 **"three quarters of the working public":** Lou Cannon, *President Reagan: The Role of a Lifetime* (New York: PublicAffairs, 2000), 8.

159 **The Rolling Stones agreed:** Naomi Klein, *No Logo: Taking Aim at the Brand Bullies* (New York: Macmillan, 2002), 47.

160 **She was found wandering the streets:** Andrew Glazer, "LA Targets Hospital in Alleged Dumping of Patient on Skid Row," Associated Press, November 17, 2006.

161 **"The United States does not have an automatic call":** Louis Uchitelle, "U.S. Businesses Loosen Link to Mother Country," *New York Times,* May 21, 1989.

161 **"master instruments of civilization":** Cited in Adolph A. Berle and Gardiner Coit Means, *The Modern Corporation and Private Property* (Piscataway, N.J.: Transaction, 1997), 4.

161 **"had no organ to sense the dangers":** Karl Polanyi, *The Great Transformation: The Political and Economic Origins of Our Time* (Boston: Beacon Press, 1944), 133.

162 **"It is a vision which fascinates":** Edmund Wilson, *To the Finland Station: A Study in the Writing and Acting of History* (Garden City, N.Y.: Doubleday, 1940; Anchor paperback edition, 1953), 290. Citation is to the Anchor edition.

162 **"Unless he could be persuaded":** Frederick Lewis Allen, *Only Yesterday: An Informal History of the 1920's* (New York: Harper & Row, 1931), 140.

163 ***Harper*'s politely refused:** David M. Potter, *People of Plenty: Economic Abundance and the American Character* (Chicago: University of Chicago Press, 1954), 169–170.

163 **"Advertising was considered an embarrassment":** Stephen Fox, *The Mirror Makers: A History of American Advertising and Its Creators* (New York: William Morrow, 1984), 15–16.

163 **One study found:** Potter, *People of Plenty,* 169–170.

163 **began to move away from such articles:** Richard Hofstadter, *The Age of Reform* (New York: Vintage Books, paperback edition, 1955), 195–196.

163 **"The family circle":** Fox, *Mirror Makers,* 152.

164 **unprecedented 7 percent:** Geoffrey Perrett, *America in the Twenties* (New York: Simon & Schuster, 1982), 337.

164 **"The making of one general will":** Potter, *People of Plenty,* 183.

164 **"instrument of social control":** Ibid., 177–178.

165 **"may not be the primary authority":** Ibid., 64.

165 **"broad changes in social conditions":** Ibid., 191.

165 **the "organization man":** William H. Whyte Jr., *The Organization Man* (New York: Simon & Schuster, 1956).

165 **David Riesman, in his book:** David Riesman, *The Lonely Crowd: A Study of the Changing American Character* (New Haven, Conn.: Yale University Press, 1950).

165 **"Even before American children":** Max Lerner, *America as a Civilization,* vol. 1 (New York: Simon & Schuster, 1963), 309.

165 **"For 'totalitarian' is not only a terrorist":** Herbert Marcuse, *One Dimensional Man* (Boston: Beacon Press, 1964), 3.

166 **"in everyday life a widespread rebellion":** Walter Lippmann, *The Essential Lippmann: A Political Philosophy for Liberal Democracy* (New York: Random House, 1963), 389.

166 **"as though they were clergymen":** Henry Adams, *The Education of Henry Adams: An Autobiography* (Cambridge, Mass.: Riverside Press, 1918), 32.

167 **the most prominent social scientists:** Richard Hofstadter, *The Age of Reform* (New York: Vintage Books, paperback edition, 1955), 154–155.

167 **"The unorganized public":** Quoted in ibid., 216.

167 **"divinely planted instinct":** William Allen White, *The Old Order Changeth: A View of American Democracy* (New York: Macmillan, 1910), 63.

167 **Franklin Roosevelt lent support:** Arthur M. Schlesinger Jr., *The Coming of the New Deal* (Boston: Houghton Mifflin, 1959), 362–364.

168 **"against the crass materialism and the shallowness":** M. L. Wilson, "The Place of Subsistence Homesteads in Our National Economy," paper read before the twenty-fourth annual meeting of the American Farm Economic Association, Philadelphia, December 29, 1933, available from the Agricultural and Applied Economics Association, Milwaukee, Wisconsin, http://www.aaea.org/.

168 **Eleanor Roosevelt directed:** Schlesinger, *Coming of the New Deal,* 365–367.

169 **"we justifiably charge off":** The American Presidency Project Document Archive, Franklin D. Roosevelt, Address at Arthurdale, West Virginia, May 27, 1938, http://www.presidency.ucsb.edu/ws/index.php?pid=15647.

169 **Even more antithetical:** Don Adams and Arlene Goldbard, "New Deal Cultural Programs: Experiments in Cultural Democracy," 1995, http://www.wwcd.org/policy/US/newdeal.html.

170 **The purveyors of these products:** Schlesinger, *Coming of the New Deal,* 356–357.

170 **"laying the basis for a new type":** Ibid., 364.

170 **"weeded out the over-privileged":** Franklin D. Roosevelt, Annual Message to Congress, January 4, 1935, available from the American Presidency Project, http://www.presidency.ucsb.edu/ws/index.php?pid=14890.

170 **"hotbeds of Communists":** Don Adams and Arlene Goldbard, "New Deal Cultural Programs: Experiments in Cultural Democracy," 1995, http://www.wwcd.org/policy/US/newdeal.html.

172 **"We had school libraries with wonderful books":** Author interview with Peggy Charren, November 24, 2006.

173 **"He took off his jacket":** Ibid.

173 **"The program was full of sales pitches":** Ibid.

173 **"We believe . . . that the broadcaster's":** Children's Television Report and Policy Statement, 50 FCC 2d 1, 5 (1974), affirmed, *Action for Children's Television v. FCC,* 564 F.2d 458 (D.C. Cir. 1977).

174 **a "vast wasteland":** Cited in Newton M. Minow and Craig L. LaMay, *Abandoned in the Wasteland: Children, Television and the First Amendment* (New York: MacMillan, 1996), 3.

174 **"We find this pattern disturbing":** Tom Englehardt, "The Shortcake Strategy," in Todd Gitlin, ed., *Watching Television: A Pantheon Guide to Popular Culture* (New York: Pantheon Books, 1987), 75.

174 **A study by the FCC's Children's Television Task Force:** Brian F. Fontes, *Television Programming for Children: A Report of the Children's Television Task Force,* vol. 4 (Washington, D.C.: Federal Communications Commission, October 1979), 4.

175 **an exhaustive study of the impact:** Tracy Westen, "Government Regulation of Food Marketing to Children: The Federal Trade Commission and the Kid-Vid Controversy," *Loyola of Los Angeles Law Review,* April 2006, 477–489.

175 **The finding painted a disturbing picture:** Ibid.

176 **"I don't know where his head was":** Charren interview.

177 **"If people wanted [the shows] to be better":** Jonathan Rowe, "Advertising and Children's TV," *Christian Science Monitor,* January 29, 1987.

177 **"The marketplace will take care of children":** Fred M. Hechinger, "About Education," *New York Times,* February 28, 1990.

177 **jettisoning the low-rated educational:** John J. O'Connor, "Leaving Children to the Mercy of the Marketplace," *New York Times,* October 17, 1982.

177 **An FCC study found:** David Burnham, "Congress Debates What to Require of TV Stations," *New York Times,* November 7, 1983.

178 **"better things to do":** "Farewell to the National Nanny," *Washington Post,* April 6, 1981.

179 **paid no net federal income tax:** Peter Ajemian and Joan Claybrook, "Deceiving the Public: The Story behind J. Peter Grace and His Campaign," *Public Citizen,* August 1985.

179 **"traditional family values":** David Burnham, "Questions Rising over U.S. Study and Role of Company Executives, *New York Times,* September 28, 1982.

179 **"The implicit philosophy":** Ajemian and Claybrook, "Deceiving the Public."

180 **"Wherever at the head of some new undertaking":** Alexis de Tocqueville, *Democracy in America* (New York: HarperPerennial, 1969), 513.

180 **Charities themselves stood to lose:** Carole Shifrin, "Charities Pessimistic of Philanthropy as Economic Savior," *Washington Post,* January 10, 1982.

181 **"it is unrealistic to expect us to fill":** Robert Pear, "Social Programs: 'A Chasm,'" *New York Times,* January 10, 1982.

181 **"We've been deluged":** Kathleen Teltsch, "Nonprofit Groups Call on Industry to Replace U.S. Aid," *New York Times,* July 6, 1981.

181 **"Higher education and the arts are visible":** Tamar Lewin, "Corporate Giving Fails to Offset Cuts by U.S., *New York Times,* February 15, 1985.

182 **"What does it mean then":** Michael Brenson, "Museum and Corporation: A Delicate Balance," *New York Times,* February 23, 1986.

182 **"an All-Star roster of corporate sponsors":** John Ward Anderson. "This Papal Visit Is Brought to You by . . . ," *Washington Post,* January 22, 1999.

183 **An exhaustive study by the *Philadelphia Inquirer:*** Gilbert M. Gaul and Neill A. Borowski, "Warehouses of Wealth: The Tax-Free Economy," *Philadelphia Inquirer,* April 18–24, 1993.

184 **A 2001 study found that 350,000 hospital beds:** Ibid.

184 **grossly violated federal tax law:** Ibid.

184 **"They were more concerned with doing":** Robert Pear, "Health Care Units Will Lose U.S. Aid," *New York Times,* April 18, 1982.

185 **A study by Physicians:** Michael Lasalandra, "Study: Nonprofit HMOs Are Superior: For-profit HMOs Offer Lower Quality of Care," *Boston Herald,* July 14, 1999.

186 **"Physician shall agree":** Cited in Paul Gray, "Gagging the Doctors," *Time,* January 8, 1996, 50.

187 **"In all the history of Central Park":** Jimmy Breslin, "Rudy Helps Slick Disney Turn Us All into Suckers," *Newsday* (city edition), June 11, 1995.

CHAPTER 8: THE SPOILS OF REVOLUTION

189 **In late 1989, a widening scandal:** The sorry history of HUD's Moderate Rehabilitation Program in the Reagan administration, including what took place at the Seabrook Apartments, is laid out in detail in the final report of a congressional committee that investigated the affair; see Committee on Government Operations, U.S. Senate, *Abuse and Mismanagement at HUD* (Washington, D.C.: U.S. Government Printing Office, 1990).

191 **"The technical term for what we do":** Ibid., 12.

192 **"widespread abuses, influence peddling":** Ibid., 2.

193 **Meese himself narrowly—and some would say unfairly:** Lou Cannon, *President Reagan: The Role of a Lifetime* (New York: PublicAffairs, 2000), 718–720.

193 **By the end of Reagan's two terms:** Haynes Johnson, *Sleepwalking through History: America in the Reagan Years* (New York: W. W. Norton, 1991), 184.

194 **the president dozed off:** Cannon, *President Reagan,* 719.

194 **"lured by the crumbs":** Dale Russakoff, "James Watt and the Wages of Influence," *Washington Post,* May 4, 1989.

194 **"I make no bones":** Committee on Government Operations, *Abuse and Mismanagement,* 21.

194 **"Thanks, you are a man of your word":** Ibid., 23.

195 **"people appointed to positions of responsibility":** Ibid., 68.

195 **She had meandered her way:** Michael Kranish, "Probe's Silent Figure Has Everyone Talking," *Boston Globe,* June 27, 1989.

197 **"This is the board of directors":** Bill McAllister and Chris Spolar, "The Transformation of HUD: 'Brat Pack' Filled Vacuum at Agency," *Washington Post,* August 6, 1989.

197 **"It's common knowledge on the Hill":** Leslie Maitland, "Focus of H.U.D. Inquiry: A Woman of Influence and Ambition," *New York Times,* May 31, 1989.

198 **"was set up and designed to be a political program":** Nancy Traver, "The Housing Hustle," *Time,* June 26, 1989, 18.

199 **"I said I can't fund it":** Committee on Government Operations, *Abuse and Mismanagement,* 30.

199 **"To my knowledge, there was no one else":** Ibid.

200 **"What I looked at more or less":** Ibid., 65.

200 **"I received a call":** Ibid., 58.

200 **"She liked power":** Philip Shenon, "Ex-Housing Secretary Says Aides Were at Fault in Disputed Program," *New York Times,* May 26, 1989.

200 **"I very strongly objected":** Kranish, "Probe's Silent Figure."

201 **"Your contribution to this administration":** Leslie Maitland, "The Dean Files: Flattery in the Quest for Power," *New York Times,* July 23, 1989.

201 **"O.P.M.," she said, "has never":** Ibid.

201 **"I know that you'll be the best":** Ibid.

201 **"Carter Bell might call":** Ibid.

201 **"She has a lot of political support":** Ibid.

201 **she used it for personal expenses:** Dan Fesperman, "Dean: At Center of HUD Mess," *Los Angeles Times,* July 28, 1989.

202 **"Thank you very much for the splendid lunch":** Maitland, "Dean Files."

202 **An internal HUD audit:** Committee on Government Operations, *Abuse and Mismanagement.*

202 **was nicknamed "Robin HUD":** Page Boinest, "'Robin HUD' Pleads Guilty to Stealing HUD Money," United Press International, January 29, 1990.

202 **"It was a pathetic operation":** Bill McAllister and Chris Spolar, "The Transformation of HUD: 'Brat Pack' Filled Vacuum at Agency," *Washington Post,* August 6, 1989.

203 **"provide credible proof":** Robert SanGeorge, United Press International, March 22, 1983.

203 **"the most embarrassing thing I ever":** Jonathan Lash, Katherine Gillman, and David Sheridan, *A Season of Spoils: The Reagan Administration's Attack on the Environment* (New York: Pantheon, 1984), 43.

204 **"top-level officials of the Environmental Protection Agency":** Committee on Energy and Commerce, Subcommittee on Oversight and Investigations, U.S. House of Representatives, August 30, 1984, *Investigation of the Environmental Protection Agency: Report on the President's Claim of Executive Privilege over EPA Documents, Abuses in the Superfund Program, and Other Matters* (Washington, D.C.: U.S. Government Printing Office, 1984), 9.

204 **"All the elements at work":** Johnson, *Sleepwalking through History,* 178.

CHAPTER 9: THE GREAT ENABLER

205 **"avert its eyes from the heart of darkness":** Eric Alterman, "Where's the Rest of Him," *The Nation,* March 27, 2000, 12.

206 **"it would be better for him":** Leonard Lurie, *Senator Pothole: The Unauthorized Biography of Al D'Amato* (Secaucus, N.J.: Carol, 1994), 380.

206 **"Al D'Amato was the sole architect":** Ibid., 384.

207 **"relationships with village officials":** Michael Winerip, "Inquiry Is Ordered on HUD Fund Use in D'Amato's Town," *New York Times,* June 9, 1989.

207 **installed a special button on his phone:** "Senator D'Amato's HUD Connections," *New York Times,* September 29, 1989.

208 **One HUD audit of the New York:** Michael Winerip, "H.U.D. and D'Amato: Hopes for Grants Prompted Gifts," *New York Times,* July 28, 1989.

208 **"Pierce explained to subcommittee staff":** Committee on Government Operations, U.S. Senate, *Abuse and Mismanagement at HUD* (Washington, D.C.: U.S. Government Printing Office, 1990).

209 **"We have a problem concerning Sam Pierce":** Ronald Reagan, *The Reagan Diaries* (New York: HarperCollins, 2007), 584.

209 **"bumped due to higher priorities":** Committee on Government Operations, *Abuse and Mismanagement,* 28.

209 **It stated that the staff member:** Ibid.

209 **"In spite of all our cutting back":** Gwen Ifill, "Pierce Invokes Fifth Amendment: Ex-Secretary Says Panel Regards Him as 'Target' of HUD Probe," *Washington Post,* September 27, 1989.

211 **"Then Ronald Reagan came on the phone":** Author interview with Dan Sullivan; also see Harold C. Schonberg, "Reagan Asks Coast Critic to Plug Show," *New York Times,* March 19, 1981.

212 **"I'm ashamed of you":** Schonberg, "Reagan Asks Coast Critic."

214 **"vulgarization which has been the almost invariable":** Arthur M. Schlesinger Jr., "The Highbrow in American Politics," *Partisan Review,* March-April 1953, 162.

214 **"We have every kind of mixture":** Associated Press, "Watt Remark on Coal Panel Offends 4 Groups," *New York Times,* September 22, 1983.

214 **"The poor homosexuals":** Jerry Schwartz, "Hemophiliacs, Homosexuals Forced to Make Difficult Choices," Associated Press, June 28, 1983.

214 **"Trees cause more pollution than automobiles do":** Martin Schram, "Nation's Longest Campaign Comes to an End," *Washington Post,* November 4, 1980.

214 **"the moral equivalent of the Founding Fathers":** Lou Cannon, "Reagan Orders Review of Policy on Nicaragua," *Washington Post,* April 27, 1985.

214 **"eliminated the segregation that we once had":** R. Gregory Nokes, "Reagan South Africa Comments Gets Listener Sympathy," Associated Press, August 28, 1985.

215 **"mahogany and marble and crystal chandeliers":** Phil Gailey, "For Senator Hawkins, a Debatable First Year," *New York Times,* December 15, 1981.

215 **"Deck the halls with Commie corpses":** Dudley Clendinen, "After 20 Years, Young Conservatives Enjoy a Long-Awaited Rise to Power," *New York Times,* August 22, 1981.

216 **"In the wee small hours of election night":** John Dillin, "Final-Exam Time for Senate Freshmen," *Christian Science Monitor,* October 24, 1986.

216 **According to the Center for Responsive Politics:** Center for Responsive Politics, *OpenSecrets,* http://www.opensecrets.org/politicians/contrib.php?cid=N00006983&cycle=2004.

216 **top contributor to Hunter's campaigns:** Ibid.

217 **"Reagan influenced a whole generation":** Nick Anderson, "Devotion of 'Reaganauts' Undiminished," *Los Angeles Times,* June 7, 2007.

217 **"I need a campaign manager":** Richard Simon, "Political Payrolls Include Families: Dozens of Members of Congress Have Paid Relatives for Campaign Work, Records Show," *Los Angeles Times,* April 14, 2005.

217 **"Our FY-96 budget does not operate":** David Kramer, "Panel Cuts DOE Programs by $1.3 Billion," *Inside Energy/with Federal Lands,* June 12, 1995, 1.

217 **"There are almost no great debates":** Elizabeth Drew, *The Corruption of American Politics: What Went Wrong and Why* (Secaucus, N.J.: Carol, 1999), 27.

219 **"We insist, of course, that people are qualified":** Hedrick Smith, "Conservatives Cite Gains in Top Posts," *New York Times,* March 8, 1981.

220 **Reagan, in an interview:** November 24, 1981, interview with ABC's Barbara Walters, cited in "Reagan Calls Capital Leaks His Biggest Disappointment," *New York Times,* November 27, 1981.

221 **"the producers of eggs, milk and meat":** Michael deCourcy Hinds, "Over 900 Federal Publications Halted," *New York Times,* November 16, 1981.

221 **Joe McGinniss's *The Selling of the President:*** Joe McGinniss, *The Selling of the President, 1968* (New York: Trident Press, 1969).

222 **"The whole thing was PR":** Mark Hertsgaard, *On Bended Knee: The Press and the Reagan Presidency* (New York: Schocken Books, 1989), 6.

222 **"If we understand the mechanism and motives":** Edward Bernays, *Propaganda* (New York: Ig, 2004), 71.

223 **"Ronald Reagan enjoyed the most generous treatment":** Hertsgaard, *On Bended Knee,* 4.

223 **"This is an eerie campaign":** Elizabeth Drew, *Portrait of an Election: The 1980 Presidential Campaign* (New York: Simon & Schuster, 1981), 269.

224 **"All across the land":** Ibid., 268.

CHAPTER 10: "THE MAN WITH THE BADGE"

225 **warned that their school was on "lockdown":** The events in the classroom are described in the civil complaint in *Shenona Banks v. Wagner School Board, Case 4:02-cv-04158-LLP, United States District Court, District of South Dakota, Southern Division;* the lawsuit resulted in a settlement in which the Wagner police agreed to have no more canine searches in areas where students were present.

227 **"There has been this notion":** Lincoln Caplan, *The Tenth Justice: The Solicitor General and the Rule of Law* (New York: Knopf, 1987), 107.

227 **The underlying criminal case:** See *New Jersey v. T.L.O.*, 469 U.S. 325 (1985), Docket No. 83-712.

229 **"It's not an Orwellian leap":** Diane Steinle, "Treading on Student Rights," *St. Petersburg Times,* September 24, 2000.

230 **A recent survey by *Family Circle:*** Ibid.

232 **"tell her why the life of the man":** Michael Grunwald, "Kerry and Weld Strike Sparks," *Boston Globe,* April 9, 1996.

233 **"My bottom line on three-strikes laws":** William Kleinknecht, "Felon Could Give Three-Strikes Law Its First Chance," *The (NJ) Star-Ledger,* November 6, 1996.

233 **"however plain it may be":** Robert Cohen, "Justices Back Net Registry of Molesters," *The (NJ) Star-Ledger,* March 6, 2003.

233 **"jump-off-the-cliff-with-the-flag-flying conservative":** Nancy Reagan, *My Turn: The Memoirs of Nancy Reagan* (New York: Random House, 1989), 240.

234 **"a stick-to-itiveness that can sometimes drive you up a wall":** Lou Cannon, *Governor Reagan: His Rise to Power* (New York: PublicAffairs, 2003), 359.

234 **"Now, Ed, don't lose this one":** Laurence I. Barrett, *Gambling with History: Ronald Reagan in the White House* (New York: Doubleday, 1983), 104.

235 **"had considerable information":** Associated Press transcript of remarks, *New York Times,* December 15, 1983.

235 **"Poppin' Fresh, the doughboy":** Larry Speakes and Robert Pack, *Speaking Out: The Reagan Presidency from Inside the White House* (New York: Avon Books, 1989), 90.

235 **"a blatant attempt to distort":** Edwin Meese III, *With Reagan: The Inside Story* (Washington, D.C.: Regnery, 1992), xvi.

236 **"When someone talks to Ed":** Martin Schram, "Streetwise: Inside Ed Meese Runs a Law-and-Order Streak," *Washington Post,* March 15, 1981.

236 **"We must increase the power":** Christian Parenti, *Lockdown America: Police and Prisons in the Age of Crisis* (New York: Verso, 1999), 47.

236 **a "criminals' lobby":** Michael Putzel, "Meese Remark Linking ACLU to 'Criminals Lobby' Said to Be His Own," Associated Press, May 14, 1981.

237 **"The thing is," he said:** "Reagan Seeks Judges with 'Traditional Approach,'" *U.S. News and World Report,* October 14, 1985, 67; cited in Howard Kurtz, "Meese Says Few Suspects Are Innocent of Crime: New Attack on *Miranda* Draws Criticism," *Washington Post,* October 11, 1985.

237 **"bad choice of words":** Merrill Hartson, "Attorney General Admits 'Bad Choice of Words' in Miranda Comment," Associated Press, October 16, 1985.

237 **"Let us have an end to the idea":** Cannon, *Governor Reagan,* 216.

239 **"utopian presumptions about human behavior":** Marc Mauer and the Sentencing Project, *Race to Incarcerate* (New York: New Press, 1999), 60.

240 **"The war against drugs provides":** Eva Bertram, Morris Blachman, Kenneth Sharpe, and Peter Andreas, *Drug War Politics: The Price of Denial* (Berkeley and Los Angeles: University of California Press, 1996), 56.

240 **"Restoring a strong federal law enforcement":** Dan Baum, *Smoke and Mirrors: The War on Drugs and the Politics of Failure* (New York: Little, Brown, 1996), 137–138.

241 **"It's high time that we make":** American Presidency Project Document Archive, Ronald Reagan, Address before a Joint Session of the Congress on the State of the Union, January 25, 1983, http://www.presidency.ucsb.edu/ws/index.php?pid=41698.

242 **"It now appears that the Court's victory":** *United States v. Leon et al.,* No. 82-1771, Supreme Court of the United States, 468 U.S. 1250; 105 S. Ct. 52; 82 L. Ed. 2d 942; 1984.

243 **One Kentucky man:** Ibid., 243–244.

244 **"collective incapacitation":** Mauer and the Sentencing Project, *Race to Incarcerate,* 64.

245 ***Time* and *Newsweek* each featured cocaine:** Baum, *Smoke and Mirrors,* 232.

245 **"the gravest domestic threat":** George H.W. Bush, Address to the Nation on the National Drug Control Strategy, September 5, 1989, American Presidency Project, http://www.presidency.ucsb.edu/ws/index.php?pid=17472&st=gravest+domestic+threat&st1=.

246 **"Hold it right there, buster":** The copy boy related the incident to the author at the time.

246 **"Mayor Frank Graves is leading the search":** The author was the one holding the notebook.

246 **"I personally believe that anyone":** William Kleinknecht, "In Need of Correction," *The (NJ) Star-Ledger,* January 25, 2004.

247 **New Jersey's prison population:** Kathy Barrett Carter, "Judge Says Mandatory Sentences Have Lopsided Effect on Minorities," *The (NJ) Star-Ledger,* April 5, 2001.

248 **"shared many characteristics":** Description of Operations Pipeline and Convoy, U.S. Drug Enforcement Administration, http://www.usdoj.gov/dea/programs/pipecon.htm.

248 **More than twenty-seven thousand state highway:** William Kleinknecht, "U.S. Program Helped Give Birth to Police Profiling," *The (NJ) Star-Ledger,* April 4, 1999.

249 **eight of every ten people searched:** Brian Donohue, "Minority Stops Are Highest on Pike," *The (NJ) Star-Ledger,* June 28, 2000.

249 **"The contents of one's bladder":** Baum, *Smoke and Mirrors,* 234.

252 **"In short, much of what has gone awry":** William Julius Wilson, *The Truly Disadvantaged: The Inner City, the Underclass, and Public Policy* (Chicago: University of Chicago Press, 1990), 37.

252 **"In other words," William Julius Wilson wrote:** Ibid., 38.

253 **A Justice Department study found:** Andrew Lang Golub and Bruce D. Johnson, *Crack's Decline: Some Surprises across U.S. Cities* (Washington, D.C.: National Institute of Justice, July 1997).

254 **The usual benchmarks of ghetto pathology:** Steven A. Holmes, "Quality of Life Is Up for Many Blacks, Data Say," *New York Times,* November 18, 1996.

255 **"Drugs are part of our culture":** William Kleinknecht, "Are Low-Level Drug Arrests a Bust?" *The (NJ) Star-Ledger,* December 8, 2002.

255 **one in three black males:** William Kleinknecht, "Turning Cons into Pros: If Jobs Don't Follow Jail, It's Not Just the Ex-Offenders Who Will Suffer," *The (NJ) Star-Ledger,* August 1, 1999.

CHAPTER 11: THE SECOND-RATE SOCIETY

260 **"I found Rome of clay":** Cassius Dio, *Roman History,* vol. 7 (Cambridge, Mass.: Loeb Classical Library, 1924), 69.

260 **"wild speculative paradox":** Quoted in Arthur M. Schlesinger Jr., *The Cycles of American History* (Boston: Houghton Mifflin, 1986), 221.

261 **"If there is a prize":** Joseph A. Califano, "What Was Really Great about the Great Society," *Washington Monthly,* October 1, 1999, 13.

261 **"condemned by law and opinion":** Alexis de Tocqueville, *Democracy in America* (New York: HarperPerennial, 1969), 278n.

261 **"It is common sense to take a method":** Schlesinger, *Cycles of American History,* 20.

263 **"Why should some steel worker":** David A. Stockman, *The Triumph of Politics: How the Reagan Revolution Failed* (New York: Harper & Row, 1986); Michael Mumper, *Removing College Price Barriers: What Government Has Done and Why It Hasn't Worked* (Albany: State University of New York Press, 1996), 94.

263 **"Then you come down to waste":** "Reagan's Rx for Beating Inflation," *U.S. News and World Report,* August 14, 1978, 23.

264 **"By and large, the amendments have been":** James W. Singer, "Without Friends," *National Journal,* March 14, 1981, 455.

264 **"There's just no constituency for the program":** Ibid.

265 **"At a time when one in 13":** Alexander L. Taylor III, "A Shortage of Vital Skills: America Is Running Out of People Who Can Do Essential Work," *Time,* July 6, 1981, 46.

265 **"The more that government gets involved":** Ibid.

266 **"restoration of apartheid schooling":** Jonathan Kozol, *The Shame of the Nation: The Restoration of Apartheid Schooling in America* (New York: Three Rivers Press, 2005).

266 **"convert power into form, energy into culture":** Lewis Mumford, *The City in History: Its Origins, Its Transformations, and Its Prospects* (New York: Harcourt Trade, 1968), 571.

268 **William Julius Wilson has amassed evidence:** William Julius Wilson, *The Truly Disadvantaged: The Inner City, the Underclass, and Public Policy* (Chicago: University of Chicago Press, 1990), 93–106.

268 **In 2008 testimony before a House subcommittee studying economic inequality:** Jared Bernstein testimony before the Subcommittee on Labor, Health, and Human Services, and Related Agencies, Committee on Appropriations, U.S. House of Representatives, February 13, 2008; available from Economic Policy Institute, http://www.epi.org/content.cfm/webfeatures_viewpoints_testimony_20080213.

INDEX